Nothing Fr̶ ̶ ̶ ̶ ̶ ̶ ̶ in the Vicinity

My Patrols on the Submarine USS Guardfish during WWII

Claude C. Conner

BLUEJACKET BOOKS

Naval Institute Press
Annapolis, Maryland

Naval Institute Press
291 Wood Road
Annapolis, MD 21402

Library of Congress Cataloging-in-Publication Data
Conner, Claude C., 1925–
     Nothing friendly in the vicinity: my patrols on the submarine USS Guardfish during WWII / Claude C. Conner
     p. cm. — (Bluejacket books)
     Originally published: Mason City, Iowa: Savas, 1999.
     Includes bibliographical references and index.
     ISBN 1-59114-130-3 (alk. paper)
     1. Conner, Claude C., 1925– 2. World War, 1939–1945—Naval operations, American. 3. World War, 1939–1945—Naval operations—Submarine. 4. World War, 1939–1945—Personal narratives, American. 5. United States. Navy—Biography. 6. Guardfish (Submarine) 7. Extractor (Ship) 8. Radar operators—United States—Biography. I. Title. II. Series.
D783.C66 2004
940.54'26—dc22

2004049875

Printed in the United States of America on acid-free paper ⊗
11 10 09 08 07 06 05 04   9 8 7 6 5 4 3 2 1

To Greg, Cathy, Christine, Michele, and John:

My longtime wish to give you a momento of me
ultimately led to my writing this book

USS Guardfish returning to the States after WWII

U.S Navy

TABLE OF CONTENTS

continued. . .

TABLE OF CONTENTS (CONTINUED)

PHOTOS & ILLUSTRATIONS

MAPS

Foreword

Claude Conner's *Nothing Friendly in the Vicinity* is an enthralling story of an enlisted man and his short navy career, the greater part of which was spent as a Radar Technician on the submarine *Guardfish* (SS-217) during World War II. Claude summarizes the highlights of *Guardfish's* early operations and details his experiences in its operations as a crew member.

His first patrol made him a participant in one of the war's most outstanding patrols, for which *Guardfish* was awarded its second Presidential Unit Citation. Only two submarines were so recognized during the entire war.

On Claude's second patrol, he witnessed *Guardfish's* commitment of a tragic error, the misidentifying and sinking of *USS Extractor* (ARS-15) in a torpedo attack. This tragic incident and its follow-on investigation, fully covered in this superb narrative, tainted *Guardfish* for the remainder of her career. After two subsequent patrols it was relegated to a "training boat" status. At war's end it sailed to the east coast of the U.S. for decommissioning.

And, on this trip the author met his wife-to-be.

Norvell G. Ward
Rear Admiral USN (Ret)
Ex-CO, *USS Guardfish* (SS-217)

Introduction

As thoroughly chronicled by Clair Blair in his monumental history of US submarine operations in World War II, *Silent Victory*, the submarine war against Japan was a relatively little known war-within-a-war. It was waged by an initially small but growing force of American boats, which eventually made more than 1,400 war patrols and sank almost 1,400 Japanese merchant and naval vessels.

These totals are astounding when one considers the handicaps under which these boats labored. The entire American submarine force was plagued by poor torpedo performance, indeed by a series of torpedo design deficiencies that revealed themselves successively, like layers of a peeled onion, over the first two years of the war. Unfortunately, solving one problem only served to expose the next one in line. Although all such enigmas were eventually resolved, torpedo firing results remained far below par until the end of September 1943.

Yet U.S. submarines compiled an amazing record. They sank almost five million tons of Japanese merchant shipping. This amounted to 55% of Japan's total shipping losses, or more than 1,100 ships. Essentially, all north-south movement in Japan's newly-acquired empire ceased about December 1944. While the freighters and tankers were being sent to the bottom, our submarines were also whittling away at Japan's navy. During the course of the war, we sank the following major warships:

1 battleship
4 aircraft carriers
4 escort aircraft carriers
4 heavy cruisers
8 light cruisers
38 destroyers
23 submarines

Particularly noteworthy are the sinkings of Japanese destroyers (38) and submarines (23). In the first instance, this was a prime example of the hunted overcoming the hunters. We did not exactly hold Japanese destroyers in contempt, but would take them on it if became necessary or desirable. In fact, for several months during 1944, destroyers were given top sinking priority by the submarine command, in order to "thin down" the escort protection provided to enemy convoys and heavy ships.

During this period, Sam Dealey in *Harder* sank three destroyers and damaged two others in the vicinity of the Japanese fleet anchorage at Tawi-Tawi in the southern Philippines. Moreover, intense American submarine activity in the vicinity forced curtailment of essential aircraft-at-sea training operations, and increased the steady attrition of exposed Japanese forces. All this took place as these forces were assembling for the Battle of the Marianas.

As noted above, American submarines sank a total of twenty-three Japanese submarines. By way of comparison, only one American sub was confirmed sunk by a Japanese boat. Even if all the "cause unknown" losses are ascribed to Japanese submarines—which is unlikely—the total would only be six boats lost in this manner, truly an enormous disparity.

Some U.S. submarines also played a major role in the various fleet engagements, beginning with the Battle of Midway, although the results were mainly incidental. An abortive attack by *Nautilus* on *Kaga*, one of the three then-burning Japanese carriers, caused no real damage but added to the general confusion of abandoning ship. Later, in the early morning hours of the following day, *Tambor's* unexpected presence near a bombardment group of cruisers was the direct cause of a collision between *Mogami* and *Mikuma* that ultimately resulted in the sinking of the latter.

During the Marianas landings, in what is sometimes referred to as the First Battle of the Philippine Sea, our submarines were very active and succeeded in picking off two Japanese heavy carriers. *Albacore* got the new carrier *Taiho*, while *Cavalla* sank the veteran carrier *Shokaku*.

The last real naval engagement of the war was the Battle for Leyte Gulf, in connection with General MacArthur's landings in the Philippines. Here, the coordinated advance of several widely separated Japanese forces was supposed to culminate in a pincer-like movement to annihilate the American landing force and its ships. Where possible, our submarines attempted to intercept and destroy these gathering enemy forces. *Dace* and *Darter*, waiting in Palawan Passage under the command of the *Darter's* skipper, attacked in succession. *Darter* sank heavy cruiser *Atago* and badly damaged *Takao*. *Dace* was also successful when her torpedoes ripped apart and sank the heavy cruiser *Maya*. Later that night while in hot pursuit of the enemy, *Darter* ran high and dry at 19 knots on Bombay Shoal, in the Dangerous Ground in the South China Sea; she remains there today. *Dace* was called to the scene and took aboard *Darter's* crew, returning them to safety in Australia.

Our successes were not without sacrifice. Destroyer-killer Sam Dealey and *Harder* were lost off Caiman Point in August of 1944, one of 52 submarines which are still on patrol. More than 3,500 American sailors lost their lives waging this "war-within-a-war."

One of the submarines which left and returned with her crew more than a dozen times was *USS Guardfish*, the subject of Claude Conner's engrossing memoir. Although *Guardfish* missed participating in the Battle of Midway as well as the First Battle of the Philippine Sea (she was in the navy yard being overhauled between her seventh and eighth war patrols), and was assigned elsewhere during the Battle for Leyte Gulf, she nevertheless compiled an enviable record.

Her first two skippers, T. B. Klakring and Norvell Ward were both outstanding commanders. As a result of their accomplishments, *Guardfish* was one of only two U.S. submarines twice awarded the Presidential Unit Citation. In addition, she ranked eighth overall in the number of ships sunk (19), and was thirteenth in total tonnage sent to the bottom (72,424). Conner's reminiscence of his several patrols aboard *Guardfish* contains his recollections of the tragic friendly-fire sinking of *USS Extractor* and the Court of Inquiry that followed, including rare firsthand accounts with several survivors of that unfortunate tragedy.

I know readers will enjoy *Nothing Friendly in the Vicinity* as much as I have. Claude Conner has carefully researched all relevant aspects of the tale he has to tell, and has skillfully woven them into a fascinating story.

Ralph M. Metcalf
Rear Admiral USN (Ret)
ex-CO, *USS Pogy* (SS-266)

Preface

When I originally made my request to the U.S. Navy for a copy of the Court of Inquiry Record regarding the World War II sinking of *USS Extractor* by the submarine *Guardfish*, I had no intention of writing a book. Since I had given testimony at that hearing, I wanted to give my children a memento by providing each with a copy of the court record. It took the Navy more than a year to locate, declassify and mail me the huge transcript, which totaled 110 pages and 40,000 words.

To my surprise and delight, I found the record so interesting I felt compelled to share it with others by getting it published in one form or another. My initial plan was to add explanatory addenda to it to clarify technical and naval jargon for the general reader. I also hoped to locate some of *Extractor* survivors to get their personal stories to include with the court record. It took me another year just to find the first member of the *Extractor* crew. Fortunately, he knew the addresses of a couple of others, they knew of others, and I ended up with about a dozen names and addresses. All of these survivors happily supplied me with both written and oral histories, most of which are included in this book.

I shared my plans with my old friend and shipmate, author-historian Clay Blair. Clay, who served with me for a time aboard *Guardfish,* has written several excellent books on submarine warfare during WWII. He offered to read my manuscript and provide help along the way. Before long Clay pointed out that the court record was too repetitive and technical to be of interest to a general audience. He suggested instead that I write an autobiography about my service on *Guardfish* and incorporate the fascinating stories told to me by crewmen who survived the *Extractor* tragedy. I took Clay's good advice and started over.

As I was writing my manuscript I enlisted the help of my first *Guardfish* skipper, Rear Admiral (Ret) Norvell G. Ward, who willingly read through my manuscript and penned the Foreword. His suggestions improved my book significantly in all respects, especially regarding the accuracy of my presentation of World War II submarine naval terminology and practices.

My publisher Theodore P. "Ted" Savas suggested that an Introduction consisting of a basic overview of American submarine service in the Pacific Theater was in order, and I readily agreed. Thankfully, Ted had become acquainted over the years with Rear Admiral (Ret) Ralph M. Metcalf, the distinguished WWII submarine commander of *USS Pogy*. In addition to providing his fine Introduction, Admiral Metcalf read the manuscript twice and made several valuable suggestions.

Even though *Nothing Friendly in the Vicinity* correlates historical events in World War II to the activities of *Guardfish*, and much of it is based on or supported with official documents from the U.S. Navy and other sources, my purpose was not to write just another history book. I simply wanted to tell about my experiences aboard one of the most famous (and infamous) boats of World War II. My goal was to present the story largely from the viewpoint of enlisted men (something rarely done in submarine books) in a way that will interest layman curious about life aboard a wartime submarine. In order to make the terminology easier to understand, I have included an extensive glossary of terms, as well as an index of personal and ship names for those who have a background in naval and submarine activities. I am confident that the chapters regarding the Court of Inquiry, which includes extensive quotations from the official record, will fascinate not only those who are naval and military history aficionados, but general readers as well.

I would never have successfully completed this book without the professional guidance of my mentors, Clay Blair and Admiral Ward. You will meet them, along with many other former shipmates, in the pages of this book. All of them have personal stories to relate about their World War II experiences, and I am indebted to each of them. I also appreciate the help of the Operational Archives Branch of the Naval Historical Center in Washington, D.C., who supplied me with invaluable background information and reference sources.

Of course, any mistakes, errors, or omissions are mine alone.

Claude C. Conner
Rancho Cucamonga, CA

Chapter One

Navy Training

I have come to realize that sea water probably flowed in the veins of some of my ancestors. Their memories of ships, raging seas and high adventure lay buried with them. It is my family name, Conner, that gives me that clue. A few years ago, as I thumbed through an old unabridged dictionary, I stumbled across the word "conner." It means "ship pilot," one who conns, directs or steers a ship. As a child I had no idea that I was to briefly relive some of my seafaring ancestral past.

Born in Redwood City, California on November 24, 1925, I was the only child of Claud March Conner and Dolores Cullen Conner. My father, a motion picture projectionist, died a few days before my tenth birthday. A year or two later my mother married a long time family friend, Joseph Manuel Faso. He owned and operated an automobile repair business in Redwood City. I never called him "father," even though I gradually felt that way toward him; instead, I simply called him Joe. Joe's son by a previous marriage, Leon Faso, also lived in Redwood City, but with Joe's brother, Charles Faso. Leon called his uncle "Charlie" but he called Joe "Dad." Even as a child I thought it was sad the way divorces mixed up kid's lives.

When I was twelve years old, I became intensely interested in radio communication. I earned my Class "B" Amateur Radio License a year later, and proceeded to build my own short wave receiver and very low power CW (code) transmitter. Joe helped me put up a wire antenna from the roof of our house to the flag pole, and before long I was on the air.

My station call was, and still is, W6SXA. Very quickly I became totally immersed in ham radio, to the detriment of my high school grades. Because of the war in Europe, the government prohibited American hams from "working" any foreign countries. Amateurs were allowed to communicate only with stations in the United States and her possessions. I made contacts all over the United States, the Territory of Alaska, the Hawaiian Islands and other American possessions throughout the Pacific, as far away as Guam. I never dreamed that I had a future in some of those distant places.

My hobby developed rapidly and I became rather skillful as a radio telegraph operator or "brass pounder," and developed a basic knowledge of radio circuits and radio wave propagation. Late in 1941, at the age of sixteen, I upgraded to the Class "A" Amateur Radio License, which is now called the Advanced Class.

A frantic wave of near hysteria swept the nation when Japan attacked us on December 7, 1941, and dragged us into war. Many in this country had a fear of enemy spies, and within days after the attack on Pearl Harbor, the government banned all amateur radio transmissions. The bombing also caught my attention and like most citizens, I too succumbed to the war frenzy. I became interested in world news for the first time. However, I felt a terrible loss, because of the "death" of my obsessive hobby, ham radio.

Joe lost his car repair business shortly after marrying my mother and we went on relief (welfare), as a result. Although he hated them, Joe was forced to take on miscellaneous government sponsored "make work jobs." When wartime employment hit the labor market, he got a job in San Francisco, twenty-five miles north of our home in Redwood City. His position was foreman of the diesel engine repair shop at the navy's Bethlehem Submarine Repair Base.

Then came the war time labor shortage. During my summer vacation my mother saw an ad in our newspaper about manufacturing jobs in Palo Alto, a nearby town, and pushed me into applying for one of them. A little company called Fisher Research Laboratories hired me to do electronic assembly work, and the bosses quickly embroiled me in the daily work routine. After vacation was over I continued at Fisher part time. Since my occupation was helping with the war effort, I received school credit for it.

With everything going on in the world, High school soon became boring for me. I started dropping out of school activities, even from the radio club. My mother gave me a lot of grief about my absenteeism, failing grades, and "poor attitude." The best way for me to escape from all the stress and hostility seemed obvious, even to a teenager, and thus I decided to join the navy.

Joseph Wetzel (W6HKO), a ham radio friend of mine, was also a retired sailor. The navy called him back to be a recruiting officer some time after the Pearl Harbor attack. I visited Wetzel at his downtown office to talk about enlisting, but he said that I had to be seventeen years old and get my parents' permission. He talked at length about his prior navy duty aboard submarines. I found his stories utterly fascinating. Wetzel strongly recommended that I take the "Eddy Test" to get into the new, "secret" *radar school. Although submarines interested me, I had had my fill of school.

As I approached my seventeenth birthday, I pleaded with my mother to let me enlist. She repeatedly refused my entreaties, saying that, after my father's death, she could not cope with losing me, too. Ultimately my stepfather talked my mother into letting me enlist. On December 15, 1942, I quit my senior year of high school and joined the navy. My goal was to become a radio operator, and I figured I would have no trouble getting that assignment because of my ham radio background. I would soon be back on the air, "pounding brass" to my heart's content aboard a ship or at a navy base.

A special train brimming with recruits transported us directly to Farragut, Idaho, where we were to get our naval training. For a California kid, it was as if I had been transported to Antarctica. The temperature hovered continuously around twenty degrees below zero during the first two weeks there, and sheets of ice flowed from the roofs of all buildings down to the ground, where they piled up in huge mounds. The Naval Training Station was on the shore of Lake Pend Oreille. The base held something like 50,000 recruits at a time, with about 100 men to a barracks. The navy gave all new recruits the rating of Apprentice Seamen, but they called us "boots" because we spent our twelve-week training

---

* An asterisk (*) preceding a word or phrase indicate that this item is listed and defined in the Glossary, found on page 213.

period wearing the khaki colored canvas boots (leggins) that identified us as recruits.

Several weeks into the training the instructors asked us what kind of assignment we wanted after completion of boot camp. Of course, I selected radio operator's school as my first choice. I did not think there was any point in filling in second and third choices, since I had told them I held a Class "A" Amateur Radio License. But I followed the instructions, and put down sonar school as my second choice (It sounded sort of "electronic" to me.) I entered music school as my third choice, since it was common knowledge that they never had openings for that navy school. (During high school I played saxophone and oboe in the band and orchestra.)

Repeatedly the company commander, a chief petty officer, suggested that we consider taking the Eddy Test, named after its designer. According to the chief, those who passed the test would be, upon completion of boot camp, advanced to the petty officer rating of Radio Technician third class. Our next assignment would be to radio materiel school, to learn how to repair radar and other types of electronic equipment. The prestige and extra pay that went with a petty officer rating were really attractive to me. However, after failing so badly in high school, I was afraid to try for it. Every time the announcement was made about the Eddy Test, word went around the barracks that there was no use taking the exam because "only a genius could pass it." Tests frightened me, and I did not want to get over my head again. I just wanted to be a radio operator—nothing else.

The rumors did not scare off everyone, however. A couple of the guys (whom I thought were among the company's least intellectually gifted) had not only taken the test but passed it! Their success convinced me that I should at least give the test a shot. As it turned out the test was comparatively easy, and I looked forward to sewing my petty officer rating badge onto my dress blue uniform. (I also thought the badge would impress the girls when I was on liberty after completing boot camp.)

When our boot training was over the chief posted our new assignments on the barrack's bulletin board. We were an excited flock; cackling, pushing, elbowing up around the lists, fingers pointed, tracing from our names to our new posts. I finally found my name, traced my finger across the page and found my new assignment: music school! When I complained to the chief about my assignment, he checked his records and found there was a mistake. My music school assignment came from an instructor who did not know that I had passed the Eddy Test.

After release from the Farragut Training Station I was transferred to the Navy Yard at Bremerton, Washington. My assignment there lasted for about a month, as I waited for an opening at one of the several radar schools. During that time I spent many liberties in Seattle, where I found that the girls were not impressed with my petty officer rating badge, after all.

In May 1943, I was transferred again, this time to the naval base on Treasure Island, California. T.I., as it was called, is a man-made island attached to Yerba Buena Island, located at the midpoint of the San Francisco-Oakland Bay Bridge. The Radio Materiel School I was about to attend was located at three successive sites. The first was called Pre Radio School, and mine was located there on T.I. It was one month long and consisted of preliminary math and lab classes to prepare us for the balance of the schooling.

The next part of my training was called "Primary School," and there were several different locations with the same curriculum. The one that I attended was run by the Texas A & M College's Engineering Department. It was an excellent program. We lived in brand-new, four-story brick dormitories, two men per room. Since we were there during the middle of the summer, from June to September, the weather was extremely hot and humid. Neither the dorms nor the classrooms were air conditioned. The curriculum consisted of cram courses in algebra, trigonometry, electricity theory, radio theory and laboratory classes. They promoted the top ten percent of the graduating students to the rating of "Radio Technician second class." Despite my aversion to school, I made the cut—although only by the skin of my teeth.

Secondary School was back at Treasure Island, looking out over beautiful San Francisco Bay. Everyone who kept his grades in the top ten percent of the class was rewarded with liberty each weekend. Since I qualified, I spent a lot of time in "The City." I found that the extra chevron on my arm and the extra money in my wallet helped me find girls, but my bashfulness was an impediment.

My first four months at T.I. were spent studying electronic circuit theory. To my dismay, the circuits we studied were strange and amazing to me—with no connection to radio at all. The instructors hinted to us that those weird circuits had something to do with "radar." Some scientifically oriented laymen at that time were familiar with the name radar. They understood that it was a radio wave device that the military used to detect airplanes, but its operation was a mystery to them. A few knew that Marconi, the inventor of radio communication, suggested to the world's radio engineers in 1922 that reflected radio waves could be used to detect ships and planes. However, most people were not aware that the United States, England, France, and Germany, late in the 1930s, independently and furtively developed experimental military models of VHF and UHF radar systems. Even fewer people realized that precision radar installations were limited to land stations and large ships because they required large antennas.

What the public did not know was that early in the war, scientists in England invented and developed a "secret weapon," the multi-cavity magnetron. It was a source of very efficient, very high power, super high frequency (*SHF) radio energy that was ideal for use in radar transmitters. The use of SHF radio signals required the development of a range of completely new microwave devices for use in the associated radar. The British magnetron enabled the design of powerful, sensitive, and precise radar systems small enough to fit into airplanes. An SHF radar could detect not only other aircraft and surface ships, but even the protruding periscopes of submerged submarines. It was a critical development that played an important role in turning the tide of the Battle of the Atlantic. Great Britain shared her secret developments with the United States, beginning in late 1940. The United States then embarked on its own secret SHF radar developments, which we in turn shared with England.

The navy taught us about this new microwave technology during our last two months at T.I. All radar classes were held inside a compound surrounded by a high barbed wire fence, its gates patrolled by armed marine guards. The school issued large hard bound notebooks to everyone studying this new technology. For obvious reasons, we had access to them only while we were inside the compound. I was introduced to a variety of radar types. Some were in current use; others, the latest types, were not yet being used in the field.

It was not a simple task to keep microwave radar working properly. During World War II, the average operating time of this type of radar before it failed was only fifty to one hundred hours. Thus, some failures occurred after only a few hours of operation, while at other times the gear performed for a couple of hundred hours before going down. It took twenty to thirty years of post- war radar development to make radar reliable. Its unreliability meant there was a great need during the war for trained people to keep the radar working. The critical need for radar technicians resulted in the navy's massive electronics training program. Nevertheless, technicians were scarce throughout most of the war. Initially, the candidates for the Radio Materiel Schools came from the navy's radiomen (radio operators). Later, they skimmed candidates from the ranks of new recruits. (The name of the rate, "Radio Technician," changed to "Electronic Technician's Mate" late in the war.) Their priority assignments after school were typically to first-line combat ships, or to radar repair teams aboard service and support vessels, or to shore stations.

My graduation standing in the top ten percent of my class resulted in a promotion to first class petty officer, as well as a choice of duty assignments. I learned from magazine articles during the war that many sailors in the surface navy returned from the war zones as "living dead people," with their bodies burned, maimed, and mangled. Since I would rather die than live in that condition, I chose submarine duty. To my way of thinking, the majority of submariners came back in one piece—or not at all. But that meant that I needed more schooling, since none of the radar gear used on submarines was covered at T.I. Thus in early March of 1944, I found myself on another long distance train trip, this time to New London, Connecticut—in time for more snow and ice!

The navy's policy was to have all potential submarine crew members attend Submarine School, to learn about the intricacies of a sub before assignment to one. However, radar technicians were so desperately needed that the navy did not send us technicians to Submarine School. Instead, we were dispatched to a Submarine Radar School, which was also located at the New London Submarine Base.

Even though it was situated inside the heavily guarded New London Submarine Base, armed guards were assigned to protect the Submarine Radar School building. For two months we studied and worked on the five submarine radar types, only two of which were generally installed on any given boat. I spent my weekend liberties in the dingy dance halls of Hartford, Connecticut, a town filled with fun-loving girls, many of whom worked at the plethora of insurance companies based there. After graduation from the Submarine Radar School in May, I was transferred to the naval base at Mare Island, California, for reassignment.

My new assignment disgusted me. Instead of being ordered to a front-line boat, I was assigned to a submarine relief crew. "All this talk about how desperately techs are needed on the subs, and I'm to be filed away in a relief crew on a noncombatant ship or base," I complained to myself. "Oh well," I remember thinking, "it will be great to go to San Francisco on liberty again to look up my old girlfriend." Since Redwood City was only about sixty miles south of Mare Island, my new assignment would make it easier to visit my family as well.

It really pleased me to see my parents again. My mother did not seem to be angry anymore. I enjoyed being able to sit around and talk with my folks. Before I went into the navy we rarely did that. Of course, I mentioned to Joe how disappointed I was about not getting assigned to a submarine. He told me his son, Leon, was going out on the *USS Salmon*. Joe sympathized with me and asked if I would like to visit the Submarine Base to see where he worked. He suggested that the commanding officer of the base might even put in a good word for me. "Fat chance an officer would do anything for me," I thought, but I answered, "Sure, when can I come over?"

I visited Joe at the Sub Base some time during the following week. He showed me around the repair shops, particularly around his diesel shop. Then he took me outside, where there were two submarines tied up alongside the piers. One boat had completed its overhaul, and the other was about to undergo the lengthy procedure. Joe was as good as his word, and he took me in to meet Capt. Frank C.L. Dettmann, the commanding officer of the base. I remember that Joe's face glowed when he introduced me to the CO. Captain Dettmann was very friendly and we visited for about ten minutes, talking about navy life, how I liked New London, and my hope to get a berth on a submarine. After we said our good-byes, I left and returned to Mare Island.

The word we had been waiting for finally came over the Mare Island barrack's P.A. system: "Now hear this," boomed the announcement. "All members of Relief Crew Eighty-Two, prepare to board ship at 1600 hours." Our new assignment was to the *USS Fulton*, a submarine tender preparing to sail in a few days. The barracks broke out into a buzz of activity as men packed their belongings into their seabags, rolled their mattresses, and stuffed it all into their big mattress bags.

Shortly after I had finished my packing, the master-at-arms walked over and told me I was wanted at the duty officer's shack. Wondering what I was called for, I hustled over and identified myself with a salute. The officer turned, picked up and handed me a large manila envelope. "Here are your transfer papers and records. Go get your gear on the double and get into that Jeep out there. The driver is going to take you to your new assignment, the *USS Guardfish*, SS-217." The news left me dumbfounded. "Wow, Captain Dettman came through for me after all," I thought.

The jeep seemed to fly over the highways and across the Bay Bridge. We arrived at the Bethlehem Submarine Repair Base less than sixty minutes later and drove down onto the pier alongside *Guardfish*. My head was reeling as I walked across the gangplank. I saluted the ensign, and then the deck officer. "Radio Technician first class Conner reporting for duty," I said proudly, handing him my papers. This was the first time I had ever set foot on any navy ship. A chief petty officer led me below into the crew's space and showed me where my bunk was located. It was immediately clear to me that I had to discard some things. My tiny personal locker had a one-foot square door.

The following morning, May 25, 1944, after chow I went topside to the main deck and "shot the breeze" with a group of off-duty crewmen. Suddenly, *Guardfish's* engines roared to life. Sailors withdrew the gangplank, cast off the mooring lines and the boat backed down away from the pier. It seemed unbelievable that we were on our way out into the Pacific. Suddenly I heard my name called, and there, walking toward the end of the pier as the boat moved, was "my Dad," Joe. He waved and his voice cracked with emotion as he called, "Good luck, sonny." I choked back tears and waved back to him until I could no longer see him. I wondered if I would ever see good ol' Joe again.

* * *

More than one thousand miles east, Mary Angela Rahm knelt at St. John Berchmans' shrine in Gran Coteau, Louisiana. "Dear Lord Jesus," she prayed, "please save some serviceman's life so that we can marry and work our way to heaven together."

USS Guardfish at her Commissioning, May 1942.

National Archives

Chapter Two

Life on a Fleet Boat

Guardfish maneuvered northward through the Bay and then west around the tip of the San Francisco peninsula. Although I wanted to have one last look at the City's skyline, a chief petty officer ordered us all below. I slowly walked back around the conning tower to the after battery hatch, following the others. Then, mimicking them, I dropped through the hatch, lowered myself down the ladder into the innards of the boat by sliding my back along the stainless steel well-wall between the upper and lower hatches. The ladder landed me in the crew's mess section of the after battery *compartment. I watched as the chief closed and dogged down the two hatches. All benches around the four mess tables were full. Everyone already seemed to be waiting for chow. Much like an awe-stricken immigrant, I stood there not knowing what to do next.

We probably reached the anti-submarine nets around 10:00 a.m. Eventually the nets were opened, the boat glided through, and we passed under the Golden Gate Bridge. The boat began to pitch and roll as we dieseled out into the open sea. "Secure the maneuvering watch," came over the loudspeakers. "Man your watch stations."

The lights went off in the crew's quarters soon after setting the watch. A few men straggled into the darkened room and dropped onto their bunks to wait for food or their watch. A card game was already going at one of the mess tables. That game, with varying participants, seemed to go on for the rest of the war. Music from a San Francisco station flowed from a radio on the wall. The radio station, our connection with home, faded out after a couple of days at sea. Of course, under water we could not receive any radio broadcasts.

About an hour after passing under the Golden Gate Bridge the diving alarm sounded throughout the boat: AH-OO-GAH, AH-OO-GAH filled our ears and roused the entire crew to a high state of alert. The thunderous alarm sent a chill running up and down my spine. What is happening? Have we had an accident? Are we in an emergency? Swishing and gurgling sounds came from above as the roar subsided. I felt the deck moving under my feet, tilting forward and down, then slowly rolling from side to side. Gradually things became quieter, and the boat's motion smoothed out. We were submerged and safe.

The new fellows on board who had attended Sub School recognized the sounds and knew that this was a "trim dive," the first submergence of the day. It was later that I learned the source of the eruptive diving sounds. They begin when the fourteen large, hydraulically operated vent valves, located on the tops of the seven main ballast tanks, exploded into their open position. The trapped air inside the ballast tanks rushes out through the open vents at the top, allowing seawater to flood into the tanks through their open bottoms. The filling of the main ballast tanks produced a net "negative buoyancy," which in turn causes the boat to submerge. The diving officer in the control room "trims the boat" to compensate for the submarine's changing balance and weight as fuel burns, torpedoes are fired, and so on. Sea water is pumped between the forward and after trim tanks to level the deck. Water is also pumped from the ballast tanks to or from the sea to establish the subsidence or settling rate of the submarine. If not properly trimmed, a submarine could become uncontrollable during an emergency "quick dive."

But I learned all of this only after experiencing my first trim dive. Once *Guardfish* was deemed trimmed the boat rose to the surface, decks rolling, as we steamed ahead toward Pearl Harbor. Lieutenant William J. "Jerry" Howarth, the communications officer, found me in the crew's mess. He guided me forward to the radio room and introduced me to Chief Radio Technician Reid A. Dudrey, my leadman. Dudrey was a pleasant and mildly mannered fellow with a slight build and a Texan twang in his voice. It was obvious that he was proud to be a *Guardfish* sailor. He quickly pointed out that she was a famous submarine—one of the top scoring boats in the fleet. She also was the unidentified *fleet boat that made nationwide news early in the war.

Guardfish, he informed me, made nationwide news by operating so close to the Japanese mainland that the crew watched, and bet on, horses racing at a track! I remembered hearing that news item before I joined the navy. Dudrey also admired Lieutenant Commander Norvell Gardiner Ward, the current captain of the boat. Ward was impressive for a number of reasons: he was handsome, courageous, and intelligent—and, so far, all of his patrol missions had been completed successfully.

When I mentioned that I had never been aboard a sub before, Dudrey offered to walk me through the boat, explaining that *Guardfish* was a Gato-class submarine, since she was built to the same plans as an earlier boat with that name. We started the tour in the forward torpedo room (also called the Forward Room) and then worked our way aft. The boat's overall length, Dudrey pointed out proudly as we walked in single file, was almost 312 feet. Her beam, the maximum width over the outside of the ballast tanks, was a little over twenty-seven feet. Those ballast tanks were wrapped up and around the steel pressure hull, much as a bun surrounds a hot dog. The narrow weiner-shaped pressure hull, inside which we lived, was only about eighteen feet in diameter. A flat, horizontal deck stretched through every compartment except the torpedo rooms. The clearance height above the deck, to pipes and valves that suspended from the overhead, ranged from about six to eight feet, from side to side. The hull, fabricated from welded 3/4" steel plates, tested safe to a depth of 300 feet. The hull's entire inner surface was covered with a one-inch thickness of cork to minimize water condensation from the moisture-ladened air.

The boat's interior had been freshly painted a greenish-white during her overhaul in San Francisco, and there was no escaping the fumes. (As I would soon experience, the smell of the paint gradually diminished and was replaced with diesel oil "perfume," which permeated the entire vessel.) Dark green linoleum, outlined and spaced with stainless steel strips, covered the decks throughout most of the craft. Heavy watertight partitions, or bulkheads, divided the pressure hull lengthwise into eight compartments. A small oval-shaped watertight door of heavy cast steel connected each of the bulkheads. The bottom of each door was about a foot and a half above the deck. For safety, the watertight doors were generally kept closed while at sea.

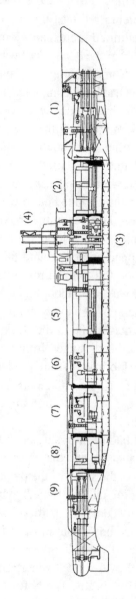

Gato-Class Fleet Submarine Cross-Section

See glossary for compartment descriptions

Although I listened carefully to Dudrey's explanations as we coursed our way through the narrow boat, I was really more intent on watching him. After opening a bulkhead door with a deft turn of the long lever handle, he slipped through the small opening like a trackman jumping a hurdle. One arm and one leg went through first, followed by his lowered head and chest, then his other leg and arm. I tried my best to imitate him, and then slammed the heavy doors behind me.

The complexity of the boat overwhelmed me, and despite Dudrey's best efforts, it was impossible to take it in all at once. Of particular interest to me was the radio room and the conning tower compartment. Dudrey informed me that the conning tower was to be my watch station. One other thing caught my attention as we passed aft through the bulkhead door into the forward engine room. Dudrey, who was about 5' 6", "hurdled" through the oval door, straightened up and continued walking aft with an almost unbroken stride. When I attempted the same "hurdle" through the door and straightened up, I smashed the top of my head into the boat's air conditioner compressor unit. The bottom of the compressor was about 5' 10" above the deck, allowing Dudrey free passage. I, however, was an inch and a half over six feet tall. I hit my head on that compressor unit almost every time I had reason to go back to the engine room.

Off Watch

Everybody considered Dudrey and me, along with the four radio operators, to be part of the radio "gang." The radio shack was where I stayed most of the time when I was off watch. The room was bright and cheerful, and each of us enjoyed the others' company. The standouts in the "gang" were "Brink" and "Ojay." Our lead radioman was Malcolm P. "Brink" Brinkley, a tall skinny kid from Tennessee. "Brink", whose 6' 2" frame often required him to stand slightly hunched over, wore a mustache and goatee and constantly chewed tobacco or snuff; which was always dripping out of the corner of his mouth along with his rich Southern drawl. He presented himself as the personification of the lady's man, a genuine Lothario. Orin R. "Ojay" Johnson was from New Hampshire. He was a talkative, friendly sort; outgoing and cocky.

Whenever the boat was on the surface at sea, one of the radiomen was always on radio watch, listening for messages for us. The sound of

Morse code filled the room; it was music to my ears. But it was a foreign music. My code experience was entirely in plain English, which I could even "copy" in my head without writing it down. These operators, however, copied everything on a typewriter, mostly in neat columns and rows and in five-letter groups of *ECM-security-coded gibberish. Messages in plain English occasionally came through, but they were rare.

Brink liked to practice on transmissions at higher speed than the navy's Fox (Fleet) schedules provided. He often sat at the second operator's position when he was not on duty and copied an English language, commercial high speed station operated by the International News Service or one of the other syndicates. Afterward, he edited his typed copy into "Home News" and "War News," and pasted it on a page with the title heading "G-Fish Herald." (The crew usually referred to *Guardfish* in casual conversation as the "G-Fish.") Brink often added cartoons and shipboard editorials that others supplied to him before posting the pages in the officers' wardroom and crew's mess. His "newspaper" was the only way the crew was able to keep up with what was transpiring in the outside world. Old hands tell me that the first publishing of the "G-Fish Herald" occurred before the boat's first war patrol, and that successive radio operators continued producing it throughout the war.

Blowing The Head

The heads (or toilets) on the boat provided many articles and cartoons for the ship's newspaper. "Blowing the head" (flushing the toilet) was a complex and unnerving experience for newcomer and old hands alike. To dispose of the contents of the toilet, the user washed it down into a small holding tank directly below. Compressed air was then used to blow the tank's contents into the ship's sanitary tank. While the user blew the head, he had to place his foot firmly on a flapper valve between the toilet stool and the holding tank. If the flapper valve's actuating lever was not tightly closed, or if the valve was not seated properly or if the valve gasket was defective, the waste contents of the holding tank would blow back all over the user! The force of the spray was proportional to the air pressure setting. When the sanitary tank was full, it was necessary to blow the contents of the holding tank overboard to sea. If the boat was submerged, however, the user had to utilize higher air pressure—higher than the operating depth's water pressure—to accomplish the same task. The valves and pressure gauges in the head compartment enabled the user to do all these things. And he could blow the head without getting a smelly bath—if everything went right.

Qualification

A "submarine-qualified" enlisted man could always be recognized by his swagger. But when he was in his dress uniform you could also see his "Dolphins;" his embroidered Qualified Submariner badge, worn on his right forearm. The insignia looked like a submarine's bow, faced by two dolphin fish (not the mammalian porpoise) one on each side. An officer wore his gold Dolphin pin on his chest.

When I came aboard the boat there were eighty-two men in the crew, seventy-three enlisted and nine officers. Through the balance of the war the crew size was relatively constant. However, with each new patrol about twenty percent of the men got reassigned and replaced by newcomers. Some of the new men were qualified submariners, but many were not. For safety reasons, it was imperative that most members of the crew be intimately familiar with the workings of the boat. Toward that end, qualification training classes, called "school of the boat," took up much of each unqualified man's off-watch time. Qualified officers and enlisted leadmen in each compartment instructed the classes. Finally, the boat's engineering officer gave each man an oral and practical qualification examination, as they walked together through the boat. The candidate had to show that he could operate all the boat's machinery and answer questions put to him by the officer. It took me several patrols to complete my qualification, receive my Dolphins—and learn to swagger.

Scuttlebutt

Each time the duty radio operator received a security-coded message addressed to *Guardfish*, he informed the communications officer over the ship's telephone. The officer then came to the shack, sat down at the ECM and without a word to us, decoded the message and took it to the captain. Unless we had a "need to know," as they called it, the officers kept us in the dark about the substance of these messages. Since we were tightly packed in a small area, however, we managed to glean the substance of many of these messages by listening to "private" officers' conversations. The boat was a virtual scuttlebutt (gossip) factory.

Field Days

I suspect that, from its beginnings, the halls of the Naval Academy joyously reverberated with the words, "A clean ship is a happy ship." I can attest to the fact that the motto caused much griping aboard our ship. Every couple of weeks the announcement blasted throughout the darkened submarine, "Field day: Clean sweepdown, fore and aft." Then all the lights came on and a groggy, disgruntled crew "turned to" and cleaned the boat. I think the voice over the loudspeaker belonged to the chief of the boat. He was the number one enlisted man, the officers' mouthpiece to the rest of the crew. The chief assigned enlisted men's watch stations, watch times, bunks, cleaning details, and so on.

Our harping and complaining echoed throughout the boat every time the chief announced field day. As we went to work, some men spouted out mock announcements like, "Secure from battle stations. Clean sweepdown, fore and aft." We did more than sweep, however. Buckets of dear, fresh water were used to wash painted surfaces and swab the decks. This was a point of contention with many of us, particularly during the summertime or in the tropics. Enlisted men could take an unlimited number of salt water showers, but that was like showering in sugar water. The boat had a very limited supply of fresh water produced by the onboard sea water distillation plant. The chief of the boat allowed enlisted men to have only one fresh water shower per week. The officers, though, could shower with fresh water anytime they wanted. They always looked neater and cleaner than the rest of us.

As I became more familiar with the informality of the submarine arm and had the opportunity to visit other boats, I discovered that some skippers did not require much cleanliness. Their submarines rightly earned the nickname "pig boats." Even though field days ticked me off, I was pleased that I was assigned to a clean boat.

Food

The Submarine Service had a well-deserved reputation for providing excellent cooks and food for the crews. I do not remember them ever serving powdered eggs or powdered milk, as was common in the surface navy. We submariners got the real thing, and the best that was available: steaks, chickens, hams, holiday turkeys, even ice cream. Most of us, however, developed poor appetites after a few weeks at sea, largely as a result of little or no exercise or fresh air; in addition, nearly everyone smoked cigarettes. The distance from my bunk to my watch station was only about seventy-five feet. The radio shack was around the half-way point, and I rarely had reason to go elsewhere in the boat. If I was in my bunk trying to sleep when chow call came over the loudspeaker, I usually ignored the announcement. I snoozed until the below decks watchman came and woke me to go on watch.

Surface Watch

My Station

The conning tower was a small, cramped compartment. The fact that its hull was about eight feet in diameter and its inner deck some ten feet long, gives a distorted image of its working space. My watch position on the *SJ radar was immediately aft of the portside hatch that led up from the control room. When I stood by the radar, I could touch the hull overhead without stretching, and while sitting on one of the radar stools, could touch the shield surrounding the periscope hoist motors located on the starboard side of the room. The two periscopes, lined up on the deck's centerline, were between the radar and the hoist motors.

In addition to the radar, there were two other watch stations in the conning tower; the helm and ship's log. The helm (or steering wheel) was at the forward end of the compartment, where the helmsman stood facing forward into the bulkhead. He received steering instructions from the officer of the deck on the bridge by way of the intercom. The helm's metal rim was about thirty inches in diameter and was wrapped with a fibrous cord. A gyrocompass repeater was at chest level to the right of the helmsman. That device showed the heading of the ship in degrees, relative to true, as opposed to magnetic, north. A rudder deflection indicator was located directly ahead of the operator. Two-hand operated, electrical signaling devices called annunciators, located ahead of the helmsman and on his left, told the controllermen at the motor room's maneuvering panel what speed and direction settings to use on the port and starboard propulsion motors (such as "stop," "ahead full," "back 1/3," etc). The annunciators also revealed whether the motor controllermen had responded to the annunciator commands.

The ship's log position was at the chart desk on the starboard side of the room, slightly aft of the ladder that led through the upper conning tower hatch to the bridge. The watchman who sat on a stool beside the tiny chart table had two duties: making log entrees, and operating the *1MC intercom control station. The ship's log was a small, hard covered, book with ruled pages in which the watchman recorded the time of every change in course or speed. He also wrote the time and type of every visual or radar sighting. The 1MC operator communicated with the bridge and other individual locations throughout the boat over each compartment's loudspeaker. He could also set the 1MC equipment to broadcast one-way voice announcements throughout the boat, simultaneously.

As I mentioned earlier, the SJ radar watch station was on the port side of the compartment, aft of the lower conning tower hatch. There were two deck-mounted stools at the radar. The one closest to the lower hatch enabled the operator to sit hunched over as he looked down at the *PPI radar screen. The operator used the PPI to look for potential targets. A few feet farther aft, the other stool was at the *A-scope. That viewing screen, used for precise measurement of target range, was mainly used for *fire control during battle.

The Routine

At night, while on surface, the conning tower and the control room were illuminated only by red lighting. That was because red light, reflecting up through the hatches, was not as visible as white light to an outside observer. Red lights also protected the night vision of our lookouts as they prepared to go on duty. Conning tower watchstanders usually came up the conning tower ladder with a cup of hot coffee in hand.

As soon as we relieved the previous watchman and settled down at our positions, our cigarette packs came out. Shipboard regulations did not allow us to use matches because of the flare of light they produced. Instead, we used a homemade electric cigarette lighter located at the chart desk.

The radar watch was a boring, sleep-inducing job. We often went for days, sometimes for weeks, at sea without seeing anything on the hypnotic radar screen except waves, rain squalls, or whale spouts. The conning tower watchmen had a longstanding agreement that pleased me; after every thirty-minute period, we rotated to another's watch position: radar to chart desk to helm to radar.

The ship's log/1MC position was nearly as boring as the radar, but I found the helmsman job to be a challenge. Steering a ship is not at all like steering a car. The boat's slow reaction to the wheel, and then over reaction, particularly at slow speeds, required the helmsman's complete attention at all times. I became sufficiently competent to do the job in the open sea. However, I learned to have great respect for the maneuvering watch helmsman as we went in and out of port. During that watch the boat often operated at slow speeds while in tight quarters. I recall an occasion after the war, as we worked our way up the Mississippi River, the maneuvering watch helmsman was slow in getting up to the conning tower to take over the wheel from me. Before he relieved me I almost ran the boat aground.

San Francisco to Pearl Harbor

Training

Guardfish's crew went through numerous training exercises before I came aboard in San Francisco. Each separate watch section continued to be trained as we made our way to Hawaii. Captain Ward was particularly intent on perfecting the coordination of our "quick dives." He stood in the conning tower with a stopwatch in hand and at random times instructed the officer of the deck over the intercom to "take her down." When the diving alarm sounded, the captain clicked his stopwatch and stepped back out of the way.

A "quick dive" resembled an organized stampede. The officer of the deck shouted to all the lookouts, "Clear the bridge." Then he yelled, "Dive, dive" over the boat's loudspeaker system and immediately hit the diving alarm's actuating switch two times in succession: AH-OO-GAH, AH-OO-GAH. The chief of the watch in the control room closed the *main induction valve operating lever and watched closely the red-green lighted "Christmas Tree" panel. When all the lights had turned green, he knew the hull openings were all closed and that it was safe to submerge. He called out loudly, "We have a green board!" Immediately, he raced to the hydraulic manifold and opened all main ballast tank vents, thus initiating the submergence of the boat. As this was transpiring, the port, starboard, and after lookouts dropped from their posts and ran across the bridge deck to the conning tower hatch. They jumped into the hatch in rapid succession, their hands sliding down the ladder side rails, their toes barely tapping on the ladder rungs as they fell. They bounced onto the conning tower deck, whipped around and lunged for the lower hatch and repeated their toe-tapping fall into the control room. Two of the lookouts took their positions as *bow plane and stern plane operators and threw the planes into "hard dive." The quartermaster, who shared the forward bridge position with the officer of the deck, dropped down the hatch into the conning tower as soon as the lookouts cleared the bridge. He stood by in the conning tower, waiting for the officer of the deck. The junior officer of the deck, who was the high lookout up in the crow's nest at the top of the *periscope shears, finally climbed down and cleared the bridge. He went all the way down into the control room, where he took his position as the *diving officer adjacent to the base of the ladder.

The officer of the deck impatiently waited for the junior officer to get down from the high lookout position. Then, as last man down, the officer of the deck climbed into the conning tower, grabbed the lanyard attached to the hatch cover, and pulled the cover closed with a metallic bang. He held the cover down, the weight of his body hanging on the lanyard, as the quartermaster climbed up the ladder to the hatch. The quartermaster dogged the hatch cover down with a clockwise spin of the ten-inch diameter wheel at its center. As the boat submerged, we heard waves pounding on the conning tower fairing and water swishing, bubbling, and gurgling over the bridge.

The captain repeated the training dives over and over until he was satisfied with the time it took to take the boat down to its keel-depth of forty-eight feet. That was the depth at which the periscope shears were completely submerged. He stopped the exercises for each watch section after they repeatedly submerged the boat in forty seconds or less.

Crew Cuts

It did not take me long to realize Captain Ward's impatience with imperfection and his admiration of confident, self-assured people. At the earliest opportunity, he sacked anyone in the crew who exhibited poor coordination, timidity, or fear, and that applied equally to officers and enlisted men. On the way from San Francisco, I personally witnessed one poorly coordinated, ranking officer fall in a quivering heap on the deck of the conning tower after clearing the bridge. He fell directly at the feet of the embarrassed captain. The captain obtained replacements for that officer and four enlisted men when we reached Pearl Harbor.

Submerged Operation

Since I was a member of the radio gang, my submerged watch assignment was at one of the passive *sonar equipments. There were two independent underwater sound positions; one was in the conning tower and the other in the forward torpedo room.

The ultrasonic *QC in the conning tower was simple to operate. You wore earphones and stared at an azimuthal direction scale, as you hand trained the motor driven sound head through 360 degrees and back. As you did that, you listened for the enemy's *sonar pinging or the sound of a ship's screws (propellers). There was usually only a small amount of noise from marine life.

The sonic *JP in the forward torpedo room was more physically demanding, but much more fascinating than the QC. The operator had to stand and stretch upward to reach the handle on a twelve-inch diameter lever-wheel as he listened on a pair of headphones. He had to manually force the sound head rotation, and usually dripped with perspiration because of the work involved. The equipment was very sensitive to the cavitation noise, or the faint "swish, swish, swish" of a ship's screws. The enemy's asdic pinging could not be heard on the JP because of its operating frequency range, but you could hear a lot of marine life. One could easily identify snapping shrimp, croakers, and whales, but there were many other mysterious organic sounds we were unable to identify. The sounds built up to a peak at sunrise and sunset, like those in a tropical jungle. It was a wonderful cacophony of discordant whistles, howls, hoots, rumbles, belches, snaps, crackles, and pops.

Surfacing

While traveling over great distances from home base to and from their assigned patrol areas, World War II submarines spent much more time on the surface thán submerged. The primary reason for this was that submarines were much faster on the surface, where they were powered by diesel engines, than submerged and running on electric motors. After arrival at their duty stations, the boats ran submerged during most daylight hours, and surfaced at night to recharge the electric batteries.

Surfacing a WWII submarine was almost as complicated as diving. It was also very dangerous, since a submarine was completely vulnerable to attack when it breached the waves. When the "Prepare to surface" announcement came over the speaker system, I secured (stopped) my sound watch and warmed-up the SJ radar. The officer of the deck usually called for the waiting radioman to actuate the SD radar in the control room at the same time, and to raise its periscope-like mast. The officer of the deck rang the surfacing alarm a short time after the "Prepare to surface" announcement: AH-OO-GA, AH-OO-GA, AH-OO-GA. The *hydraulic manifold operator immediately slammed all the vent valves closed and valved high pressure air from the *air banks into the ballast tanks. We heard the heavy hiss of air rushing into the ballast tanks and the swish and gurgling of the water ballast blowing out through their open bottoms. As the boat lifted, we felt the deck's upward tilt and its lifting pressure on our feet. As we approached the surface, the boat began to pitch and roll.

The raised search periscope, operated by the officer of the deck, broke the surface as our keel-depth passed sixty feet. He then spun around with the scope several times, searching the sky for enemy aircraft at different elevations. The SD radar's nondirectional antenna broke through the water shortly after the periscope. Sometimes the radar spotted a high-flying airplane, alerting the officer of the deck to "dunk" the boat again before we were detected. I actuated the SJ radar when we rose to forty-five feet. Its PPI showed targets (low-flying planes and surface craft) the SD radar could not "see." As the conning tower broke the surface, the officer of the deck ordered the quartermaster to crack the hatch open a little, and then, if no water poured in, to throw it wide open. The officer of the deck, quartermaster, and lookouts clamored up through the dripping hatch to take their posts.

Lookout Duty

During patrol on the surface, we usually ran with the boat's main deck awash, at about water level. We ran that way, with only the conning tower sticking out of the water, to create the smallest possible target. However, whenever we needed high surface speed, we ran with the deck out of the water. To attain that posture, the officer of the deck ordered activation of the low pressure blower. It pumped low pressure air into the ballast tanks and blew the residual water from them. During its operation the low pressure blower sounded like a screaming banshee from hell. It produced a loud, piercing, high frequency, pulsating scream which continually increased in pitch as if it were ultimately going to explode. The sound amplitude decreased as the tanks blew dry.

I only stood one lookout watch while I was on board *Guardfish*, and I do not know why the chief of the boat selected me to do it that time. It was quite a memorable experience. I had the high lookout position and was apprehensive about being up in that crow's nest. I breathed a sigh of relief when the low pressure blower's screaming subsided. Even then the roar of the four diesel engines and the sound of the wind and the ocean were almost deafening. I remember clearly that the boat's pitching and rolling made it difficult to keep my binoculars trained on the horizon. Dark and thick distant clouds exacerbated the matter, since they made it almost impossible to distinguish for sure exactly where that boundary line was located.

Suddenly there were fourteen simultaneous claps of thunder and I saw steam-filled air-streams blasting out of the boat, high into the air. I remember screaming to myself, "We are submerging, and I did not hear the diving alarm!" I rushed down as fast as I could, jumped to the bridge deck, and ran to the conning tower hatch—just as it closed in my face. I called and banged on the hatch-cover with my binoculars, and to my eternal relief it quickly opened wide. The officer of the deck said, with a sheepish look on his face, "What are you doing up there?" I jumped down through the hatch, and the water splashed over it as it closed.

"Hey guys," I jubilantly proclaimed to my shipmates in the conning tower, "I almost went for a swim."

Chapter Three

Sea Stories

My long hours in the confined space of the conning tower enabled me to learn about the previous exploits of *Guardfish* from the other watch standers. (In reality, most of their sea stories were about their shore-time "sexploits," but they also shared with me information about the boat's previous patrols.) I doubted the authenticity of some of their accounts, as none of them were aboard the boat during her early war patrols. Also, I did not completely understand some of their narratives, because I did not know the background of the stories; nor, apparently, did they.

As I began to pen my recollections I realized it would be impossible for readers to fully understand the boat's accomplishments without an appreciation of her history. Thus, I decided to fill in these gaps in my knowledge with formal records and firsthand recollections from crew members who had actually served on *Guardfish's* early patrols.

The First Skipper

Lieutenant Commander Thomas Burton Klakring had a reputation for being an outstanding musician while he was at the Naval Academy. He was an excellent piano player, a composer, and the leader of a locally popular dance band. As a result of post-graduate work at Annapolis and the University of California, he received a Master of Science degree in marine engineering. His first submarine command assignment was early in 1941 to the *USS S-17*. He took command of *USS Guardfish* at her commissioning on May 8, 1942, took her directly into the Pacific Theater, and proved to be a bold and aggressive combat leader. Men told me that both officers and enlisted men greatly admired him—but also feared him because of his violent invective, blustery demands, and unbelievable bravery.

Frank Medina served under Captain Klakring on the early patrols as an enlisted man. I met Frank for the first time at a recent *Guardfish* reunion, and then read about him in a newspaper story after the banquet. A few days later I talked to him on the telephone, fleshing out his impressions of Klakring and recording his recollections of events during the boat's first patrols.

According to Frank, he came aboard *Guardfish* right out of Sub School and boot camp as a third-class Torpedoman, but he had to stand lookout rather than a watch in the torpedo room because there were too many Torpedomen on board. "I'd be up on the bridge, late at night," he remembered, "I could see the sun coming up, lighting up the nearby mountains on Japan. I'm up there shaking in my boots, wondering when the old man was going to dive the boat. And he's as cool as a cucumber. I used to say, 'There is one guy who's got some guts.'"

Frank recalled a particularly harrowing event when Klakring took *Guardfish* deep into the heart of a Japanese convoy. "One time," he began,

we were submerged right in the middle of a convoy of Japanese transports. I was on the wheel in the conning tower and depth charges were going off all over the place. Klakring said, "Well, this seems like a good spot, those Japs can't hit us, they're blind anyway." He was as cool as cool can be, but when he ordered, "Ten degrees left rudder," I was so petrified I couldn't even answer "Aye, aye, sir." To me he really exemplified somebody who was brave. The battle stations alarm hadn't gone off yet, because he was waiting until he closed range. I had the helm, but I wasn't the battle stations helmsman; I was hoping for him to relieve me. . . .All the action was up in the conning tower and I was there observing Klakring's coolness. It was a real pressure situation. *Sonar was reporting all kinds of contacts. You could hear the lead Japanese escorts dropping depth charges everywhere. And he still hadn't called battle stations. You know, battle stations is when the regular helmsman comes up. . . .

Klakring left a lasting impression on Frank Medina. "I observed the captain several times on the bridge where, in my opinion, we should have long before gone under the water," continued the former Torpedoman. "Other times when we were making a run on some ships, I thought the range was close enough for us to fire torpedoes and get the hell out of there. He still wanted to sneak in closer. Another thing that was amazing about Klakring; he didn't look like a guy who should be that brave. He looked to me like an old country doctor. He had little old spindly legs. When it came to making the right decision at the right time, though, he was the man."

Another submariner who served under Captain Klakring was Eugene G. "Sam" Brewer. He was a *Guardfish* "plank owner," which means he was aboard at the time of the boat's commissioning. He also made eleven war patrols on *Guardfish*, more than any other individual who served on her. Brewer is known to this day by *Guardfish* crewmen as "Sam" because during an early patrol a fellow Torpedoman called him "Sam the Brewer," after a prohibition-era alcohol brewer the shipmate had known by that name. "I was a lookout until I became a rated Torpedoman," Sam explained,

I had exceptional vision and on the second patrol I spotted [a] Japanese bomber. Down through the years someone else was given credit for that, but I definitely spotted it and reported it. Klakring was a little stubborn. He had to spot that bomber himself. It was turning toward us and the duty officer. . .called out, "I have it, Captain, its coming at us." So we dove. They dropped a little calling card on our stern. It blew a section of the deck plate out, that's all. It was not a depth charge, it was a surface bomb, but we weren't that deep."

The Minefield Story

Naval Intelligence probably cautioned submarine skippers that Japanese coastlines were mined—or maybe Intelligence only suggested it as a possibility. With minefields protecting the inshore shipping lanes,

Japanese vessels could travel between them and the shore, safe from submarine attacks. I told Frank Medina that I had heard scuttlebutt that Klakring made a practice of going through minefields to get at those ships that ran close to the shore. "I've heard the same story, but I can't verify that," he replied. "Usually as soon as I got relieved after my watch I went back aft, where I used to live, back in the after torpedo room." But a friend of Frank's, a Quartermaster who spent most of his time in the conning tower, told him, "You know what that fool [Klakring] was doing? You know there were minefields up there, you could almost hear the wires scraping, but he's still trying to sneak in there closer."

Clay Blair, Jr., in his monumental book on American submarines in the Pacific during WWII, quoted Klakring's version of what may be "the minefield story."[1] According to Klakring, he maneuvered *Guardfish* in the dark (without surface *search radar) into what he described as the "safe zone," the area between the close-in shipping lanes and the shore:

> In the early morning, after we got our battery charge in, we made a high-speed run at the beach, sort of groping toward the mountainous coast in the pitch dark. There were tricky currents—some northbound, some southbound. We got so we could time it just right. Get right in there on the beach just about daybreak when we had to submerge. Then we were in ideal position.

Klakring, it seems, traveled *over* rather than *through* submerged minefields—if they were there at all. We may never know for sure, however, for Klakring made no reference to minefields in his war patrol reports. Nevertheless, he had to be truly fearless to perform such blind moves in the dark.

The Horse Race Story

Following the Japanese attack on Pearl Harbor, some people predicted that the war would be over in a few months. But for month after

---

[1] Clay Blair, *Silent Victory: The U.S, Submarine War Against Japan* (J. B. Lippincott Company, Philadelphia and New York, 1975), p. 323.

Guardfish War Patrols
One Through Four

Map 1

month throughout 1942 we heard a lot of grim war news from the Pacific. The Japanese war machine continued to roll on, conquering the Philippines, Malaya, Burma, the Dutch East Indies, New Guinea, many south-Pacific and central-Pacific islands, plus some islands off Alaska. At the time, our government did not reveal to the American public that the Pearl Harbor attack had put much of our navy's surface fleet out of business. Fortunately, the Japanese failed to attack the Pearl Harbor submarine base. This failure allowed our "Silent Service" to be active against the enemy from the onset of the war. But the public did not hear that, either.

Guardfish left Pearl Harbor on her first war patrol on August 6, 1942, three months after her commissioning. She returned to Pearl on November 28 after completing two spectacularly successful patrols. The Commander of Submarines, Pacific (ComSubPac) decided that the time was ripe to go public with Guardfish's exploits. He invited newspapers, news services, and Life magazine to interview the boat's captain and her executive officer, Lt. Herman J. Kossler. Life, a weekly magazine at that time, had a larger circulation than any other magazine in the States. The admiral probably gave censored copies of the boat's two war patrol reports to the reporters. However, the event that caught their imagination was Kossler's reference to the "horse track" incident. Before long, newspapers and radio stations nationwide were announcing that "an unidentified American submarine" had operated so close to the heart of the Nipponese Empire that the crew watched, and bet on, some horse races.

Life, however, dug deeper. The magazine published a feature article entitled, "West To Japan: U.S. Sub Patrols The Jap Coast, Watches Jap Horse Races and Sinks 70,000 Tons Of Jap Shipping."[2] The article was fairly faithful to the patrol reports, but with some embellishments. For example, it referred to the two patrols as "a single cruise." In fact, the boat had almost been on one continuous cruise, from the time she left Pearl until she returned. She stopped at Midway Islands after the first run to get more torpedoes, fuel, and supplies. Guardfish left on her

---

[2] Life, article by John Field, March 15, 1943, pp. 84-96.

second run after some minor repairs but without the usual R&R—rest and recuperation—training, and checkout periods.

The first run was along the coastline of northeastern Honshu, a Japanese island south of Kyushu. Captain Klakring's actual tonnage claim for the two patrols was 65,400. Up to that time no other submarine had even made such a claim. *Life* rounded the figure to 70,000 tons. Although the article included photographs (with names) of Klakring, all of his officers, and one enlisted man, it did not name the submarine. *Life* claimed that the boat attacked eleven ships and sank eight. In reality, *Guardfish* attacked eighteen ships and claimed to have destroyed eight using torpedoes, plus two smaller vessels that she sank with her deck guns. What the magazine article did not mention was the sheer magnitude of the Japanese shipping activity Klakring encountered. The boat made contact with seventy-seven vessels—fifty-eight of which were potential torpedo targets. With that kind of activity teeming around it, *Guardfish* was like "a fox in a hen house." According to *Life*, after Klakring chased two ships into a shallow harbor, it took only one hour (Klakring's report says two hours) for him to sink four other vessels. Klakring would have destroyed more enemy shipping if it were not for *Guardfish's* slow submerged speed, her lack of a surface-search radar, and the malfunctioning of one or two torpedoes. (American torpedoes had gross design defects that were not corrected until later in the war.)

The navy gave Lieutenant Commander Klakring two Navy Cross awards for "extraordinary heroism. . .alert skill and courageous efficiency." It awarded the ship and crew the Presidential Unit Citation for their first two war patrols. The Horse Racing story gave a needed boost to the American public's morale and the New York State Racing Commission awarded Burt Klakring an honorary membership in their group.

The irony of all this is that the horse race story was false and everyone on *Guardfish* knew it. It developed when reporters asked Lieutenant Kossler, *Guardfish's* executive officer, how close the boat had operated to the Japanese coast. Close enough, replied Kossler, to watch a railroad train traveling down the track. He also said in passing that someone in the conning tower mentioned that the train's passengers might be going to the race track that was identified on their navigational chart. Klakring joined in at this time, joking with the reporters that the crew made some bets on the races. The result of that wisecrack is indelibly linked to *Guardfish's* "history."

Sam Brewer tried to correct the horse racing story when the boat went to New Orleans for Navy Day, shortly after the war. Sam was the only man left who was aboard *Guardfish* during the first run. Reporters from the local newspaper interviewed him and asked if he saw the famous horse races. "I told them that it was purely an exaggeration; that we were demonstrating how close we had been to the Japanese coast, but that we had not actually seen the race track," explained Sam. The reporters took a photograph of Sam looking through one of the boat's periscopes. The resulting front-page article included Sam's picture, with the caption, "Torpedoman Eugene Brewer, posing at periscope, as he watched horse races on Japanese coast during height of war." "I had not even been a Torpedoman at the time; I was a striker, a Seaman. I was not about to get to look through the periscope."

The Harbor Entry Stories

I had often heard different stories about how Guardfish penetrated into an enemy harbor in some strange place I had never heard of before. The story sounded so much like a trumped-up Hollywood movie that I had a hard time believing it. In fact, I dismissed it as fiction until many years later, when I read *Guardfish's* third war patrol report. It seems incredible that anyone could have such raw courage as Klakring displayed during that patrol.

The boat left Pearl Harbor on January 2, 1943, initially assigned to a patrol area near the island of Truk, a Japanese Naval stronghold about 1,400 miles east of the Philippines. From there, she traveled about 800 miles south and west to traverse the front lines of the Japanese conquests. The war front at that time ran from the big island of New Guinea through an arc of smaller islands distributed 1,000 miles to the east. Those islands are about 900 miles north of Australia.

The heavy concentrations of Japanese air and naval combat forces at the front repeatedly put *Guardfish* in peril. Most of the twenty-four enemy airplanes encountered during the patrol attacked her. Some of the planes dropped depth charges with terrifying accuracy. During her first two runs, enemy ships submitted the submarine to relatively light and ineffective depth charging, but the third run made up for that in spades.

Guardfish detected forty potential torpedo targets. Klakring broke the boat through the antisubmarine defenses of four ships and sank three—two of which were warships. He used *Guardfish's* newly installed SJ radar, with its antenna sticking out of the water while submerged, to sink one of those combat ships during a night attack. That was one of the first submerged radar approaches made during the war.

During daylight, while submerged, Klakring spotted smoke from six ships located inside the harbor of Rabaul, a Japanese stronghold on New Britain island about 400 miles northeast of New Guinea. The skipper decided to make a submerged foray into the harbor to attack the ships early on the morning of January 28, 1943. He placed the boat in *silent running mode and stole through the harbor entrance toward the city. Maneuvering point-by-point into the harbor using geographical features shown on a navigational chart was a meticulous, gut-wrenching procedure. Klakring's entries from his war patrol report tell the story well (the numbers on the left are the local times):

0547 Submerged off Watom Island for another attempt to get down to Rabaul. During the morning we got past one echo ranging patrol and had a good scare at 1000 when six monoplanes were seen at a distance of one mile headed right for our periscope.

1032 Commenced approach on ship. . .but discontinued at 1103 when it was seen to be a small disreputable looking coastal freighter of 2000-3000 tons. During the approach period a. . .destroyer passed five miles west of us, pinging [with sonar] constantly.

1103-1513 The sea became glassy so we ran deep approaching Blanche Bay. We passed at least three, possibly four, echo ranging patrol vessels off the entrance. An erratic set made it necessary to check our position every quarter hour with sets of bearings taken quickly on account of the patrols around us and the numerous planes that were seen each time we raised the periscope. We finally got a good set up on six vessels anchored in the lower reach of Simpson Harbor. These ships presented an overlapping target which I computed to be 1,750 feet in length. The six bow tubes were made ready for low speed shots and we had just a mile to go to the 8,000 yard range circle. So I raised the periscope for a final fix preliminary to steadying on the firing course and, as I did, the periscope was zoomed by a small plane and the shore battery on either Raluana or Praed Point opened up and fired rapidly. The light explosions of the shells were heard close aboard and I observed two patrol vessels head over toward us. At this point the forward torpedo room reported that we had been struck over the wardroom. We abandoned the attack, turned around and went deep.

1513-2100 Cleared Blanche Bay entrance and retreated to the north with a surface escort of several vessels which were unable to locate us accurately despite a continuous chorus of pinging. Only two depth charges were felt that were close enough to cause real concern but the boat was a mess from the heat and sweat of our almost full day of silent running and the several inches of pressure which had accumulated made the atmosphere so oppressive that I decided we were getting nowhere that way, so we surfaced and cleared out on four engines. On surfacing two patrols were seen, one on the port bow and one just abaft the port beam about two miles away. It was quite dark and I doubt they saw us for we outdistanced them quickly without being fired on. Thus, we missed our day of glory by just ten or fifteen minutes—a heart-breaking experience. . . .

Three days later, *Guardfish's* captain moved his boat's patrol station to the vicinity of the city of Wewak, New Guinea. At about noon on the first of February, Klakring spotted masts of two ships through his periscope. The ships were at anchor well inside Wewak harbor, and he decided to go in and get them. He carefully maneuvered the boat though the harbor entrance, again using charted objects for navigational fixes. Three and a half heart-palpitating hours went by. Suddenly *Guardfish* lurched and with a grinding crunch, heaved upward, throwing men to the deck throughout the boat. With her bow sticking out of the water, she was set solidly on an uncharted reef. Klakring described the harrowing event in his report:

I backed down immediately but then grounded aft. . . .We then resorted to an old river boat trick and went ahead on the port side with right full rudder and twisted the stern out 30° using the grounded bow as a pivot. . . . When it first became apparent that we were grounded both fore and aft, the confidential publications were assembled for destruction and preliminary arrangements were made to abandon ship in case we were badly holed by bombing, as was very likely under the circumstances. But in spite of the exposure of twenty feet of the submarine above the surface in full view of the beach for a period of about five minutes, we came off unmolested, which I gratefully consider a remarkable escape. . . .Both sound-heads were flooded and the pitometer log was damaged. I made no further attempt to get inside the harbor but stood out to seaward and surfaced at 2034.

"This third patrol of the *Guardfish* has been an exhaustive one in many ways," wrote Klakring as he closed out his report:

During one two week period the ship was depth charged six times and attacked by gun fire on the surface three times at night. Enemy submarines were encountered twice at night during this same period. The abortive attempt to penetrate Rabaul—and its aftermath were distressing physically and mentally. But overshadowing all the rest, the almost utterly helpless situation where the ship was grounded in Wewak harbor proved the mettle of the ship's company and convinced the commanding officer that we can't lose this or any war as long as our ships are supplied with men like them. . . .

For his courage and heroism during the third war patrol, the navy gave Lieutenant Commander Klakring his third Navy Cross award. The crew's reward, as the third patrol ended on February 15, 1943, was R&R at Brisbane, Australia—in itself a wild and woolly adventure.

The Missing Story

Nobody in the conning tower watch ever mentioned the fourth war patrol of *Guardfish*. The reason was that the navy officially classified the fourth run as "unsuccessful." A "successful" patrol was one in which the submarine achieved her assigned mission. In most cases, a sub's assignment was unrestricted warfare; that is, its mission was to seek out and destroy enemy shipping. Success was usually defined as sinking at least one ship, but the ship had to be considered of significant tonnage to be counted. That definition was a loose one, but seems to have been, at a minimum, around 200 to 1,500 tons.

When a boat completed a "successful" patrol, navy officials awarded every member of the ship's company his silver Submarine Combat Pin, which looked like a wartime submarine. Then officials added a gold star to the pin for each subsequent successful run. All submariners wore their combat pins with pride—and all were chagrined by an "unsuccessful" patrol, such as the fourth run of *Guardfish*.

It began March 9, 1943, when *Guardfish* departed Brisbane and traveled directly north, up the eastern coast of Australia to Bougainville in the Solomon Islands group. By that time forty-eight enlisted members of the original sixty-six had left the boat for other duties; many to man new submarines. "Thus with this large enlisted turnover and with only two qualified officers remaining on board besides the commanding officer," explained Klakring, "*Guardfish* began her fourth war patrol with a ship's company so inexperienced as to approach the danger point.

Spending a great deal of time in training exercises, the boat moved north and west to patrol supply lines flowing from Truk and the Philippines to the Japanese-controlled war front. Finally she went to New Guinea, before being ordered to return to Brisbane. She arrived back at port on April 30.

During the patrol Klakring spotted a total of thirteen enemy ships. He attempted two bold attacks, but broke off both when the Japanese discovered the boat and attempted to sink her. *Guardfish* suffered some light damage from the depth charging, and was lucky to escape relatively unscathed. Burt Klakring, the holder of three Navy Cross awards for his valorous command of *Guardfish*, was transferred back to the States after returning to Brisbane. He left the war front for about a year, assigned as an instructor of officers at the Submarine School, New London.

The famous boat was assigned a new skipper: Lieutenant Commander Norvell Gardiner Ward.

Chapter Four

More Sea Stories

The New Skipper

Thirty-one year old Lieutenant Commander Norvell Gardiner Ward was a calm, cool, steely-eyed professional. He had the self-assured movements, erect posture and lean build of an athlete. In fact, Ward—known as "Bub" by his friends and admirers—had been an All-American lacrosse player at the United States Naval Academy. His heroism was not limited to sports, however. He once carried a mortally wounded shipmate off the submarine *USS Seadragon* during a Japanese air attack on the Cavite Naval Base in the Philippines, a couple of days after the onset of the war. The shrapnel that killed Ensign Samuel H. Hunter also wounded Ward, who recovered and made five war patrols on *Seadragon*. He went to the submarine *USS Gato* as executive officer for two war patrols. His first command was on *Guardfish*, two weeks after his promotion to Lieutenant Commander.

Ward indoctrinated his *Guardfish* officers with a philosophy that endeared him to his enlisted crewmen. Jerry Howarth, who was the communications officer when I boarded *Guardfish*, recently told me about his initial instruction from the captain. "If you want respect from the enlisted men," Ward advised "you have to give them respect." I personally heard Ward repeat that motto, with the emphatic addition, "but do not accept inefficiency." Ward added, "If it were not for chiefs

Guardfish's War Patrols Five Through Seven

Map 2

[chief petty officers], the navy would not be able to function." Members of his old crew revere Ward—no, idolize him—to this day.

The Native Rescue Story

One of the sea stories that I heard on watch had to do with Ward's first (and *Guardfish's* fifth) war patrol, when she rescued a group of natives from a Japanese-held island. Nobody in the conning tower watch could satisfactorily explain the circumstances that led to the event. I could understand it if the boat had been assigned to evacuate Australians or Europeans, but why natives? Other than an entry in the boat's fifth patrol report that *Guardfish* performed "a special task," nothing more was mentioned about it. I was unable to find a copy of the secret report that the captain wrote about that mission. Sam Brewer, however, referred me to a book that related much of the intriguing story.[3]

Most of the island chains north of Australia were protectorates of Great Britain. Australia, a member of the British Commonwealth, was responsible for the governing and policing of those islands. Members of the Australian government became apprehensive when Japan invaded China in 1937 and declared that all of "greater southeast Asia" was in their interest. The Aussie response was to install special agents throughout their islands, because they suspected the Japanese might invade them as well. The agents, called Coastwatchers, were provided with short-wave radio equipment with which they could directly report any Japanese activities to headquarters in Australia. The government assigned two men from its navy to the island of Bougainville (a lieutenant at the northern end of the island, and a petty officer at the southern end), located in the northern end of the Solomon Islands group about 1,300 miles due north of Brisbane, Australia. High mountains cover the island, which has more land area than the American state of Delaware. The native population, Melanesians, are black-skinned and have bushy, tightly curled hair.

The Japanese occupation of Bougainville began in early March 1942. They also took over the remainder of the Solomon Islands, which stretch about 400 miles in a southeasterly direction past Guadalcanal.

---

[3] *The Coast Watchers,* by Eric A. Feldt (Doubleday, New York, 1979).

American marines launched an attack against Guadalcanal from New Zealand on August 7, 1942, the first Allied ground offensive of the Pacific War. The Japanese initiated and supported their counter-offensive against the marines from their bases at Rabaul and Bougainville. The Coastwatchers in Bougainville were thus able to give advanced warnings of some Japanese air and naval attacks launched against the Guadalcanal area. The opposing forces engaged in a fierce land, sea, and air warfare for many months for control of Guadalcanal. Finally, in February of 1943, after six months of violent combat, the Japanese admitted defeat by withdrawing from Guadalcanal. Fifteen months after the Pearl Harbor attack, the tide of the war had finally turned.

Few of the Melanesian natives on Bougainville cooperated with the Japanese during their first few months of occupation. As the Japanese wreaked vengeance on them, however, they grudgingly offered cooperation. Some of the Melanesians actively joined the Japanese and fought against not only strangers on the island but their uncooperative native brothers as well.

The Japanese and Melanesians finally succeeded in disorganizing the Coastwatcher's activities on Bougainville. Almost the whole island was pro-Japanese after fifteen months of occupation, and the lives of the plantation owners, merchants, missionaries and their families were in jeopardy. The Coastwatcher Australian lieutenant arranged by radio to have some of the endangered people evacuated. With Lieutenant Norvell G. Ward serving as executive officer and navigator, *USS Gato* was the first submarine to be assigned to the rescue. On the night of March 29, 1943, under the noses of the Japanese, she picked up fifty-one evacuees in Teop Harbor on the northeastern side of the island.

The Coastwatcher lieutenant finally succeeded in contacting the remainder of the imperiled inhabitants. He had these people travel to the west side of the island from their various locations and meet at Empress Augusta Bay. Their trips were rigorous and dangerous because of the long distances over rugged mile-high mountains, Japanese patrols, and enemy natives. In fact, two of the natives were killed by the Japanese while they were en route to the rendezvous. As the weary fugitives arrived at the coast, the lieutenant transmitted his request for another submarine to pick them up.

The Fifth War Patrol Rescues

Guardfish, now under the command of Norvell G. Ward, left Brisbane May 25, 1943 assigned to the same areas she patrolled during the
previous "dry" run under Klakring. However, this time she came across
twenty-three enemy ships and attacked two of them. Although *Guardfish*
was severely depth charged, Captain Ward managed to sink one freighter
and damage another. It was near the end of the patrol when the high
command diverted *Guardfish* to perform a special mission.

Ensign Kenneth G. Curtis, *Guardfish's* gunnery officer, led the first
of the rescue landings. He was what we called a "mustang," an officer
who had been an enlisted man before he obtained his commission. "On
our fifth patrol we were directed to go to Tulagi, about twenty miles
north of Guadalcanal," Ken recalled from his home in Wolfeboro, New
Hampshire. "We were to off-load torpedoes there to make room for extra
people. Then we were to go up the Slot [a passageway between two
chains of islands leading between Bougainville and Guadalcanal] to pick
up survivors of the cruiser *USS Helena*, that the Japanese had sunk."
When *Guardfish* reached Tulagi, however, the mission was changed and
the boat was ordered to pick up a group of people at Empress Augusta
Bay on Bougainville.

Ken recalled the mission as if it had happened yesterday. "We arrived at Empress Augusta Bay and sighted the prearranged visual signal,
which was a large sheet facing toward the sea," he began:

> I was directed to pick three men and a signalman to go ashore with me on
> the first boat. Later that evening the evacuees lit a signal fire and *Guard-
> fish* closed the beach to a safe distance. When we launched our rubber
> boat, I had a .45-caliber pistol and the four enlisted men were armed with
> Thompson submachine guns. *Guardfish* then hauled out, as we paddled
> toward the signal fire.
>
> Beyond the breakers we called out for identification and, when we were
> assured it was the correct, we landed and sent a signal back to the boat
> with a light-gun. *Guardfish* then moved in and launched the rest of the
> rubber boats.

It was not an easy task. "The breakers were high, and our first
boatload of people capsized," continued Ken, who remembered:

The following boatloads were launched using friendly natives to bring the boats through the surf by hanging on the sides until they were free of the surf. We had about six rubber boats and evacuated Coastwatchers, downed Australian aviators, native policemen of New Guinea, Chinese civilians, Australian Commandos. There were also two well-armed, very large New Zealand Maoris. In all we got sixty evacuees and transferred them to a small surface craft near Tulagi. We then returned to Bougainville for another sixty evacuees. The second landing, farther north, was led by Lieutenant (junior grade) James D. Schnepp.

When the first group of evacuees came aboard, all hand grenades were collected in a pillowslip and thrown overboard for safety. When I made my inspection of the boat, before I went on the 12:00 p.m. to 4:00 a.m. watch, I heard a bumping noise in the after battery compartment. It was a loose hand grenade. After that we really thought we had them all. However, the next morning I went into the mess hall—and one of the Australian Commandos was busy disarming a hand grenade as a souvenir for a crew member!

The evacuees bunked throughout the boat, even in the after room. "Some slept in the torpedo rooms, some in the crew's quarters," Sam Brewer explained. Many crewmen gave their bunks to evacuees while they used bunks of other men who were on watch. "We had a Chinese merchant from the islands. He had a little strong box with him that had all his earthly possessions. We also had one of the most famous New Guinea policemen. He was quite an individual, a truly brave man." The evacuees had never been to sea, and "they were all sea sick. The odor, the aroma, was terrible. They were in the bunks and they upchucked all over the torpedo racks and we had a tough time of it," Sam reminisced. "When we got back to Australia [August 2, 1943] about a week after we dropped the last people at Tulagi, the boat still smelled bad."

The Marine Landing Story

Another story I often heard discussed concerned the landing of a group of marines on Bougainville. I discovered that the true story is more complicated than the versions I heard so many years ago. In fact, there was not one but several landings, and marines were not the only ones put ashore.

Guardfish's sixth war patrol, her second long patrol in succession, lasted seventy-one days, from August 24 to November 3, 1943. She spent a total of twenty-five days on two special missions to Bougainville, and twenty-nine days on a normal patrol against enemy shipping between Truk and Rabaul. Thirty-three enemy ships were sighted, and the four attacks that followed resulted in the sinking of two freighters. Captain Ward decided not to attack some of the ships in order to avoid jeopardizing the secret operations in progress.

Guardfish's missions to Bougainville were in preparation for the American invasion of that island, which followed closely in her wake. The endorsement letter by the commander of Submarine Squadron Eight, attached to *Guardfish's* sixth war patrol report, revealed that Norvell G. Ward's reputation as a fearless submarine skipper was growing. "*Guardfish* was handpicked for the two hazardous and highly important special tasks because of her previously demonstrated ability to handle such assignments," read the report. "The choice was amply justified by the results obtained."

The first secret landing, which took place shortly after leaving Brisbane—probably early September—was made in order to determine the location of Japanese outposts and to find a good site for an airfield for fighter aircraft. A total of about twenty-five men were in the scouting party, including native police who acted as guides. The field was to be built near Empress Augusta Bay by navy SeaBees (Construction Battalion) shortly after the invasion. The field's purpose was to put fighter planes within reach of the main enemy base at Rabaul.

Ken Curtis, *Guardfish's* gunnery officer, remembered a close call during this mission:

On the sixth war patrol we took a scouting party to Empress Augusta Bay. It was composed of American marines, SeaBees, New Guinea native police, and one New Zealand Maori. After a couple of days we picked up the same party. When we left to return them to Tulagi the captain decided to bombard Cape Torokina, on the north end of the bay, at night with our 4"-50 deck gun. Japanese troops were located there. We were going to sort of hide behind a small island and lob shells over it and ladder our shots, by varying our elevation and deflection, to hit Torokina. Captain Ward and a marine lieutenant colonel, in charge of the landing party, were on the bridge and ready. The captain was about to give the "commence firing" when the radar operator reported the radar was out. So the skipper said, 'Well forget it, we won't fire because we can't tell the range.' Just as well. We determined later that the nearby island was heavily fortified with 88mm guns. If we had fired we probably would have been blown out of the water by those guns, because we were so close.

About a month later on October 19, *Guardfish* picked up essentially the same group of men at Tulagi. Captain Ward's secret report about this voyage to Bougainville has some interesting details:

Approached Cape Torokina. . .arriving. . .at dawn [October 27]. Submerged and proceeded directly to Atsinima Bay [north of the cape], arriving at 1000. Sat on bottom until dark; surfaced and disembarked First Party, the last boat leaving the ship at 2020. Remained in position until 2100, to ascertain that party reached shore safely. Then headed north, arriving off Kiviki River at 2345, where it was planned to disembark Second Party. A fire was noted burning in vicinity of Sipai Mission, so sent a boat of natives ashore to reconnoiter. They reported the landing could be made safely as planned. At 0248, the Second Party disembarked, the *Guardfish* remaining in area until 0325 to cover landing, then departing to carry out survey mission. . . .

Included in the landing parties were members of Ferdinand, the code name for the Coastwatcher organization. "With poetic justice," explained Eric Feldt, the head of that organization and the author of a book called *The Coastwatchers*, "Ferdinand's return to Bougainville was made in the U.S. Submarine *Guardfish*, the ship that had spirited away the harried coastwatchers, soldiers, and natives three months before." Ferdinand's return was "no quixotic gesture," Feldt continued. "It was a well-laid plan for covering the landing of U.S. Marines at Torokina on the west coast of the island."

The two landing parties did not return to *Guardfish*. Their task was to infiltrate the island and establish contacts with friendly native groups. After dropping off the final landing party, the boat continued last minute preparations for the American invasion. She made a submerged reconnaissance of the sea floor off Empress Augusta Bay near the proposed invasion landing sites, using the ship's onboard *fathometer. The purpose of the depth readings was to determine the profile of the bay's bottom, looking for shoals that could give trouble to surface ships and to identify suitable landing sites. Another objective was to establish a site for a proposed U. S. minefield.

Guardfish surfaced after dark on October 28 and transmitted invaluable, last minute landing information to headquarters by radio before departing for Brisbane early the next morning. The invasion of Bougainville took place three days later, when the Third Marine Division established a beachhead. After about four months of heavy battles, the United State's forces brought the island and the surrounding sea under American control. The starving Japanese garrison, however, did not surrender until the end of the war.

The Ramming Story

While many stories circulated while on watch, the most frequently discussed event concerned the ramming of *Guardfish* by an American ship. The incident occurred late at night as the boat was on the surface heading out from Australia on what was supposed to be her seventh war patrol. Everyone I ever heard talking about the event, whether in or out of the conning tower, enlisted man or officer, was convinced that the American ship had purposely rammed *Guardfish*. "Friendly" ships and aircraft frequently attacked American submarines during the war.[4] The rule about submarine contacts seemed to be "shoot first and ask questions later." Still, neither *Guardfish* radar nor the boat's lookouts detected the approaching ship soon enough to take evasive action. Why?

Captain Ward began his report on *Guardfish's* seventh war patrol by first describing the situation that led to the collision:

Underway 2 December 1943 on seventh war patrol. . .to wage unrestricted warfare in the Bismark Archipelago-Palao-Truk area. . . . .Conducted sound tests and firing of guns in Moreton Bay and proceeded to training area for independent exercises. Rendezvoused with [Australian ships] *HMAS Stuart* and *Cowra* at 1800, 3 December 1943 for joint training. . . .

---

[4] At least thirty-two incidents of accidental or aggressive actions against American submariners by friendly forces occurred during World War II, including depth charging, torpedoing, gunfire, and ramming. Thirteen boats suffered significant damage. Three submarines, *Dorado*, *S-26,* and *Seawolf*, went down with 221 men.

Around midnight, *Guardfish* was at battle stations engaged in a simulated night surface attack on the *Stuart* in an area some fifty miles north and 100 miles east of Brisbane. The radar operator trained the antenna back at the friendly destroyer some six miles directly astern of *Guardfish* and fed a series of range and bearing readings to the *TDC (Torpedo Data Computer) operator. Grinding away noisily, the dials on that mechanical monster's panel kept track of the target's course and speed, as well as our torpedo firing conditions. The attack plan was developing nicely. Suddenly, a ship ahead of *Guardfish* emerged from the murky darkness on a deadly collision course, forcing Captain Ward to take immediate evasive action. When he realized that the impact was unavoidable he sounded the collision alarm, which instructed the crew to lock down all the watertight bulkhead doors. Seconds later the attacking ship rammed *Guardfish's* starboard side aft of the conning tower. The submarine immediately took on a starboard list and settled down by the stern. The ship did not stop, as a friendly ship would, but instead disappeared into the night. Although Ward called for every compartment to issue an immediate damage report, nothing was heard from those compartments aft of the conning tower. Ward feared the worse: it looked as though the rear of the boat had flooded.

"When no reports were immediately forthcoming from the four after compartments," Ward wrote a few hours later in a detailed "Statement Of Commanding Officer" regarding the collision, "I ordered the word passed for the men in the forward compartments to lay up on deck through the conning tower, at the same time ordering the Quartermaster to train his searchlight around. . .to signal the *Stuart* of the collision." The crew interpreted Ward's order to go topside differently than the captain intended.

"My recollections are rather vivid," explained Sam Brewer, who offers this recollection of the harrowing event:

> We were at a drill situation and the collision alarm went off and we felt the ramming. The escape hatch in the after torpedo room was filled with potatoes. We had put cloth across the bottom of the escape hatch, filled it with potatoes on the top side, then secured the outer hatch. When the collision alarm went off, we were told to come topside. We rather hurriedly cut the potatoes loose and they went all over the place. There was no ladder through the hatch, so Larry [Laurence B.] Hall pushed me up and I

opened the escape hatch topside. Then the five of us in the after room at the time, went up. The boat was decidedly setting down aft, the main deck was only slightly above the water line. There was no panic and there was no sign of immediate sinking. . . .We were somewhere in the order of 100 or 200 miles off the coast, in what was called a Secure Area, a practice area. After that night's drills we were to go off on our own, head north to our patrol area, but naturally we had to reverse course and go back into Brisbane. At the time we did not know how much damage had been done. Luckily, it hit between the forward engine room and the after engine room at the heavy bulkhead. That probably saved us from the inner hull being penetrated. We were not unhappy to go back to Brisbane. It was a great liberty town."

Paul D. Snyder, the ship's baker, tells a similar story. He was in the after-battery compartment at the time of the collision. When word came over the battle telephone for men to go topside, crew members opened the after-battery hatches and, in the process, spilled potatoes everywhere. Most of the crew gathered forward of the conning tower in the dark and awaited further orders. According to Paul, someone on the bridge trained the searchlight back toward the stern to determine the extent of damage. He remembers being amused by the first thing the brilliant light revealed: the stern end of one of the crew members, whose only clothing was some badly torn undershorts.

"After the ramming we thought we were sinking, sinking by the stern," recalls Jerry Howarth, who was promoted to assistant engineer and communications officer. "It turned out it was a ballast tank on the starboard side, aft, that was ruptured and then flooded. That caused the stern to go down." As I remember it, he continued,

Captain Ward gave the word for all hands to come topside. . . .Now I was down below at that time and our executive officer, Dick [Richard H.] Bowers, grabbed hold of me. He said, 'Come on Jerry, let's go aft and see what damage we have.' So I never did get topside. I remember going back through the compartments from the control room. I'm not too sure what enlisted man was with us, but I'm sure there were one or two. We went back through the compartments and when we hit the engine room we found there was damage to a starboard engine.

Guardfish, photographed after she was rammed at sea by YO-20, an oil transport ship.

According to the patrol report, which was produced after returning to Brisbane to assess the total damage inflicted on the boat, "The sixth main ballast's starboard tank was ruptured, starboard main induction line was crushed, the number one main engine muffler and topside piping were demolished, the pressure hull was dented and the number two main engine crankcase was cracked."

The ship that rammed *Guardfish* was eventually identified as the YO-20, an oil-transport ship of the United States Army Transport Service. I recently asked "Bub" Ward (who retired as a Rear Admiral) if the army ship had intentionally rammed *Guardfish*. He thought not. "The small army oiler was headed into the approaches of the Brisbane River, and no one knew it was there," he explained. "As far as I was concerned," continued Ward,

it was not supposed to be in the area. My bridge watch doped off. We were out exercising with an Australian destroyer. It was at night and we were in the process of conducting a night surface attack, simulated of course, on the destroyer when the accident occurred. I believe, and I can say I'm quite sure, that all the lookouts were concentrated more on the destroyer than they were in maintaining an active watch in their sectors. The radar was probably, at my direction, not in the search mode at the time. In those days we didn't have *PPI on the *Guardfish*. In order to take a range, the radar antenna had to be stopped and focussed directly on the target. Then, after it had the range, it would resume its slow search. I'm guessing now, that it took thirty seconds or so for the antenna to make a revolution. . . .

Lieutenant Commander Ward, the consummate professional, was not one to blame others for his difficulties, and he certainly was not one to get into an inter-service controversy. If he encountered a problem, it was his responsibility to recognize it and take care of it. In order to avoid being blind-sided again, Ward determined to get a PPI for the ship's radar as soon as possible. Also, after navy specialists and Australian shipwrights at Brisbane repaired the collision damage, and before the real seventh run, I am confident Ward had a new set of lookouts assigned for battle stations.

Two days after Christmas 1943, following her repairs at Brisbane, *Guardfish* sailed out to patrol the shipping lanes between the islands of Truk and Guadalcanal. Although I didn't hear any sea stories about that run, it was another grand success for Captain Ward and his crew. A total of thirty-six enemy vessels were sighted, although only two attacks were able to be launched. The result was well worth the effort, for Ward sent both an oil tanker and a Japanese destroyer to the bottom. After serving briefly as a "lifeguard" ship off Truk, *Guardfish* arrived at Pearl Harbor on February 18, 1944. Nine days later, she left Pearl and returned to the States for a major overhaul at the United States Navy's Bethlehem Submarine Repair Base in San Francisco. Shortly before I became a crew member in May, the repair base's radar repair group finally installed that PPI-scope Ward was intent on getting.

Chapter Five

Off to Convoy College

We wound our way through the entrance to Pearl Harbor about noon on June 1, seven days after leaving San Francisco. The devastation from the surprise December 7, 1941 attack was still visible more than two years after it was delivered. Everywhere I looked, twisted hulks of warships protruded from the water. I admit seeing the wreckage in that manner was rather unnerving.

There was no visible damage at the Submarine Base. Fresh supplies poured aboard *Guardfish* for the first four days following our arrival, including food, fuel, fresh water, deck gun ammunition, and torpedoes. The flurry of activities impressed me; there were men scurrying everywhere. An officer with a clipboard in hand documented food storage locations, as his team stuffed packaged and canned items into every nook and cranny, into every pigeonhole throughout the boat. Base personnel, with their fuel and water tanker-trucks on the dock, draped large hoses over to the boat. The main deck was covered with those snake-like hoses and the smell of diesel fuel was everywhere. Another loading crew carried live ammunition by hand across the deck to topside watertight lockers and down the after-battery hatch into the ship's magazine.

Torpedo loading was the most impressive of all. Transfixed on the pier, I watched as the crane lifted a torpedo from the carrier vehicle on the dock and swung it into the air over *Guardfish*. The 2,000-pound underwater missile had a warhead containing 600 pounds of high explosive. The crane operator slowly lowered the fish toward the submarine's

main deck, as a torpedoman guided it down onto the sloping skids that
led through the loading hatch. For the torpedo crews, loading twenty-
four torpedoes into the boat was a time consuming, backbreaking, nerve-
wracking job.

We faced ten days of sea trials and training before *Guardfish* left for
her eighth war patrol, so there was no time for liberties. Everything was
strictly business. Well, almost everything. The pending reentry into the
war arena by such a famous submarine as *Guardfish* did not go unnoticed in the social circles of Pearl Harbor. A couple of days before our
departure, the entire ship's company received an invitation to a party, to
be held in our honor.

The gathering took place in a large white Colonial mansion on a hill
overlooking the harbor. It was a glittering gala, with officers in their
dress whites and ladies in their jeweled finery, dancing and toasting and
eating. I felt completely out of my element, and I don't think I was the
only enlisted man who felt that way. However, this celebration was an
indication of the democratization that was infiltrating the navy, albeit
little by little.

Our departure day, June 14, 1944, finally arrived. Shortly after we
reached the open sea, the captain told us over the speaker system that our
patrol area was to be north and west of the Philippine Islands, from the
Straits of Luzon into the South China Sea. He also announced that our
mission was "unrestricted warfare against the enemy." We were to be
part of a coordinated attack group, or "wolf pack" (as similar German
operations in the Atlantic were known) with United States submarines
Thresher, *Piranha* and *Apogon*. The commander of the group's operations, Captain William Vincent O'Regan, was aboard *Guardfish*. O'Regan's nickname was "Mickey," so he named his wolf pack "Mickey·
Finns." Our patrol area was the eastern sector of "Convoy College,"
bounded by the coasts of northern Luzon, southern Formosa (Taiwan)
and China.

Four days after leaving Pearl we made an eight-hour refueling stop
at those small mounds of coral sand known as Midway Islands. A
number of submarines and other vessels went aground on the reefs
adjacent to Sand Island's very narrow channel, and the wreckage served
to remind skippers of the danger of entry. In addition to the remains of
vessels, the islands of Midway were a home for thousands of "Gooney
Birds," large, seagoing albatrosses that patrol much of the Pacific Ocean.

We left Midway and resumed our westward voyage toward our patrol area, staying on the surface most of the time. We were in company with the other submarines, though we rarely saw them. The nearest boats were usually over the horizon, but we occasionally picked up their *radar indications. After finishing our watch, those of us in the conning tower often got permission, one at a time, to go topside for a quick smoke on the cigarette deck. The weather, sea, and sky were beautiful. A couple of Midway's "Gooney Birds" flew behind us for days. Flying fish and porpoises were our constant companions. It was a beautiful, and often breathtaking, scene.

The war front was no longer around the Solomon Islands. American forces had captured the Gilbert and Marshall Islands during and after *Guardfish's* seventh war patrol. The fighting for control of New Guinea by Allied forces began during the boat's overhaul in San Francisco and continued during the entire eighth run. The American invasion of Saipan, the first island in the strategically important Marianas group, began as *Guardfish* set out on patrol number eight. The critically important island chain was only 1,500 miles east of the Japanese-controlled Philippines, and 1,400 miles south of Tokyo, Japan. Violent land, sea, and air battles for control of Saipan were in full swing as we passed about 800 miles north, on our way to "Convoy College." It was only then that we got our first inkling that a war was in progress.

Twice on June 28 we were attacked by planes, each of which forced us to dive to escape destruction. The second plane triggered our *IFF transponder several times as it made a bombing run on us, which indicated that the aircraft was a friendly plane checking us out. Nevertheless, it continued its hostile approach as our boat labored to get under the water.

The boat's slow submergence probably had something to do with a sticking vent valve on one of the ballast tanks, but the captain was not certain. He made a submerged periscopic examination of the boat's topside to see if he could spot anything else. I remember hearing him comment to the officer of the deck, in a matter-of-fact voice, "There are air leaks all over the place." I did not realize the seriousness of the situation at the time.

Our lives changed radically just four days later when we reached our patrol area. Each morning at dawn we submerged as normal, not merely for a trim dive but to stay down all day. A pall of quiet slumber fell over

Guardfish's War Patrol Eight

Map 3

the boat. The deck was motionless, and all we heard was the quiet background hum of electric motors and muted speech. We manned the underwater sound equipment continuously, both submerged and on the surface. Our submerged patrol depth was usually around 100 to 120 feet. Every fifteen minutes the officer of the deck in the conning tower called down the hatch to the diving officer to have him bring the boat to periscope depth. When we reached 60 feet, the officer of the deck raised the search periscope, made a quick spin around to look for airplanes, then slowly and methodically scanned the horizon for smoke from enemy ships. After he was satisfied that all was clear, we returned to 120 feet.

Wolfpack leader O'Regan's instructions called for all boats in the pack to listen for coded radio transmissions from the others during the first few minutes of each hour. We did that by sticking our periscopic SD radar masts out of the water, with our radio communication equipment connected to the mast, using it as a radio antenna. Thus, any of the boats could report enemy contacts to the others, even though we were all submerged.

The Straits between the northern tip of Luzon and the southern end of Formosa are relatively shallow and filled with small islands. There are two major east-west deep water channels between those islands. Bashi Channel, the northernmost one, was our first patrol assignment. The boats in the pack, spaced about twenty miles apart, patrolled below surface, north and south, across the channel. *Guardfish* spent the fourth of July dodging twenty fishing sampans. O'Regan did not want to reveal the presence of a pack of American submarines, so the pack skippers were ordered to avoid contact with and not attack the sampans.

Very early the next morning our sound operator picked up sonar pinging from our first ship contact, an anti-submarine patrol boat. Our radar detected him forty minutes later at a range of about six miles. We tracked and avoided him for a couple of hours. Then, after we submerged at dawn, we changed course and headed for the nearby southern tip of Formosa. Nevertheless, the patrol boat's pinging stayed with us. We heard distant, mysterious underwater explosions shortly before I came on watch at 8:00 a.m.

My Radioman friend Anthony (Tony) Ubriaco relieved me at the end of my watch on the sonar, and I moved to the stool at the inactive SJ radar. As the officer of the deck, Lt. Donald C. Bowman raised the periscope to make an observation. At that moment an earsplitting, bone rattling, explosion rocked our starboard side. Another explosion followed immediately on our port side. The source of the explosions became quickly apparent: an unseen airplane had straddled us with bombs.

"Take her down, flood negative!" the officer of the deck shouted to the control room. "Rudder amidship, all ahead full!" he ordered the helmsman.

"Rudder's amidship, all answered ahead full, sir," came the reply.

"Make the depth two hundred feet. Check for damage," Bowman ordered.

The bow and stern plane operators in the control room had their planes at full dive. Normally, full speed would take us to about seven knots, submerged, but not this time. Our stern probably broke out of the water because the boat took on a steep downward angle and we were slow to get down. I had to hold on to the radar cabinet and brace my feet against the inclined deck. Seconds after the explosions I looked down and saw Captain Ward climbing into the conning tower through the lower hatch. He surprised me when he laughed and had a big grin on his face as he spoke to Lieutenant Bowman. "Those SOB's caught me in the head. I stumbled and hopped my way into the control room trying to pull my pants up." A third bomb exploded overhead as we went down, but it was not as close as the first two.

The captain took the conn and had us reverse course to evade the attacking airplane. A short while later I heard him lecture the diving officer about broaching the stern, which caused us to lose propulsion during submergence. After a couple of hours at 200 feet, we went up to periscope depth and found the sky clear. The captain left the conning tower and the officer of the deck resumed normal patrol duties.

After finishing my turn on the sound gear, I was back at the inactive radar, killing time. When I remembered that I had not finished filling out my radar maintenance log, I asked the officer of the deck for permission to go down to the radio shack to complete it. I promised to come right back to take over the sound watch at the appropriate time. When he agreed, I climbed down to the control room, walked aft to the shack and sat down at the *ECM. The seat that we used was the metal spare-parts box for the SJ radar. It had a thick, green cushion on top. I sat there, straddling the box with the logbook and pencil in my hands. Suddenly, I heard another bomb splitting through the water directly overhead:

swishshshshsh. . .BOOM! The boat rolled violently, almost throwing me off the box. The sharp vibration from the depth charge caused the hull, piping, and bulkheads to crash together loudly for several seconds before merging into discordant musical tones. Cork particles from the hull coating showered the deck. My ears rang, my pulse raced, and I felt like running—but there was no place to hide. The airplane had found us again, even though we were 120 feet below the surface. For years I thought that the pilot must have seen us through the crystal clear water. It was not until recently, when I read the patrol report, that I realized he must have seen our track of leaking air bubbles Captain Ward had commented on several days earlier.

After hurriedly completing my logbook entries, I went back to the conning tower to take over the sound watch. Captain Ward was there and he had us going deeper. As we passed 230 feet, another bomb exploded, but it was far away and barely rocked the boat. Back at the sound gear, I had only been listening on the *QB for a few minutes when I heard the rapid screws of a patrol boat. It was coming directly at us from the south, probably in response to a call from the airplane. I reported the sound contact to Captain Ward. He immediately ordered, "sound battle stations." The helmsman reached to his right and actuated the battle stations alarm contactor: bong, bong, bong. . .went the alarm, softly, seventeen times.

"Rig for depth charge," the captain said calmly. "Rig for *silent running." He also called down the hatch to the diving officer, "Close all vents." Closing the vents prevented air that was leaking into our ballast tanks from marking our location on the surface.

Brink Brinkley, whose battle station was *QB/QC sound gear, quickly relieved me and I ran to the forward torpedo room. My station was with the torpedo reloading crew—about which I knew absolutely nothing. I sat on one of the torpedo racks and watched Ojay across the room. He had the *JP sound operator station at the after end, starboard side of the room, regularly reporting the patrol boat's bearing over the chest-mounted battle telephone hanging around his neck. After noting the bearing, he cranked the sound head 360 degrees to look for other possible targets. When he got back to the patrol boat, he again reported its bearing, then continued his search. Operating on silent running (with fans and air conditioning off) was really stifling. "Ojay" stripped his clothes off down to his undershorts. Cranking the sound head was a strenuous job and rivulets of sweat poured off him, soaking his shorts.

Eight minutes after we detected the patrol boat, the first depth charge exploded far astern. First we heard a "thud," as if someone outside hit the hull with a ten-pound sledge hammer (not a "click," as is often heard in the movies), followed a few seconds later by the explosion. Then we heard swishing and gurgling sounds, as water rushed through the superstructure supporting the boat's main deck. The time interval between the "thud" and the explosion, swishes, and gurgles, became shorter and shorter as the depth charges got closer: Thud. . . . boom! Thud. . .boom! Thud. .boom! ThudBOOM! I quickly learned that if no "thud" was heard, the depth charge was disastrously close to the boat. As the explosions became more violent, the ship's piping and other structures vibrated and clattered together for several seconds. No submarine movie I have ever seen has portrayed accurately the cacophonous racket brought about by a depth charge explosion.

The patrol boat stalking us dropped thirteen charges over a three or four minute period. Luckily, none of them was close enough to cause serious physical damage, but the strain on the nerves was real enough. Eventually the patrol boat left, but we stayed deep for the rest of the day. The damage control party found that either the aerial bomb or the deep dive had caused some flooding of several electrical circuits leading up to the bridge. One of the boat's three *air banks was found to be leaking. Damage Control spent the following day attempting repairs, and ended up bleeding all the air out of the damaged air bank, thereby preventing its use to surface the boat for the rest of the patrol.

The next five days were relatively uneventful. All I could think of was the oppressive heat and humidity in the conning tower while we were on the surface at night. I discovered why they called an experienced sailor an "old salt." The salt-ladened air caused salt crystals to encrust on my bare neck, back, arms, and chest. Boy, did I long for my weekly shower! The monotony was broken one day by a couple of enemy aircraft. One of them closed for an attack and forced us to make a quick dive to safety. We found out much later that the ferocious battle for American control of Saipan successfully came to an end that week.

One of the submarines in our patrol group broke radio silence on July 11 at 10:41 p. m, waking the Mickey Finns from almost a week-long slumber. *Thresher*, the westward boat, had made a radar contact twelve miles west of her position, as the pack was in the process of moving on the surface to new hunting grounds about ninety miles to the south. The target was soon determined to be a convoy of nine large ships steaming in three columns. It was surrounded by five escort vessels. *Guardfish* changed course and went to full speed on four main engines to assist *Thresher*. We picked up the convoy on our radar at a range of about fifteen miles. Our fire control party tracked the convoy on radar while we tried to get into an attack position on the port side of the Japanese ships. Visual contact was made around midnight, when our starboard lookout spotted the convoy ahead of us in the bright moonlight.

Captain O'Regan, the commander of the group's operations and stationed aboard *Guardfish*, was pleased with the way the situation was developing. "The attack doctrine at this time was working beautifully," he later explained in his report of the action. "The situation resolved itself into this: the *Thresher* was trailing astern and reporting movements of convoy. The *Apogon* was working up the starboard flank and the *Guardfish* the port flank. The *Piranha* was kept informed of the convoy's movements and was closing from the northwest at four engine speed."

O'Regan directed the *Apogon* to open the attack. At 2:30 a.m., she made a submerged radar approach (that is, with only her radar antenna out of the water). Shortly after 3:00 a.m., we heard ten sharp explosions. The blasts caused a ripple of speculation in *Guardfish*; some of us thought that two of the explosions had been torpedoes, and that the rest depth charges, while others were unsure of their origin. *Guardfish*, meanwhile, soon reached a position about nine miles ahead of the convoy, at which point we were ordered to battle stations and dived for a radar approach.

Fire control party personnel packed the conning tower. Captain Ward was working the periscope, while Ensign Curtis, with red flashlight in hand, stood on the opposite side of the scope reading its bearings and operating the lifting motor. Lieutenant Schnepp was on the *TDC at the after end (port side) of the room. Lawrence F. (Larry) Teder, the enlisted Fire Controlman, stood behind him as relief TDC operator, with his back to Brinkley, who sat at the sonar on the starboard side. The SJ radar operators, Chief Dudrey and Lieutenant Howarth, sat on the port side with their backs to the captain and Ensign Curtis. The executive officer, Lt. Comdr. Alexander K. Tyree, was there as well, as a backup for the captain. Two enlisted men manned the ship's log and helm positions. I was a relief radar operator, but since I had no deck to stand on, I straddled the lip of the lower hatch—and waited.

The dark room glowed softly with a low intensity red lighting. The two radar screens illuminated the faces of the operators with an eerie radiance; green light from the A-scope, yellow from the PPI. We were tracking the leading ship in the convoy, trying to obtain firing solutions on the TDC. It wasn't working, however, because we were too far away. Closing the distance meant we had to get past the convoy's two forward escorts without being detected by their sonar. It was a dangerous proposition because of the bright moon, and Captain Ward was concerned the enemy lookouts might see our radar antenna and the sizable phosphorescent wake stirred up by it and our periscope shears. Instead, he decided to go deep to avoid the escorts.

"Make the depth one hundred feet," Ward said.

"One hundred feet, aye."

"Right full rudder, steady on course zero one six."

"Zero one six, aye."

"All ahead one third."

"All answered ahead one third, sir."

"QB sound, keep a sharp watch," Ward intoned coolly. "Tell me if either escort switches to short-scale pinging [which indicates that the enemy may have a sonar contact at short range]. Keep the escort bearings coming to me. Tell JP sound to maintain a continuous 360 degree search."

We were barely creeping through the water at about two and a half knots, but the convoy's closing speed was nearly thirteen knots. We all held our breath while the first escort passed down our starboard side to the east of us. One down and one to go.

"QB, now give me continuous bearings to the escort on the port side," Ward ordered.

Ward's gamble paid off. After we passed the second escort undetected, the captain resumed the submerged radar attack.

"Make the depth sixty feet"

"Make ready all bow tubes."

"Up 'scope"

"Plane up to forty-two feet."

"All ahead two-thirds."

"We have ready lights on all bow tubes, sir."

"Radar, give me a range to the nearest ship in the convoy."

"3,800 yards, sir."

"Stand by to mark the bearing," said the captain, as he trained the periscope on the target. "Mark!" The tension mounted with each passing exchange.

"Three five nine."

"TDC, how does that check out?"

"We've lost our solution light, Captain."

"Very well, keep radar ranges coming."

"Stand by to mark 'scope. Mark!"

"Zero zero two."

"Captain, it looks like they've changed course."

The convoy had made a radical course change to the southeast shortly before dawn. We went to standard speed (about six knots) and changed course, but submerged there was no way we could keep up. A short while later we secured from battle stations, surfaced in the dawning daylight, and fired up four main engines. Although we gave it everything we had and tried to again overtake the convoy as it steamed westward toward the Babuyan Channel, our effort was to no avail. By this time the convoy was covered by air as well as naval escorts. On six separate occasions we were driven down by Japanese airplanes, and we lost contact with the ships. The disappointment in the conning tower was palpable.

The probable course of the enemy ships was plotted as we traveled on the surface, over the horizon from the convoy, until *dead reckoning placed us ahead of it. The captain repeatedly sent messages to the engine room to reduce the smoke produced by our diesel engines so we would not give away our position. In the early afternoon we turned back for what we hoped would be an intercept course—but the ships were not there. We discontinued the search at 6:30 p.m., July 12, reversed course and resumed the voyage to our new patrol area. *Piranha* and *Thresher* reported by radio that they were also heading to the new station.

We repeatedly tried to contact *Apogon*, but our efforts proved futile. A chilling fear spread throughout the boat that *Apogon* had been lost. Had the enemy gotten the better of our group? The faces of the crew showed few smiles, just tightly set jaws and grim determination.

Chapter Six

A Busy Night

We received good news on the night of July 14 as we plied westward through Balintang Channel toward a new patrol station: *Apogon* was safe, although she had sustained serious battle damage. A ship in the enemy convoy she was attacking had rammed her periscope shears, destroyed her periscopes and radar antennas, and flooded her conning tower. Fortunately, no lives were lost, but it had been a close call. She informed the pack commander, O'Regan, of her abort as she blindly limped back to base. The news that *Apogon* was safe raced through *Guardfish's* narrow hull, and some of the men even woke their sleeping buddies to share the good news.

I was on my July 14th night watch when a rash of problems disabled the SJ radar. The first problem involved a serious component breakdown. Dudrey and I worked on it for over seven hours before we got it back in commission, after which I went back on an uneventful watch. Shortly after I was relieved, the radar's power source, a DC-to-AC motor generator set went out of control. The set's finicky amplidyne motor needed frequent adjustment. After a couple of shut downs, Dudrey left instructions for the conning tower watch to call me to make further adjustments. Unfortunately for me, this piece of equipment was located below the control room deck in the auxiliary room. I spent much of my off-watch time down in that oily, steamy, tightly crammed "hell hole" over the next two days. The motor-generator refused to cooperate. Every time I wanted to get some sleep, it broke down again. To this day I remember the exhaustion and frustration I experienced dealing with it.

We reached our new patrol area about midday on July 15, surfaced, and fired up all four of our diesel engines. Excitement coursed through the boat, because the roaring engines usually signaled to the crew that we were out to chase an enemy ship. According to a radio message we received, a convoy was somewhere in our general vicinity, northwest of Luzon. O'Regan had the three boats left in the pack (*Piranha*, *Thresher*, and *Guardfish*) make a coordinated search spaced twenty miles apart. *Thresher* received the order for a course change, but *Piranha* somehow missed the message and continued searching to the northeast. The mistake was our good fortune, for it was *Piranha* that made contact early in the morning of July 16. She reported a convoy of twelve ships traveling in three columns about 100 miles directly north of the northwestern tip of Luzon. She reported she was traveling on the surface trying to get into position for a submerged attack. While the news was welcomed by all of us, *Guardfish* and *Thresher* were out of position, about 110 miles to the west of the convoy's location. O'Regan ordered full speed on the surface and we moved as fast as we could to join *Piranha*.

Near the middle of my morning watch Lieutenant Bowman, the officer of the deck, sighted smoke on the horizon off our starboard bow. It turned out to be a new convoy heading south, a different one than that reported by *Piranha*. Our lookouts quickly determined that this convoy had at least two airplanes overhead acting as escorts. Bowman called Captain Ward to the bridge. The skipper immediately ordered what we referred to as an "end around," a change of course roughly to the convoy's heading in order to stay over the horizon as we pulled ahead to an attack position. Simultaneously, the captain directed Lieutenant Howarth, the communications officer, to compose a contact report and radio it to the other two boats. Twenty minutes later, one of the convoy's air escorts spotted us and banked in our direction, zeroing in for the kill. We dove for cover as fast as possible. While submerged we heard two of *Piranha's* torpedoes explode against one of the enemy ships. *Piranha's* attack, of course, revealed her presence to the Japanese and she quickly became the quarry. Her pair of torpedo blasts were soon followed by a series of forty-eight explosions. *Piranha* was taking a depth charge beating from the escorts. Knowing your fellow submariners were going through such hell without being able to assist them is a awful feeling.

We surfaced several times and tried to move ahead of our convoy, but the air cover kept driving us down, causing us to drop behind the ships. During our submerged runs we heard over twenty more underwater explosions, which meant that *Piranha* was still under attack. At 5:00 p.m. we received a message from *Thresher*. She was tracking yet a third convoy comprised of four ships and two escorts, all traveling in a westward direction. "Convoy College" (a gathering of convoys) was certainly a good code name for this place.

In spite of harassment from their planes, under cover of darkness Ward finally managed to work *Guardfish* into position ahead of our convoy. When my round of watch rolled along, I took my normal first watch position at the radar. For some unknown reason, our radar's motor generator held steady. I fervently hoped it would not decide to go out while we were tracking the enemy. The convoy was still beyond the horizon when unusual radar indications, coming from the direction of the ships we were tracking, appeared on our screen. I could tell from the width and shape of the radar pulses on the A-scope that the strange emanations were not from an American radar transmitter. I immediately reported this to the captain, who was on the bridge with the officer of the deck, Lieutenant Bowman.

The enemy's radar antenna, high atop his mast, was apparently high enough to peek over the horizon. This was one of the earliest inklings we had in the war that the Japanese had microwave radar capability. Somehow they had succeeded in copying our "secret weapon," the microwave magnetron. Captain Ward directed Lieutenant Howarth to come to the conning tower and examine the radar interference. Howarth reached the conclusion that the Japanese were attempting to jam our radar screen to make it more difficult for us to detect their ships. Actually, their signal led us right to them, and within a short time we detected the convoy on our radar screen at a range of about eleven miles.

"Battle stations torpedo," the captain ordered.

Immediately the man at the chart desk broadcast the announcement to all compartments over the *1MC and the helmsman actuated the general alarm. Men went scurrying to their battle stations throughout the boat. Dudrey climbed briskly up into the darkened conning tower and took the stool at the radar's *A-scope. Lieutenant Howarth relieved me at the PPI position. Although we were on the surface, the executive officer, Alex Tyree, took over the search periscope. The night was clear,

but there was no moon. The exec coordinated all the activities in the
conning tower. Enlisted man Larry Teder was on the TDC. Brinkley sat
at the sonar, with the equipment in standby condition. Ensign Curtis, the
gunnery and torpedo officer, was periscope bearing reader. I stood aside
until everyone was in position, then got out of their way by taking up my
familiar position straddling the lower hatch. I craned my neck to watch
the emerging picture of the convoy on the PPI screen. Lieutenant
Schnepp was in the control room plotting the target course on the *Dead
Reckoning board.

"Keep the radar rotating constantly," the captain instructed.

Initially, the radar picture of the convoy was merely a single big
blob of light, but soon we were able to distinguish *pips representing the
individual ships. Eventually, we were able to make everything out. There
were ten ships in the convoy arranged in two columns of five each. Four
escort vessels encircled the convoy; two ahead, port and starboard, and
two spread behind on the flanks. The group was traveling southwest, less
than fifty miles off Luzon's northwest coast.

"Lookouts, keep a sharp watch in your sector," I heard the captain
repeatedly call to the men topside. "Do not get distracted by the action
ahead."

When we closed range to about five miles, the captain was able to
vaguely discern the enemy ships. The phosphorescent sea was relatively
calm, rolling with long, glowing swells. He decided that we would attack on the surface and that our best approach was to let the ships pass
us so we could attack the port flank. That gave us the advantage of
having a dark background of clouds and rain squalls behind us, making
it more difficult for the Japanese to spot us. He decided on that course of
action even though "the most desirable target was leading the starboard
column." Later, one of his superiors described Ward's approach as "mas-
terful." The captain began to carry out his plan as we crept up on the
lead escort.

"Make ready all torpedo tubes, fore and aft. Open outer doors forward. Set depth at eight feet," Ward instructed.

"We have ready lights, all tubes forward, Captain."

"We have some big babies up here. A tanker leads the starboard
column, and a large AK [cargo ship] leads the port column. We will
target the lead ship in the starboard column with a spread."

Firing "a spread" of torpedoes meant that they fanned out, each one aimed slightly differently, to compensate for measurement errors and uncontrollable variations as they traveled toward the target.

The exec leaned over and studied the radar PPI. He discussed the situation with Howarth for a bit and then pointed to the pip on the radar that was our target. Each time the radar antenna swept over that pip, Dudrey and Howarth called out the target's range and bearing, which Teder then entered into the TDC. The coffee-grinder-sounding mechanical computer noisily worked away, until it's "solution light" finally came on. As Teder fed in more data, however, the light suddenly blinked off. Something was wrong.

Although the radar range measurements were very precise, the bearing readings, under the best of conditions, were not as good as optical readings. The best radar bearing accuracy could be obtained by stopping the antenna rotation and activating a bearing improvement device, called the "lobing motor." But the captain's instruction to keep the antenna rotating meant that we could not do that. The bearings had to be taken directly from the inaccurate PPI screen. A further complication was that for each measurement, Howarth had to mentally add two and a half degrees to correct the PPI observation before he called out the bearing. The exec repeatedly tried to use his periscope to get accurate bearings on the target, but there was not enough light. He reported the situation to the captain over the intercom. Ward immediately responded with a command: "Lieutenant Howarth to the bridge."

Howarth was being called topside to take optical bearings using the Target Bearing Transmitter, the *TBT, a binocular-equipped target sighting device that electrically transmitted the bearings to the conning tower. The recently installed TBT system had much better light gathering power than the periscope.

As Howarth was leaving, he turned to me and said, "Conner, take over the PPI." My head swam as I tried to read the target bearing from the PPI, add two and a half degrees and call out the corrected number to the waiting TDC operator. I stumbled and stammered and missed some observations as the antenna whizzed by the target. My mind seemed numb; I could not think straight. The exec said, "Keep those bearings coming." I stammered out additional corrected readings. The TDC solution light came on briefly, then went dark a second time.

The exec yelled at me in exasperation, "KEEP THOSE BEARINGS COMING, DAMN IT." Finally, I just called out the uncorrected readings. That kept the exec off my back until Howarth was ready.

Howarth got the TBT binoculars focused on the target ship in short order. The exec read the bearings from the TBT indicator that was mounted on the starboard side, between the periscope lift motors and the sonar. Teder fed several more sets of ranges and bearings into the TDC before jubilantly announcing, "I have a solution; it's a good one!"

The exec relayed that word to the captain. Ward responded, "Very well, fire when ready. Make a two degree spread." By fanning out the torpedoes as they went toward the target on the starboard column, the captain hoped that some of them might hit ships in the closer port column, as well.

The exec told Ensign Curtis, the mustang torpedo and gunnery officer who had been an enlisted torpedoman, to fire the torpedoes. That order elated Curtis, who had never fired a torpedo in battle. The firing panel, located on the port side over the radar's A-scope, had switches representing each of the torpedo tubes. Dim orange lights above each indicated all forward tubes were ready to be launched.

"Fire one!" called out the exec, who had a stopwatch in his hand to time the torpedo's journey to the target.

Curtis switched tube number one to the "fire" position and pushed the two-inch diameter red firing key above the panel with the palm of his hand.

Fifteen seconds passed.

"Fire two!"

Fifteen seconds more

"Fire three!"

The voice of the captain interrupted our thoughts. "New target. Second ship in the starboard column." New TBT bearings and radar ranges went into the computer.

"We have a solution," Teder called.

Tyree responded quickly. "Fire four!". . ."Fire five!". . ."Fire six!"

The captain could see the faint phosphorescent glow of the wakeless electric torpedoes as they shot out of the tubes and angled off to intercept the unsuspecting targets. At the moment of firing, Ward's attack plan came to fruition. The images of five ships in the port and starboard columns merged, forming a continuous line of vessels. It was almost impossible to miss. That is, it was impossible if the ships did not see the ghostly torpedoes coming toward them and make radical course changes to escape.

Three minutes after firing, the slow electrically-powered fish found their marks. The first hit struck a large tanker loaded with fuel. Ward's patrol report described the resulting cataclysm:

> The Tanker was loaded with gas and blew up immediately sending flames thousands of feet high. The large AK was also loaded with combustibles, commencing [sic] to burn aft and later blew up. The third ship in line, an AK, broke in two in the middle and sank, and the fourth ship in line went down bow first. The scene was lit up as bright as day by the explosions and burning ship.

The horrendous explosions and flames awed even Captain Ward, who invited each man from the fire control party to come to the bridge, one at a time, to view the spectacle. To this day I still get a chill when I think of the sight I saw that night.

Radar interference from the convoy disappeared from our screens when the first ship exploded. As the port and starboard columns of ships erupted, the forward Japanese escort sped away from us at top speed. It careened into the space between the burning columns and dropped depth charge after depth charge. The escort commander had no idea where we were. Meanwhile, we veered right and increased speed in an attempt to get set up on the next group of ships with our stern tubes. Unfortunately, we were not fast enough and the small convoy broke up, the ships scattering in all directions.

Just past midnight on July 17, we found ourselves surrounded by the remnants of the convoy. With depth charges exploding in the distance, the captain isolated his efforts against a large cargo ship and we started to track it. I remember wondering, each time a depth charge exploded in the distance, how many Japanese were killed in the water that night by their escorts.

When we reached our attack position we could see only two ships on our radar screen: an AK (cargo ship) and a small escort. Tracking went without a hitch. We turned right to bring our stern tubes to bear, as we were on the cargo vessel's starboard bow. Ensign Curtis fired tubes seven, eight, and nine at ten second intervals. The exec counted off the minutes and seconds with his stopwatch. BOOM!. . .BOOM! Two hits engulfed the big ship, which erupted in explosions and flames from stem to stern. We were dangerously close to the escort vessel at this time, and wisely pulled away when the fish hit the target. Our torpedomen worked frantically to reload the torpedo tubes while the captain continued to hunt for the residue of the convoy. The burning ship turned over on its starboard side, about four miles from us. After one last explosion, she disappeared under the water.

We searched for a little over half an hour and found another ship from the splintered convoy. The fire control party tracked the new target as *Guardfish* moved ahead to get into firing position. The target ship had an escort and was zig-zagging radically every four or five minutes. It took us about an hour and a half to get into position. The captain ordered two stern tubes fired. Just as Ensign Curtis hit the firing key the target zigged, and as a result both torpedoes passed ahead of the ship's bow.

In an effort to obtain another attack position, Ward ordered *Guardfish* "ahead flank, swing left and make two bow tubes ready." When the boat was within 1,250 yards, tubes three and four were fired. Both shots struck the cargo ship. According to the captain, the "proximity of [the] escort and rising moon induced [him] to head out fast," especially since he was "sure this ship would sink immediately." The stricken merchant freighter, however, continued steaming at about three knots although it was visibly settling by stern. According to Captain Ward's patrol report, the ship. . .

disappeared from the radar screen at 13,000 yards with escort seen at 12,500 yards at same time. Numerous lights and much activity was seen on the target as we hauled clear. It is believed this ship sank but only damage is claimed. Did not consider it possible to make another attack on any of the widely scattered targets, so secured from battle stations and pulled clear to northward on four engines. Everyone in the control party was beginning to show fatigue after six hours at battle station under constant tension; the commanding officer had not enjoyed any rest for over fifty hours. Under these conditions it was considered best to let the others go.

The captain was right. I was thoroughly exhausted and like him, had been up for almost fifty hours because of repeated radar problems and the torpedo action. We secured from battle stations around 3:30 a.m., July 17. "Amazing," I thought, "the radar didn't go out while we were at battle stations. I hope it doesn't crap out again soon." I was scheduled to go back on watch in less than five hours, so I dragged myself to the crew's quarters, climbed to my top bunk, and crashed into it with my clothes on. Sleep immediately enveloped me as the boat submerged and peace returned once again.

"Rig for depth charge! Rig for depth charge!"

The announcement blasted out through the loudspeaker directly above me. As the patrol boat headed toward us, the boat dove to a depth of 350 feet. I was too tired to move, and I did not know what I was supposed to do. Although it may seem odd today, I fell back asleep. The exploding depth charges, however, threw me wide awake.

Thud. . . .boom! Thud. . . .boom!

The explosions were far off the mark.

Thud. . . .Boom!

I turned over and closed my eyes again.

Thud. .BOOM!

That one was closer! Back to a fitful drowse. Hour after hour the attack continued, with over forty depth charges being dropped around us. Only a few were close enough to raise eyebrows, but each one woke me up with a start. Finally, the patrol boat gave up his search. Our loud-speakers blared, "Secure from depth charge!" A few seconds later the below decks watchman shook me twice to get me to wake up. "Conner, get up, its time to go on watch."

We soon learned *Thresher* had been busy as well. She had sunk her convoy of four cargo ships, expended all of her torpedoes, and was on her way back home. Now the Mickey Finn wolf pack consisted of only *Piranha* and *Guardfish*.

Chapter Seven

Battle Stations Submerged

O ur patrol station on July 18, 1944, was in the South China Sea about 100 miles west of a line drawn between the tips of Luzon and Formosa and roughly equidistant from those two islands. We were again patrolling north and south across the Bashi Channel. *Piranha* was about twenty-five miles east of us. The weather was overcast and squally, and by late afternoon we were rolling through heavy seas. In order for our bow and stern planes to keep us up at periscope depth, we had to run at a higher than normal submerged speed. The officer of the deck, Lt. James Schnepp, had to expose ten feet of the periscope in order to see over the crest of the waves. Even then, the waves sometimes swallowed the periscope glass, and he often stopped training the 'scope until he could get a clear view.

"Whoops, what is that?" Schnepp muttered. Then low and forcefully: "Stand by to mark the bearing. Damn, where did they go? Mark!"

The man at the chart desk jumped up and read, "Three zero zero."

"Call Captain to the conning tower," Schnepp snapped out as he adjusted the large black stadimeter knob at the base of the periscope. With that device, an optical range finder, he set duplicate images of the target precisely, one above the other; mast-top of one at the waterline of the other. Schnepp repeatedly checked the range readings, tracing his finger to the different mast height scales. Satisfied, he continued his 'scope search, scanning the sky for airplanes. Unbeknownst to him the operator at the chart desk accidentally left the *1MC speaker system on, and the entire crew could hear what was happening. As soon as Ward reached the conning tower, Schnepp put him in the picture:

"Skipper, we have a fast carrier force at about eleven or twelve thousand yards. I can also occasionally see some other sizable ships. There's nothing on sound. We're having trouble maintaining our depth, so we're at two-thirds speed. Course zero zero zero."

"Very well," Ward said, I have the conn. Where are they?"

"About two nine eight degrees, they appear to be moving fast. They show a large port angle on the bow."

"Up 'scope."

The captain quickly sized up the situation. He took repeated bearings and ranges and plugged them, together with target angle on the bow estimates and our course, into his *"Is-Was" circular slide-rule device. The "Is-Was," which hung from around his neck on a metal-beaded chain, was the forerunner of the torpedo data computer (TDC). He used it to see if it was possible to get into a suitable firing position.

"Battle stations submerged," Ward ordered. "Come left to two seven zero. All ahead full. Jim, get the ONI [Office of Naval Intelligence] silhouette book."

Visibility was poor and variable; different ships came in and out of view from time to time. The target group was incredibly rich. There were two aircraft carriers, two large tankers, a troop transport, seaplane tender, naval auxiliary, and several other unidentifiable vessels. But after only a few minutes of tracking it became apparent to Captain Ward that we had no hope of intercepting them. Their heading was southwest and they were moving too fast.

"All ahead two-thirds," called out the captain as he continued to pass range and bearing information to the TDC operator.

Then, amazingly, the ships changed course and several on their flank headed almost directly at us. The captain chose the closest ship, a naval auxiliary, as our target. They were closing fast and there was not much time to act.

"Make ready three tubes forward. Open outer doors."

"We have ready lights, Captain: tubes one, two and three. Outer doors are open," came the reply.

"Set the depth at fifteen feet. Four degree spread. Give me a one degree down angle on the boat. All ahead one-third. The captain paused for a moment. "This is a final setup. Standby—Mark! Standby to fire. . . Fire one. . .Down 'scope. . .Fire two. . .Fire three."

I felt an impulse of air pressure on my ears as the torpedo tubes were vented inboard after each fish was launched on its way. It had been only twenty-two minutes from the initial sighting of the ships to the firing of the torpedoes.

"All ahead standard, right full rudder; come to zero two zero. Make ready three tubes aft. Open outer doors. Standby for setup on new target. Up 'scope."

The first target was closing fast at fifteen knots. She was traveling past us, on our port side, at a distance of about one-half mile. The new target, a fleet tanker, followed the first ship. Two torpedoes hit the leading ship. The captain spun the 'scope around and saw that one of the hits was about fifty feet aft of the ship's superstructure. He immediately whirled back to the tanker for a final set of ranges and bearings—and found that the ship was rapidly turning toward us. It was only 800 yards away and traveling at a high speed in an attempt to ram us. There was no time to fire.

The captain dispatched a list of urgent instructions. "Flood negative! All ahead full! Take her down to two hundred fifty feet! Make a ten degree down *bubble!"

Ward wanted to go down fast, but without broaching the boat's stern and causing the screws to lose propulsion. He also knew there was a steep temperature gradient (a sudden change in water temperature), at the 200 to 300 foot depth. That temperature gradient acted as a barrier to an enemy's sonar and would help protect us from detection. Ward took one last look at the first target, which was settling fast, before lowering the periscope. The stricken Japanese auxiliary ship had about a thirty degree port list and her main deck was nearly awash. The captain had seen men trying to launch life boats in an attempt to get clear of the doomed vessel.

Guardfish had barely escaped into the depths when the tanker passed directly over us. We all clearly heard the ship through our hull; it's bow cleaving through the water, the sound of its propellers coming closer and closer. Shsh, shuck, Shuck, Chug, CHUG, CHUG. . . .Suddenly I realized that our boat's downward angle was increasing. I had to support myself and lean my body toward the stern to keep myself from falling forward. My battle station in the forward torpedo room was the sound-powered battle telephone, and I heard communications going on throughout the boat. The boat's depth was increasing at a faster rate than the diving officer wanted and it was not responding to his efforts to control the down angle. I heard him from his post in the control room, calling orders to the bow and stern plane operators and to the *hydraulic manifold operator.

"Blow negative," ordered the diving officer.

"Give me fifteen degree rise on the bow planes."

"Fifteen degree rise on stern planes."

"Hard rise on bow planes and stern planes."

"Pump bilges to sea."

"Pump 400 gallons from forward trim to after trim."

"Pump 800 gallons from forward trim to after trim."

We passed the assigned 300-foot safety depth and continued sinking rapidly. The diving officer's voice betrayed a note of urgency. I could feel my own pulse beginning to race.

"Blow *safety."

Apparently the accumulation of small leaks into our trim tanks and around periscopes and electric cables, plus the large deep-water temperature change, had radically affected our trim and buoyancy. I don't know how deep we went, and the captain did not record the loss of depth control in his patrol report. The control room switched to its deep-depth gauge—the one that could measure down to 600 feet. I remember holding my breath, expecting the pressure hull to crush at any moment. Slowly, however, the boat's descent came to a stop and reversed as a result of blowing the safety tank. I had nightmares about that episode for years. They were always the same, with *Guardfish* plunging down, down, down into oblivion.

The Japanese task force steamed away, but it left a destroyer behind to drop a few depth charges, none of which fell close to us. About fifty minutes after going deep to evade the attempted ramming, we struggled back to periscope depth. By then it was getting dark. The captain saw a destroyer circling around, but it was rescuing survivors from the ship we sent to the bottom instead of looking for us. We secured from battle stations. As I was going on watch an hour later, we surfaced. The high speed of the Japanese naval force, together with the increasingly heavy sea, convinced Captain Ward not to pursue the enemy. He was also concerned about our fuel supply, which was dwindling rapidly.

Radar picked up our sixth ship contact ten hours after securing from battle stations. Our heading was south and we traveled very slowly on the surface, powered only by our fuel-saving auxiliary engine (see *Compartments, forward engine room). The new contact was ahead of us and to the west at a range of 22,500 yards, or a little over eleven nautical miles. Our four main engines roared to life. An announcement came over the loudspeakers: "Fire control party, man your stations." That verified the speculation: We were on the chase again!

We reversed course and tracked the northbound target, trying to get ahead of it before dawn. Much to our satisfaction, our radar soon revealed that our target was actually a six-ship convoy protected by several small escort vessels. With dawn breaking we were forced to submerge or be spotted, even though we had not gotten far enough ahead to take up an attack position. Because of our limited submerged speed, however, we quickly fell behind the convoy. High seas and frequent rain squalls limited visibility and prevented the captain from obtaining a visual sighting of the ships through his periscope. Our underwater sound gear was not much help either and, despite our best efforts, we could not pick up their screws or pinging. However, Ward suspected that the convoy might be preparing to turn right to enter Bashi Channel. His hunch proved correct, and before long one ship after another steamed into view. They had changed course and were headed directly across our path just behind us.

"Battle stations submerged," ordered the captain. "All ahead two-thirds. Come right to one-eight-zero. Make ready four bow tubes. Open outer doors. Up 'scope."

"Tubes two, four, five and six are ready, Captain,"came the ready reply.

The captain selected a large cargo ship as our first target, the one leading the convoy's port column. The periscope reader and the captain called out bearing and range data to the TDC operator each time the skipper briefly viewed the ship. Because of the battle telephone and the active loudspeaker system, I was able to hear much that was going on throughout the boat.

"Captain, I have screws on sound at zero-eight-five degrees."

"Up 'scope."

The convoy's leading port escort was only half a mile away and headed straight toward us.

"Take her down smartly to one hundred twenty feet," the captain instructed.

"One hundred twenty feet, aye."

The loud and chilling sounds of the ship's bow waves and screws resonated through the boat and put me in a cold sweat. I braced myself for depth charges—but none came. We passed smoothly under the escort, completely undetected. It had passed directly over us without an inkling that an enemy submarine was about to thin out its flock.

The captain ordered the boat to periscope depth as soon as we were clear of the warship, but for some reason *Guardfish* stubbornly resisted. When we finally got up, Ward found that his target was at a bad firing angle, and it wasn't getting any better.

"Switching to another target. Standby—Mark! Down 'scope. Sound, give me a single ping range to the new target ship."

"One thousand yards and closing, sir. I'm also getting a weak return at 2,500 yards."

"Up 'scope." Ward liked what he saw. "Oh, yes—Down 'scope. That's an overlapping ship on the far side of our target. Maybe we'll get him, too. Prepare to fire; set depths at fourteen feet, four degree spread. Give the boat a one degree down bubble. All ahead two thirds. Take over, Alex."

The exec leaned over to the Firing Panel and selected number two, the first torpedo tube displaying a ready light. Without a word he reached up and pressed the red firing key with his left hand, simultaneously studying the stopwatch in his right. Three more fish went on their way at ten second intervals. Those were the last of the forward room's torpedoes, but it was not the last of our troubles. The boat's slow speed at firing and the severe turbulence of the twenty-foot waves caused us to lose depth control. The boat rose toward the surface, even though the skipper immediately called for standard speed after firing the last fish.

"Don't let her broach!" warned the captain. "All ahead full! That's right, keep her at periscope depth. Up 'scope. Oh, oh, right full rudder."

The next ship in line was on a collision course with us, and Ward had to again resort to evasive maneuvers to avoid being rammed. Simultaneously, Ojay Johnson, in the forward torpedo room, called over the battle telephone:

"Conning tower, this is JP sound. Three of our fish are running straight and normal, but one is. . ."

BOOM!. . .BOOM!

The boat shuddered as two of our torpedoes slammed into the nearby ship. The skipper spun the periscope around and reported that the target ship had broken completely in half. A cheer went up throughout the boat. After some of the hubbub had died down, Ojay went on:

"Conning tower, one of our fish is going way off to the right. . . ."

At that moment, a third explosion went off. According to our timing, it struck the overlapping far ship.

"I can still hear that fish," continued Ojay. "It's still going. . . ."

Brinkley, on QB sound, interrupted with a new report: "Captain, I hear fast screws coming in at one-nine-zero."

"Up 'scope," Ward said, and then after a quick look, "Down 'scope. That escort we passed under is coming back for us." Simultaneously, the battle telephone came alive with calls from different parts of the boat, lively voices shouting back and forth.

"After room here. We hear sort of a buzz coming through the hull from the starboard side. Its getting louder."

"We hear it in maneuvering."

"This is the forward engine room: We hear it, too. Its getting much louder."

"Hey, it passed directly over us. This is maneuvering. It sounded like an angry bee. Was it a Torpedo?"

"Take her down to two hundred fifty feet! Rig for depth charge," Ward ordered loudly.

The terror in all the voices stunned me. My mind spun round and round. "Where did that torpedo come from? Did it come from an enemy destroyer?" It became clear much later that the "angry bee" was in fact one of our own torpedoes—the one that had veered off to the right and made a circular run. A faulty torpedo, traveling in a circular path, sank at least one of our submarines (*USS Tang*) during the war. In all likelihood, *USS Tullibee* met the same fate. A total of 157 men lost their lives on those two boats. *Guardfish* had come within a few feet of joining them.

Before we got to our assigned depth, a second enemy escort joined the first and together both began dropping depth charges. A series of sharp explosions erupted in rapid succession over the next fifteen or twenty minutes. Two of them gave the boat a bad shaking. However, after we got under the protective temperature gradient, the charges went well off their mark and we all heaved a collective sigh of relief.

We returned to periscope depth about three-quarters of an hour after the last depth charge explosion. By then the escorts were nowhere in sight. Only a minute passed before the masts of two ships and an escort hove into view. They were to our east, traveling in a southerly direction. We tracked them for about twenty minutes until the captain realized that they were too far away for us to attack. At 9:44 a.m. we secured from battle stations, and I went onto my regular watch.

The day had still more in store for us. All was quiet until about five in the afternoon, when the officer of the deck sighted a Japanese destroyer west-southwest of us. The ship was obviously on an anti-submarine search mission, her sonar pinging the depths in the hope of latching onto an American submarine. Our fire control party tracked her for a couple of hours using both periscope and underwater sound detection. She never came closer than about three miles from us during that time. But after darkness fell, she closed in and we went back to battle stations.

The approach of the lone warship prompted Captain Ward to attack it, even though we only had three torpedoes left and were precariously low on fuel. Although he seemed to think the ship offered easy pickings, it was a very dangerous foe. In fact, this type of a ship was originally called a "submarine [torpedo boat] destroyer" for good reason.

"Make ready three tubes aft," the captain called out.

The destroyer was less than a mile away. We were in perfect position and had a beautiful firing setup. Just as we were about to fire, the destroyer increased speed, turned toward us, shifted her sonar to rapid, short-range pinging. Depth charges were dropped as she rapidly closed on our position.

"Take her down!" Ward shouted. "Flood negative, rig for depth charge!"

A palpable fear of calamity hung in the boat's atmosphere, as the destroyer violently churned the water and crossed over our sinking stern. We all waited in suspense. But then, oddly, she broke off her attack and a short while later left the area. As we secured from battle stations we contemplated our near-brush with disaster, amazed that we didn't take a beating from the nemesis of submarines. I was utterly limp from exhaustion.

It was about 9:30 p.m. when we surfaced and I went on watch. I was in the conning tower when I heard the captain say, "Let's head for home while we still have some fuel in our tanks." Those few words lifted a heavy weight from me. Home this time was to be Midway. The calendar changed to July 20 as we went eastward into Bashi Channel.

The following day, as we emerged from the eastern end of the channel, the United States invasion of Guam, south of American-held Saipan in the Marianas, was launched. Our return home was mainly on the surface. Airplanes drove us down several times over the next three days as we passed some 400 miles north of Saipan. Based on IFF signals, at least one of those planes was on our side.

We saw the last evidence of war on this patrol on July 26, when we were almost half way to Midway. One of our sharp-eyed lookouts spotted a floating mine. We circled around and our gunners mate used our dual 20 mm guns to sink it. Japanese mines regularly broke loose from their underwater moorings during storms, floated to the surface, and then followed the prevailing winds and ocean currents. We fired at floating mines on every patrol I made. It always disappointed me when gunfire only caused the mine to sink, rather than to explode.

The entire ship's company was in high spirits as we plied the surface toward Midway. Where Captain Ward was usually steely-eyed and all business, in view of our spectacular success in Convoy College, he set aside protocol and a joking camaraderie prevailed. The following announcement resounded throughout the boat: "The Cribbage Champion of the Wardroom, Captain Ward, challenges members of the crew to participate in a match for the Championship of the Boat. Anyone wishing to take his challenge should meet in the wardroom at 1300 hours."

The radio gang's representative was Ojay Johnson. I can't remember how many enlisted men from other departments accepted the skipper's challenge. A few days later, after completing a series of games, Ojay proudly strutted through the boat: he had defeated the captain!

Members of the crew demonstrated their warm regard for the skipper in a rather unusual way one day. The radioman on watch copied a plain-English message during the *Fox schedule, which announced the advancement of Lieutenant Commander Norvell G. Ward, our skipper, to the rank of full Commander. Immediately an Ad Hoc Committee formed. One of the symbols of the rank of Commander was embroidered golden filigree on the visor of his cap—something we called "scrambled eggs." Somebody, probably one of the steward's mates from the officers' quarters, obtained one of the captain's caps and furtively brought it to the galley. Paul Snyder, the Baker, cooked some real scrambled eggs and Scotch-taped them to the cap's visor. A call was placed to the captain on the ship's telephone requesting his presence aft in the crew's mess. Marvin L. ("Hobbie Dobbie") Kline, the auxiliary room machinist; Robert T. ("Hobby") Hoblitzell, the auxiliary electrician; Paul Snyder, Baker; Ojay Johnson, the Cribbage Champion; and others, formed the Presentation Committee. They showed the radio message to the skipper and, with suitable ceremony, presented him with his Commander's hat. I was not in on the gag, but I was there when Ward marched with feigned pomposity through the control room after the award ceremony, sporting his egg-dangling cap.

Commander Ward maneuvered *Guardfish* through Midway's tricky entrance channel and moored at Sand Island's pier number nine at 7:15 a.m., July 31, 1944. We had but eight hours of fuel left in our tanks. A formal navy band was blaring loudly on the pier, as they always did for a submarine returning from a successful war patrol. The commanding officer of the submarine base and members of his staff formed the greeting party. Commander Ward, with those scrambled eggs dangling from his cap, snapped a formal salute as the base commander, a captain, came aboard.

The base commander went below with Ward to hear firsthand about *Guardfish's* eighth war patrol. That run was one of the most successful of the war, with seven ships claimed sunk, totaling 58,200 tons, and one ship damaged. It resulted in Norvell G. Ward receiving the navy's highest award, the Navy Cross. They also honored *Guardfish* and every member of her crew with a second Presidential Unit Citation. Of the 258 American submarines that patrolled the Pacific Ocean during the war, only one other received two Presidential Citations: the *Tang*, the same submarine sunk by her own circular running torpedo.

Postwar Japanese records identified the sinking of four of the eight ships we torpedoed during that run. They were *Mantai Maru, Hizan Maru, Jinsan Maru* and *Teiru Maru*, which together totaled 20,400 tons. These records do not account for the ships that were damaged but not sunk.

I was proud to be a member of *Guardfish's* crew and looked forward to going ashore for R&R with the gang. We were ordered to turn the boat over to a relief crew late in the day and debark for Camp Gooney-ville. Lieutenant Howarth found me as I prepared to wash some clothes. Normally he was a very friendly, cool-headed guy, so his demeanor surprised me. He seemed rattled and would not look me straight in the eye.

"Conner, " he blurted out, "the captain said, 'Get that kid off the boat.' So pack up your gear. You're being transferred to the relief crew." Without another word he turned and quickly walked away.

The news was a crushing blow, but I figured I had it coming to me. The exec had reported to the captain my radar bearing foul-ups that had occurred during the night surface attack. Captain Ward's professional response was to get rid of me at the first opportunity.

Chapter Eight

New Assignments

eing dumped by *Guardfish* after only one patrol was an embarrassment to me and I lied about the reason why I was removed in order to protect my pride. I told everyone that I had to leave because the boat was not authorized to have both a Chief and a first-class Radio Technician (the navy referred to such a person a "supernumerary"). Captain Ward transferred eighteen other men off the boat at the same time, and a few of them were in fact supernumeraries. Most of us were assigned to Relief Crew Eighty-Two, stationed aboard the *USS Fulton* (AS-11), the same submarine tender to which I was assigned at Mare Island before being transferred to *Guardfish*.

USS Fulton

Fulton was right next to *Guardfish*, on the opposite side of that Sand Island pier, and she seemed huge to me. She displaced over 9,000 tons and was 530 feet long. Her boat deck towered over *Guardfish*. As I was preparing to carry my gear from *Guardfish* to *Fulton*, I heard my name called. "Hey, Conner!" I looked around the deck and the pier but could not find the source. "Hey, Conner, up here!" I tilted my head way back and squinted my eyes as I looked up to the top deck of the large ship, where I saw a sailor madly waving his arms about trying to catch my attention. It was an old buddy of mine, Electrician's Mate Robert E. (Bob) Bruns.

I first met Bruns at boot camp, where we were in the same company. We both went on to New London, but since we attended different schools, we lost contact for a while. When I arrived at Mare Island, we found ourselves in the same barracks, this time with our bunks side by side. San Francisco was his hometown, so he invited me to go on liberty with him there a few times.

Bruns met me at the gangplank as I boarded *Fulton*. After talking and comparing notes for a while, he showed me around the ship. It was almost a floating city, with different "business establishments" spread throughout. There were machine shops, specialty repair shops, large stockrooms, a commercial laundry and an ice cream, candy and cigarette ("Ship's Service") store. Of course, he showed me the crew's quarters and the mess hall. Our bunks were in the hold, about five decks down. The crew's mess resembled a large cafeteria with a constant buzz of activity. I was only a few seconds into my first meal on *Fulton* when I realized the food they served was far below submarine standards.

During the next few weeks a swarm of men from Relief Crew Eighty-Two took over repairs and control of *Guardfish* as the boat's regular crew rested at nearby Camp Gooneyville. Upon completion of their R&R period, *Guardfish's* crew returned to the boat, which started going out for daily sea trials. In the meantime, a number of other submarines tied up side by side at the pier. One day it suddenly dawned on me that the good old *Guardfish* was not around anymore. It saddened me.

Bob and I were not assigned to any work for over a month while *Fulton* was tied up at Midway. We reported for muster every morning, then killed the rest of the day soaking up the sun and shooting the breeze. Bob was an avid musician, and we spent many hours talking about our hobbies.

Our routine changed somewhat on September 8, when *Fulton* pulled out to sail to the still smoldering island of Saipan. Both of us had sea watch assignments; mine was monitoring the operation of the ship's radar transmitters. Less than a week later, at roughly the half-way point of our journey, *Fulton* pulled into the huge ship-filled lagoon at Eniwetok atoll of the Marshall Islands. Craters, palm tree stumps and piled debris from the massive American invasion bombardment covered the isles that encircled the lagoon. After a day or so we proceeded on to Saipan's Tanapag Harbor, where *Fulton* was to serve as a forward repair and resupply base for submarines.

F = Fulton Relocation

Guardfish's War Patrol Nine
and USS Fulton Relocation

Map 4

Saipan's mountains still had a dense growth of trees and underbrush, but the bombarded lowlands were a jumble of wreckage. The majority of the Japanese defenders died, or committed suicide, during the American onslaught, but some managed to escape and hide out in the mountains. Occasionally a few snipers fired shots at the ships in the harbor.

The weather was incredibly hot and humid. My bunk down in the ship's hold was the top one in a five-high stack, and there was no noticeable ventilation. Consequently, I never slept in my bunk while at Saipan. Instead, Bruns and I slept in the open on the ship's top deck without covers and with our clothes rolled up under our heads as pillows. One morning I awoke and found my clothes scattered about the deck and my wallet gone. Some friendly sailor had stolen about a week's pay from me.

When we arrived at Saipan, I was assigned to work with the ship's radar repair team. Usually, two to eight submarines were alongside *Fulton* for refueling or maintenance. Members of the repair team often brought the submarines' defective radar units to *Fulton's* large and well-equipped workshop for repairs. They also assigned one or two of us to go aboard small surface ships in the harbor to repair their radar. At various times I was dispatched to destroyer escorts, sub chasers, minelayers, and large landing craft. Ships smaller than a destroyer did not have radar technicians assigned to their crews. The officers and men of the ships we visited treated us like royalty.

In the meantime the front moved on. The battle to reclaim New Guinea, which had begun in April 1944, finally came to an end around September 15 while I was in Saipan. This important action set the stage for the liberation of the Philippines. Many of those preparations were concentrated at Saipan and Guam.

Guardfish to Ninth Run

Guardfish left Midway on August 23 to patrol the East China and Yellow Seas, a large expanse between Japan, Formosa (Taiwan), China, and Korea. She drew another wolfpack assignment, this time with the submarines *Sunfish* and *Thresher*. The assigned areas proved to be a disappointment, but Captain Ward again came through with a successful patrol.

Only six of the thirty-three vessels *Guardfish* contacted were sizable enough for torpedoes. Ward made two torpedo attacks, sank one cargo ship, later identified as the 873-ton *Miyakawa Maru #2*, and damaged a 1,500-ton destroyer. He also carried out two "battle surfaces" (gun actions) on some smaller craft. Poor radar performance was a possible reason for the paucity of good contacts during the first half of the time on station, when the weather was ideal. During portions of the last eighteen days on station, winds ranging up to sixty miles per hour and waves as high as twenty-five feet probably kept enemy shipping in port. Life on the boat, while on the surface at night, was miserable during these storms. The heavy weather also created another problem. Many submerged Japanese mines broke loose from their moorings and floated to the surface. During one nine-day period, *Guardfish* nearly ran into five floating mines. The boat's gunnersmates destroyed all of them. Two of the mines exploded, probably when the bullets hit the contact-detonator horns.

Since I was not with *Guardfish* on this patrol, I asked a number of former crew members to share their recollections of the boat's ninth war patrol. That run was the first for Ensign Richard U. Schock, the only officer on board whose training included radar. He had spent a few months at the Massachusetts Institute of Technology, the foremost radar research center in the United States. Consequently, Ward assigned him as radar officer, a new position on the boat.

One incident in particular remained prominent in Schock's memory. One night, after about two weeks on station, lookouts sighted a large and well lighted enemy hospital ship. It was against the "rules of war" to attack a hospital ship, but Captain Ward tracked and carefully scrutinized her. The SJ radar, however, never detected the ship's presence.

"Captain Ward was absolutely furious," recalled the ensign, "wondering how long the radar had not been working." The skipper came down on Schock with both feet. His radar training, Schock informed me, did not include maintenance or trouble shooting, but he and Chief Radio Technician Reid Dudrey nevertheless worked on the radar for two solid days around the clock in an attempt to find the source of its severe (and potentially fatal) lack of sensitivity. At the time, the equipment had no quantitative way to check for that defect. Schock and Dudrey finally found that the radar repair team at Midway had improperly installed a microwave cavity device called a "TR tube." Thus, the radar had been deteriorating from day one due to poor, slowly oxidizing contacts.

By far, the majority of comments and recollections about the ninth run had to do with the two "battle surface" gun duels. Frederick M. Jennings, another new ensign on that patrol, wrote a detailed and fascinating description of the first battle for me. It took place on September 2, 1944, in the late afternoon before *Guardfish* reached her patrol area. Fred's account of the action, which he called "The Battle of Sofu Gan," is worth reprinting in its entirety:

> In the early stages of America's submarine war against Japan, the prescribed doctrine of ComSubPac was to ignore Japanese fishing craft, such as junks and sampans, as targets unworthy of our precious torpedoes. As our losses of boats began to mount, however, the high command reassessed the menace of this fleet of small craft, now all equipped with radios. It was obvious that these small vessels constituted a major picket network and were radioing in sighting reports, which were promptly followed up by their big brothers, well-equipped for anti-submarine attack.
>
> ComSubPac amended its orders and encouraged attacking these pickets vigorously. With this in mind it was decided in early 1944 to equip *Guardfish*, scheduled for a major overhaul and refit in San Francisco, with additional weaponry for surface battle. Her basic armament, which consisted of a four-inch, 50 caliber cannon and .50 caliber machine gun mounts, was enhanced with the addition of a 40 millimeter rapid firing Bofors cannon on the cigarette deck. Two new mounts were also added for 20 millimeter Oerlikon machine cannons. The result, at least in theory, was a formidable surface gun platform. Early in patrol number nine, the great moment to pursue the noble experiment presented itself.
>
> Our course past the southern tip of Kyushu took us a few miles to the south of a Japanese outpost on the tiny island of Sofu Gan. [The island is about 350 miles south of Tokyo and 400 miles east of Kyushu.] Sofu Gan translates as "Lot's Wife," alluding to the biblical lady who was turned into a pillar of salt when she could not resist peeking back, contrary to the Lord's admonition, to see Sodom and Gomorrah going up in flames. This island pillar, however, was rock—probably the core of an ancient volcano. It is a spectacular sight, rearing up as it does two or three hundred feet above the water in the midst of the ocean. The land around the base of the pillar could not be seen well at our respectful distance, but appeared to

consist of a small low land mass, a few miscellaneous buildings and, presumably, a very small harbor. It was too small to have an air strip and beyond the range of most planes at bases in Japan, so we felt reasonably secure to pass by on the surface without danger.

As we neared the island we were surprised when our radar reported three *blips which were diagnosed as three small craft coming out to look us over. Captain Ward was delighted and concluded promptly that this was the ideal opportunity to try out his newly-acquired surface warfare capability. He wasted no time in calling away "Battle Stations Surface!" and putting all four engines on the line. Great excitement erupted throughout the boat; the calmest crewmen were running and shouting, hatches were wrenched open and the gun crews and ammunition train dashed to their stations. Guns were uncovered, loaded and trained on the targets, which were barely visible on the starboard bow but still too distant to identify.

"I was lucky, as the newest and most useless officer, to be positioned as a sort of super lookout in my usual spot," Fred remembers, which was "the safety ring at the top of the periscope shears and between the two 'scopes." Fred was equipped with a pair of binoculars, the ship's camera and, unbeknownst to anyone else, "under my shirt [was] the frontier model Colt .41 pistol my grandfather carried as an old western sheriff."

From his position atop the periscope shears Fred could see three small boats, "each perhaps thirty to forty feet long with a small deck house and carrying a crew of four or five. When they got a bit closer I could see some sort of small weapon on a tripod." The weapons proved to be light machine guns, probably .25 caliber. "The little formation proceeded toward us at about fifteen knots," recalled Fred, "probably their best speed, and at about 4,000 yards went into a formation three abreast and manned their guns."

At a range of 2,000 yards, *Guardfish* "opened fire with four 20mm and one 40mm guns, closing range to 1,200 yards," Captain Ward later reported in his official account of the patrol. Much to the dismay of all aboard the submarine, "the 40mm gasped one shot and failed to return to battery." Crewmen manned the 4" gun, remembered Ward, and the "Japs returned fire with small caliber machine guns and depth charges. After forty minutes of roundy-go-round, during which most of the time was spent repairing gun casualties, [we] broke off the engagement with all guns out of commission." The experiment had been an utter failure.

Guardfish expended nineteen rounds of 4" ammunition "for no hits, two miss fires, and poor fire control; 1380 rounds of 20mm with several jams; one round of 40mm. The most heavily gunned submarine of this type," concluded the disgusted captain, "hangs her head in shame and retires from the scene after inflicting only a little damage by virtue of a few 20mm hits."

I am sure Ward raked the gunnery officer over the coals for this miserable performance. Before the "Battle of Sofu Gan," the deck guns had received frequent maintenance to protect them from the effects of salt water immersion. The fiasco resulted in even greater vigilance. In fact, it became a nightly ritual for the gunnersmates to go topside with buckets of heavy grease, which was liberally applied to help insure gun maintenance.

The second gun battle that took place on the ninth patrol occurred on October 16, two days after *Guardfish* departed her assigned patrol area en route to Pearl Harbor. It, too, proved a disappointment. After a brief and ineffective exchange of gunfire with an armed trawler, the sub had to break off the engagement because of the arrival of enemy reinforcements.

The war took on a new complexion on October 23, when the American army landed on the Philippine island of Leyte. A few days later the Japanese Navy suffered a catastrophic loss at the Battle of Leyte Gulf, where it lost some twenty-six combat ships. The defeat effectively ended Japan's role as naval power in the Pacific Theater. The United States' surface navy almost had free passage around the Philippines from this point on—except for the Japanese submarines and land-based suicide planes.

Guardfish arrived at Pearl Harbor on October 24, thus completing her ninth war patrol. The relief crew from Submarine Division 281 took over the boat the following day, releasing her crew to take its R&R at the Royal Hawaiian Hotel on Waikiki beach. In honor of Norvell G. Ward's five successful patrols in command of *USS Guardfish*, the U.S. Navy awarded him the Navy Cross (eighth patrol); the Silver Star Medal (seventh patrol); two Legion of Merit awards (fifth and sixth patrols); the Bronze Star Medal (ninth patrol), and; the Presidential Unit Citation (eighth patrol). Ward's patrols had resulted in the torpedoing of fourteen enemy ships, which resulted in nine confirmed sinkings. On October 27, his superiors detached him from *Guardfish* and ordered him to report for duty with ComSubPac, the submarine high command. Commander Douglas Thompson Hammond took over as the third skipper of *Guardfish*.

The New Guardfish CO

When speaking among themselves, enlisted members of the crew commonly referred to the boat's captain as "the old man." In Hammond's case, the term was closer to the mark than usual. Although he was only thirty-five years old, most of the men believed he was well into his forties. His slow, deliberate walk, low energy disposition, calm, soft and gentlemanly speech, and lines in his well-tanned face fooled us. His face looked something like actor John Wayne's, with slightly bulbous, squinting eyes, although Hammond was neither particularly tall (about 5'10") nor athletically built. While he was slim overall, he carried a little paunch around his midsection. And the rumors flew! Some said that he came from a desk job in Washington, D.C. Others whispered that ComSubPac relieved him of the command of his previous submarine after two unsuccessful patrols in areas that were teeming with defenseless enemy ships. To his new command, Hammond was a big question mark.

In reality, before Hammond took command of *Guardfish* he made two successful patrols as commanding officer of *USS Cabrilla* (SS-288). Although he did not sink any ships on *Cabrilla's* first run, he did torpedo and damage a 17,200 ton *Chuyo*-class Japanese aircraft carrier while en route to his patrol area. He then successfully carried out a special mission of retrieving American army and navy men from Japanese-held islands in the Philippines. For carrying out those daring rescues, he received a Letter of Commendation from the Commander in Chief of the Pacific Fleet (CinCPac).

Hammond's second patrol on *Cabrilla* began with another special mission: laying mines in the Gulf of Siam (Thailand). The remainder of the fifty-four day patrol was in the South China Sea, off Indochina (Vietnam). During the entire patrol *Cabrilla* encountered but one Japanese hospital ship, an unidentified submarine, and two freighters. Despite this thin selection, Hammond sank one of the freighters and damaged the other. His superior officer reluctantly rated the patrol "successful," but complained that Hammond had found only three targets. Hammond was relieved of his command on February 24, 1944, and assigned to a desk job in Washington, D.C. for a few months. Later, after he was reassigned to the staff of the Commander of Submarine Squadron 46, he personally requested command of *Guardfish*, and ComSubPac approved.

Return to Guardfish

My job at Saipan during this time was rather routine. I rose early in the morning for breakfast, mustered, and then went to the radar repair shop for my work assignment. My leadman in the radar repair gang usually sent me out into the harbor by water taxi to fix the radar on one of the small surface ships. Sometimes I went alone, but usually he sent me with one of the other first-class techs in the gang. November 3, however, was unusual in two ways. First, when I arrived at work my boss greeted me with some astounding news. He had orders for me to fly to Pearl Harbor the following day to return to *Guardfish*. Later that day, my step-brother Leon's boat, *Salmon*, limped back from an epic and nearly disastrous patrol. *Salmon* looked more like floating debris than a submarine as she tied up alongside the *Fulton*.

I went down to see if Leon was alright. Visibly traumatized, he explained what had happened. After *Salmon* torpedoed a Japanese tanker, four of the tanker's escorts zeroed in and pummeled the boat with such a severe depth charge attack that it almost "did her in." Several of the depth charges, he continued, landed on the boat's deck and exploded. They blew away all of her superstructure decking aft of the conning tower, flattened her main induction, knocked diesel engines off their mounts, cracked engine blocks and ruptured her pressure hull in several places. Because she was leaking heavily and had lost depth control, she had to surface and fight it out using deck guns. Fortunately, she surfaced in the midst of a rain squall, which gave *Salmon* a fighting chance to correct a bad list and man her guns. Amazingly, her gunfire stopped one of the escorts dead in the water and drove away another. After radioing for help, other submarines from her wolfpack came to her assistance.

Salmon was so badly damaged that *Fulton's* engineers recommended she be scrapped. Later, Leon and the rest of the crew from *Salmon* went back to the States to take over a new submarine that was under construction at Mare Island, *USS Stickleback*.

After seeing what the enemy could do to a submarine, I had mixed emotions about leaving *Fulton*. I was thrilled that I would be allowed to return to *Guardfish*, but *Fulton* was like a safe home, particularly with my friend Bob Bruns aboard.

I anxiously looked forward to the following day. A motor launch was going to take me to shore, and after a ride to the airfield, I would catch a flight on an army transport plane. I heard that for the past months the army was filling the field with hundreds of the long-range B-29 "Super fortress" bombers. They were making final preparations for a massive air assault on Japan.

Bob and I got together after dinner as usual and planned to sit around on the boat deck until bedtime. Without warning *Fulton's* speaker system announced a "red alert." Radar located unidentified airplanes heading toward Saipan! Alarms went off all over the harbor and the lights aboard ships and shore blacked out. The ships' crews went to battle stations. We waited for what seemed like an interminable time, but nothing happened. Was it a false alarm? Suddenly, anti-aircraft guns erupted from the island and a handful of ships joined in as bombs began exploding around the airfield. Searchlights scanned the sky, but I never did see any enemy aircraft. The next day, I learned that the attacking force had consisted of only four or five planes. I don't know where they came from, and I've never seen any historical reference to that attack.

I arrived at the Saipan airfield the following morning to board my flight to Pearl Harbor. The large number of B-29 bombers parked on the field amazed me. I expected to see devastation from the previous night's air raid, but the damage was minimal. There were some bomb craters, but only a few of the bombers had been seriously damaged. The plane I was flying in was a military version of the DC-3, one of those that went back and forth across the Pacific with cargo. Our pilot dodged the craters as he taxied for takeoff.

The flight was long and uneventful except for the stops at Kwajalein and Johnston islands for meals and refueling. About eighteen hours after leaving Saipan, we landed at Hickam Field, Oahu. I took a shuttle bus to the Submarine Base at Pearl Harbor. Having been curtly dumped several months before, it felt good to return to *Guardfish*, especially from such a distance. I knew there were numerous radar technicians in the area whom they could have requested. I found later that it was my old lead-man, Chief Reid Dudrey, who requested my return to the submarine.

Chapter Nine

Return to Convoy College

Changes aboard *Guardfish* were evident the moment I stepped back aboard her on the afternoon of November 4, 1944. They had moved the big forward deck gun aft of the conning tower and pointed it toward the stern. Because of this deck gun transfer, the two long-wire radio antennas from the conning tower were now directed to a new short mast on the bow. The dual twenty-millimeter guns on the forward cigarette deck had been replaced by a forty-millimeter gun. I also noticed new VHF antennas atop the periscope shears; that meant they had new radio gear aboard. I also learned that the boat had a new skipper—and that I was the new lead radar technician! Everyone on board at that time was from the relief crew, so I did not know anyone. Everything seemed dull, drab, and mysterious below decks.

About a week after my return things sprang to life. The regular crew, back from R&R, brought the Royal Hawaiian Hotel's party atmosphere with them as they swept into the boat. Shortly afterward, some new faces appeared. One of them belonged to a second-class Radio Technician who was a friend of mine. We had not only attended technician school together, we had been roommates at Texas, A&M. It was Joseph E. (Joe) Masters, a 5' 6" fun-loving New Jersey kid with dark brown wavy hair.

Earl T. Beasley, a Chief Motor Machinist Mate, was another newcomer. Captain Hammond appointed him to be the chief of the boat. The crew guessed that Hammond must have known Beasley before they both came aboard *Guardfish*. He was a small, wiry sort, with a snarl in his voice. He promptly issued new bunk and watch assignments to the crew. I drew the 12:00 to 4:00 a.m. watch.

Chief Dudrey, my old leadman on the eighth patrol, spent a few days on board before his formal transfer to Relief Crew 281. He filled me in on the problems he had with the radar while I was off the boat. The ninth run, he explained, had been a technician's nightmare. Among many other things, the motor generator set continued to act up, as it had on the eighth run. It repeatedly went out of control and shut down the radar. He told me that he arranged to have the relief crew install a new motor generator while he was on R&R. I was glad that I did not have to worry about that anymore.

During the weeks of sea trials, the radar proved to be in top shape, but I still felt uneasy. On the morning of November 26, two days after my nineteenth birthday, I set about making last-minute checks on all my gear in the control room and conning tower. Thirty minutes before our scheduled departure time, the SJ radar's new motor generator set went completely dead. I found Lieutenant Schock, my new radar officer, and told him the bad news. He reported it to the captain, who dispatched an urgent message to the relief crew demanding that the motor generator set be replaced "on the double." The skill and strength of the work crew amazed me. It only took about four hours for them to remove the old set and install a new 500-lb. piece of iron, steel, and copper. They carried it down the hatches and ladders, through the tight places in the pump room and bolted it to a cramped space on the overhead. Captain Hammond looked in on the operation now and then. His agreeable nature pleased me. He showed no temper or displeasure about the incident, and when he talked to me he looked straight at me, not through or around me, as many officers did.

We finally departed at 1:30 p.m. in company with another submarine, *USS Sea Robin* and a patrol boat escort. When we released the escort at dusk, things settled down to normal sea routines. My conning tower watch assignment had a new challenge at the helm position. The gyro-compass repeater that showed the ship's heading relative to True North had a new device partially covering its face. The attachment, called a "course clock," enabled the helmsman to steer a zigzag course by following its constantly-moving course marker. Zigzagging made it more difficult for an enemy submarine to pick us off.

In the late afternoon of December 1, a number of hours after passing the International Date Line, we rendezvoused with the submarine *USS Sea Dog*. It was quite an exhilarating experience. We drew alongside the sub traveling the same steady course and speed, separated about 100 feet from each other. A sailor on the main deck of the other boat heaved a weighted line to men on our deck, over which they sent a metal container. It turned out that *Sea Dog, Sea Robin,* and *Guardfish* were forming a coordinated attack group, a wolfpack called Task Group 17.14, and the Task Group Commander was on *Sea Dog*. The container he sent to us had his orders regarding pack operations. After completion of the transfer, we pulled away from *Sea Dog* and took our assigned scouting station over the horizon, twenty miles off her starboard beam. *Sea Robin's* station was twenty miles on the other side of *Sea Dog*.

Efficient tactical communication was vital to the success of a wolfpack. Unfortunately, hundreds of miles away an enemy could easily hear our shortwave messages and locate us with his *radio direction finders. We also had a line of sight, ship-to-ship radio-telephone system, called the TBS (Talk Between Ships). The maximum line of sight distance—antenna to antenna—between fully surfaced boats over the horizon from each other, was about fifteen statute miles, or about thirteen nautical miles (26,000 yards). We also had another radio-telephone communications system, a newly installed *VHF transceiver that allowed us to listen to, and talk with, friendly aircraft.

On this tenth patrol we also had the ability to insert a Morse code key and earphones into the SJ radar. That allowed us to communicate by code with another submarine after we picked up each other's radar interference. We mainly used that method to pass "recognition signals" between boats to identify each other. However, we sometimes sent short messages using the SJ because it had the advantage of being fairly private. That was because the communication was not only limited to line of sight, but was also highly directional. The radar beams were like invisible searchlight beams that were only a few degrees wide.

As we traveled toward our destination on the surface, the weather showed signs of instability and turbulence. Black clouds on the horizon often developed conical tails that pointed downward to the sea. Without warning the tail would plunge into the water and, writhing like a snake, churn the ocean into a maelstrom. Often several waterspouts ran their courses at the same time. Once during my watch a waterspout headed right at us and we were forced to submerge quickly to avoid it. It was a rocky ride going down. Another day, while I was on the bridge having a smoke after my watch, I counted six separate twisters grinding away at once. It was an incredible sight.

On the morning of December 8, we arrived at Saipan to refuel and obtain a few minor repairs. We moored, with *Sea Dog* and *Sea Robin*, alongside the submarine tender *Fulton*, my erstwhile home. The day before, the third anniversary of our entry into the war, American amphibious forces made landings on the central Philippine island of Leyte, about 600 miles south of our intended patrol area. The following morning, December 9, *Guardfish* and her pair of companions continued on toward our destination in Convoy College under ever darkening skies and mounting seas.

One night out from Saipan we received orders to monitor the "lifeguard" frequency on our aircraft radio-telephone. An aircraft carrier assault was in progress against Japanese land based airfields on the main Philippine island of Luzon. The carriers hoped to prevent the Japanese aircraft from attacking American landings on Leyte to the south. Our assignment was to listen for information about downed American planes and, if possible, rescue their crew members.

Aircraft activity was definitely on the increase. American airplanes repeatedly drove us down, as usual, but now Japanese planes joined in the attack. Some of the Japanese aircraft had imprecise broad-beam *VHF radar. We could detect them by using our radar search receiver, the *APR. Our radio operators stood a continuous watch with the APR when we were on the surface in enemy territory. They could hear the enemy's radar signal well before the Japanese could detect us as a target on their screens.

The wolf pack leader on *Sea Dog* ordered us to be on station in the Luzon Straits, south of Balintang Island, on December 14. Because of the foul weather, the exec and navigator, Lieutenant Commander Luther R. Johnson, could not get star sights with the sextant for several nights in a row. At the start of my early morning watch, the day of our scheduled arrival on station, he came to the conning tower to see if we had any land on the radar. Although he was confident we should see land, there was nothing but water before us. After several visits he angrily insisted that I check the radar out, to see if it was working properly. I pointed out to him that the "sea returns" (radar reflections from waves) proved that it was working. In fact, the "clutter," as it was also called, was getting unusually large due to the rough sea. The sea returns went out to 4,000-5,000 yards, compared to the normal 2,000 yards. Johnson had good reason to question the radar reliability. On our way out to station the SJ failed so many times that we were already getting low on some spare electron tubes. Fortunately, the radar was rarely inoperative more than fifteen or twenty minutes at a time.

Finally, around 1:30 a.m. on December 14, we picked up land on the radar and I reported the news to Johnson. The exec climbed into the conning tower with a big grin on his face and looked at the radar screen. We had not one, but two pieces of land showing on the screen: the islands of Babuyan and Balintang. He looked at me rather sheepishly and said, "Conner, I'm sorry I doubted you. I was sure your radar was dead." Then, with a laugh, he admitted, "When I first came to you, the *DRAI [dead reckoning analyzing indicator] said we were two miles inland!" We both had a laugh at that news.

At daylight, we submerged and patrolled north and south across the Balintang Channel, one of the same areas of Convoy College we patrolled during the eighth run. But this was a completely different ball game than the last time. During run number eight, records show that we shared the entire Convoy College with only five other American submarines. During the tenth patrol we shared it with fifteen other subs—and with Task Force 38, commanded by the legendary Admiral William "Bull" Halsey.

Task Force 38 was a powerhouse. According to one participant, it consisted of fifteen aircraft carriers, eight battleships, sixteen cruisers and about fifty destroyers —a total of around ninety ships with close to 1,000 airplanes. It had a precise mode of operation. The force divided into four task groups, each of which moved to a designated launch point near the target area. Each group conducted air strike operations against enemy airfields and harbors for two or three successive days around the clock. Then, the whole task force retired to a point several hundred miles away to rendezvous with their service and supply ships. Two or three days later, after completion of the resupplying operation, the task force went back to its launch points and repeated the attack procedure. Land-based Japanese planes put up stiff opposition. Each time the task force returned to action, we stood by to act as a "lifeguard" for downed aviators.

At the time the enlisted crew on *Guardfish* did not know that all of this was going on, of course, even though planes repeatedly drove us down each night. We merely stood our watches and wished that the sea would calm down. It was getting very rough.

As we patrolled north and south across the channel, our station gradually moved west each night. Unable to get any star sightings with his sextant, the exec navigated by radar, fathometer, and charts. Each night the weather became increasingly severe, so the captain had us modify our north and south patrol headings. To stay on station and minimize the stress on the boat, we headed easterly into the winds and waves on each tack. This caused the bow of the ship to trace a circular, rocking motion, as we rose on the swells and crashed down the other side.

I remember one of those nights vividly. The below decks watchman woke me to go on duty and I had to struggle to get out of my bunk. As my feet hit the deck, the boat quivered, lurched, and threw me sprawling. I stumbled into the adjoining bunks as I dressed and again fell to the deck as I looked for my shoes. Finally, fully dressed, I cautiously held onto the bunk side rails as I made my way forward through the darkened crew's space. I opened the door into the brightly lighted crew's mess and saw one of the cooks holding a large, deep pan tightly to his chest with both hands. At that moment the boat pitched violently, the cook tumbled over backward to the deck, and the pan's contents baptized him with several gallons of jiggling Jello!

The storm's ferocity continued to get worse. On December 17, Admiral Halsey ordered his task force through the storm to the resupply rendezvous point, east of the northern tip of Luzon. The waiting service ships, Task Group 30.8, intended to provide the task force with fuel oil, aviation gasoline, airplanes, replacement parts, consumable supplies, ammunition, food, and replacement personnel. The armada, the task force plus the supply group, totaled over 130 ships. Since at that time we did not have weather satellites or long-range Doppler weather radar, Halsey unknowingly led the entire assemblage directly into the eye of a gigantic typhoon (hurricane). The violent winds, in excess of 115 miles per hour, battered the ships with waves over sixty feet high. The result was the worst storm disaster in the United States Naval history. Three destroyers capsized and sank, twenty-eight combat ships suffered structural damage, 156 airplanes washed into the sea, most from the flight decks of huge aircraft carriers, and worst of all, 798 men lost their lives. The typhoon[5] continued slowly on its heading toward us, just north of Luzon. We battled through the storm night after night, its waves crashing over our bow and battering the little radio mast and wire antennas stretching up from the conning tower. Because the antennas were under water so much of the time, radio communication was very difficult. As the storm intensity grew, heavy walls of water broke over the bridge with increasing frequency.

One night, we nearly lost Seaman John R. (Johnny) Johnson. He was at his after-lookout position, holding onto the after TBT as tightly as he could, when a wave picked him up, carried him aft about twenty-five feet, smashed him down onto the main deck, and wrapped him around a vertical lifeline support stanchion at the deck's edge. He was fortunate to escape with only a couple of broken ribs. Had he been washed overboard, we would never have seen him again.

Submerged patrol during the daylight hours was a relief from the pounding we suffered on surface at night. But even at a depth of one-hundred feet the boat pitched and rolled. At periscope depth it was like being on the surface, rolling this way, twisting that way. In reality, we were out of the water as much as in it. In addition to the periscope watch being nearly impossible, the underwater sound watches were also a waste of time since the water turbulence stirred and dispersed target ship sounds and buried them under severe water noise.

We experienced the typhoon's peak fury from December 20 through December 22. Since use of both the periscope and sonars were out of the question, the captain kept us on surface so we could at least use the radar. But even the radar was of little use. Its screen was cluttered with sea returns from waves out to the "radar horizon," some 13,000 yards away. (That is the horizon as the radar "sees" it, from the height of its antenna.) Waves regularly broke over the bridge, choking off air to the main induction. Its 30" diameter pipe carried air from the inlet, under the

---

[5] The full story of this incredible storm is related by the commanding officer of a ship from Task Force 38 in *Typhoon: The Other Enemy*, by C. Raymond Calhoun (Naval Institute Press, Annapolis, MD, 1977).

bridge decking aft of the conning tower compartment, to both engine rooms. The air-choking caused the engines to lose power and threatened to stall them. There was also severe danger of the water flooding and destroying the engines.

Faced with these prospects, the captain ordered all watertight doors to be open from the control room aft to the engine rooms. He also ordered the main induction valve closed, which meant the engine air was drawn down through the conning tower and aft through the boat. We ran that way, with wind actually whistling through the boat compartments, for two days. When the storm reached its maximum intensity, hundreds of gallons of sea water repeatedly crashed through the upper conning tower hatch, choking off the air each time. That, in turn, caused the interior air pressure to drop as the engines pumped air out of the boat like vacuum pumps. We felt the pressure change in our eyes, ears, throat, and chest. The hull and superstructure twisted and flexed as the boat cascaded through the water. She creaked, groaned and moaned. We heard the engines straining and slowing as the boat climbed the approaching water swells. When the boat reached the crest, her bow suspended in midair for a moment. Then, corkscrewing and writhing as if alive, her bow plummeted down and her stern rose out of the water. With the screws spinning in the air, the engines accelerated wildly. The boat gave a deathly shudder when her bow smashed down into the trough and through the oncoming wall of water.

The beating went on day after day and the storm took its toll. The battering caused one of the propulsion system's generator controls to burn out. In order for the electricians to make the repairs, the captain had us stay submerged one day in the calm, at a depth of 200 feet. And the port radio antenna, made of heavy bronze wire rope, broke from the constant wave bombardment. Two brave men, Brinkley and Hoblitzell, went topside during the storm, lashed themselves to the lifeline and repaired the antenna. But probably the most disturbing failures were the leaks that developed in the after battery compartment's pressure hull.

The leaks were in weld joints at the pressure hull's "soft patch," a removable section of hull through which battery cells could be installed and removed. During the refit at Pearl Harbor, the relief crew had removed and replaced the soft patch to exchange two dead electric cells. The storm-induced leaks were small and easy to control, when found. But the possibility of getting salt water into the battery sent a chill through the boat, since salt (sodium-chloride) breaks down in the acid electrolyte of a battery and produces deadly chlorine gas. The damage repair team kept a close watch on that soft patch during the remainder of the run.

On December 22, ComSubPac ordered our wolf pack and others to move west into the South China Sea to prepare for more "lifeguard" duty. As a result, a submarine from another pack, *USS Segundo*, joined us as we changed stations—and the storm went with us, too. Even so, we patrolled the Japanese shipping lanes off the coast of China as we waited for the Task Force 38 air attacks to resume. ComSubPac apparently did not know that the fleet was disabled and looking for overboard survivors. Finally, Admiral Halsey abandoned the search and directed his battered armada back to Ulithi for repairs, about 900 miles southeast of the northern tip of Luzon.

Before dawn on December 23, we received a disturbing message. *Sea Robin* contacted us by radar, told us they had lost a man overboard and asked us for help in the search. *Sea Dog* and *Segundo* were too far away to help so we quickly changed course to intercept the unfortunate boat. Battling heavy seas, it took us almost two hours to reach the search location. Using TBS radiotelephone, *Sea Robin* described the search plan and we joined with them. About three hours later a Japanese radar plane drove us both down, but we quickly returned to the surface and continued the search. Another fruitless hour went by and again we both were forced to submerge to avoid the radar plane. While we were below, *Sea Robin* communicated with us by Morse code, using their sonar equipment, and told us it was time to discontinue the hopeless search.

When Christmas day arrived we were about eighty miles east of the large Chinese island of Hainan, which is roughly 250 miles southwest of Hong Kong. The weather was still rough, but calmer than before, and the periscope watch officers were seeing signs of life; fishing boats and Japanese airplanes, but still no torpedo targets.

Our Christmas dinner, during a calm deep dive, was memorable. I still have a memento. Each place setting at the mess hall tables had a printed, folded menu. The cover page, in green Old English print, has Christmas Greetings addressed to the Officers and Men of the *Guardfish*. The menu inside lists the following items: Cream of Tomato Soup, Soda Crackers, Roast Young Tom Turkey, Giblet Gravy, Sage Dressing,

Candied Yams, Creamed Peas, Whole Kernel Corn, Stuffed Olives, Sweet Pickles, Parkerhouse Rolls, Mincemeat Pie, Ice Cream, Coffee, Iced Lemonade, Candy, and Cigars. Facing the menu, on the inside of the front cover, is the following verse that, in my sunset years, chokes me up:

> Breathes there a man, with soul so dead,
> Who never to himself hath said,
> This is my own, my native land!

Our patrol near Hainan continued for several days. We saw not a single enemy ship. Then on December 28, the fifteenth day on station in Convoy College, the captain's hopes rose. A coded message came in from United States forces located at the wartime seat of the Chinese government. Hammond wrote the following in his patrol report::

0155 Received contact report from Radio Chungking. Convoy was sighted by reconnaissance plane off south coast of Hainan on course 070° T. Reported course indicated convoy headed for Formosa. Changed course to get on estimated track.

Chapter Ten

Targets

Shortly after receiving the Radio Chungking reconnaissance report, *Sea Robin* found a northbound convoy hugging the southern coast of Hainan. The pack leader ordered *Sea Dog* toward the island, north of *Sea Robin*, and *Guardfish* to patrol farther north to catch the convoy if it slipped by the others. We approached within seventeen miles of the Hainan coast and then patrolled east and west across the assigned area for two days. Japanese planes repeatedly drove us down. Late on December 29 we received orders to move to a new lifeguard post. We traveled north and east, up around the coast of China, with the objective of being at the station south of Formosa three days later, on January 1.

As we cruised the surface about 150 miles southwest of Hong Kong, the sea was rough and visibility uncertain in the predawn December 30 morning. A crisp voice shouted out over the wind and waves from the port lookout, "Floating mine, one hundred yards off port beam!" The lookout spotted the mine as it rode into the dim light on the crest of the swells a couple of times but then disappeared. Lieutenant Howarth, the officer of the deck, reversed course and called over the loudspeaker system, "Gunnersmates to the bridge." When the gunners arrived, Howarth ordered them to set up the two twenty-millimeter guns on their common mount. He maneuvered the boat around, trying to find the mine again. Robert W. ("Gunner") Rose and Wilford W. ("Willy") Hill removed the cannons from their topside storage lockers and proceeded to put them on their twin gun mount. Howarth called to those on the bridge, "Keep a sharp lookout, men!" The search for the mine continued for over half an hour, as the sun rose and illuminated the sea and wind blown spray.

Unfortunately, the next time Howarth saw the mine it was dead ahead of the boat and too late for him to take evasive action. He held his breath and waited for an explosion as the metal explosive container traveled the full length of the boat on the port side, separated from the hull by only a few feet. After he regained his composure, he jockeyed the boat around until the gunners could get a draw a good bead on it. Hill manned the dual twenty-millimeter cannons and Rose hefted his favorite rifle, the BAR (Browning Automatic Rifle). They fired a hail of rounds and, with a little puff of smoke, the mine sank very unceremoniously. Jerry Howarth told me recently that, as he watched the mine stream past the boat, he was sure that we were goners.

Japanese planes forced us to submerge several times that day, and we apparently missed a contact report radioed by the other pack members while we were down. When we surfaced in early evening, we received messages from both *Sea Dog* and *Sea Robin*. They were southeast of Hainan, apparently making an approach on a target. Their position, course, and speed told Captain Hammond that we were too far away to join the attack.

We continued on our northeasterly course off the coast of China. About two hours before my 12:00 to 4:00 a.m. watch on December 31, the below decks watchman rousted me out of my bunk to fix the SJ radar. As we traveled hour after hour blind, without radar coverage, the watchstanders in the control room, conning tower, and on the bridge grew understandably uneasy. The radar officer, Lieutenant Schock, came by periodically and looked over my shoulder. Occasionally shipmates asked me in low voices, "How's it going, Conner?" I finally got it back in commission at 2:15 a.m. and breathed a sight of relief as I sat down in the conning tower to complete my watch.

On New Year's Day 1945, the captain reached the conclusion that Japanese planes were using our SJ radar signal to guide them to us. From then on, each time we picked up their VHF radar signal on the APR, we turned off our radar and only operated it briefly, every minute or so. He found that by operating the radar intermittently, the enemy plane often failed to locate us. After the war, investigators determined that Hammond was right. The Japanese had a simple microwave search receiver with which to track our radars.

The northeast monsoon winds and high seas prevented us from meeting our deadline of being on station January 1. ComSubPac ordered *Guardfish* to transmit nightly weather reports in order to prepare for the reentry of Task Force 38 into Convoy College, doubtless a reaction to the fleet's typhoon catastrophe two weeks earlier.

Reaching our lifeguard station a day late, we patrolled submerged east and west about 125 miles southwest of Formosa, waiting for Task Force 38 aerial sorties to begin. Japanese aircraft activity increased noticeably during the day. Lieutenant Schnepp, who had the periscope during the 8:00 a.m. to noon watch, spotted seven planes in short order: two with single engines, two seaplanes, and three twin engine bombers. Around 10:00 a.m., he notified the captain that he suspected something was happening, or about to happen, topside. His hunch proved correct.

It was 2:25 p.m., and we were submerged at 120 feet and I was on the helm, steering a due east course, when the underwater sound operator, Radioman third-class Charles B. (Ham) Hamilton, suddenly broke a long silence.

"Mr. Andrews, I have some weak pinging at one-six-oh degrees, sir."

"Put it on the speaker and let me hear it."

"Its pretty weak, sir, and there's a lot of background noise, but here it is."

We heard nothing but static, chirps, crashes, and popping sounds. But then out of the din we detected a faint pinging. It grew louder, and then faded out as the sonar beam slowly passed over us like a rotating searchlight.

"Well what do you know," Lt. Zenas B. Andrews said, "we may have some action. Captain to the conning tower. Control, come up to sixty-five feet."

Almost immediately, Captain Hammond hurried up the ladder into the conning tower. He stood erect, calmly taking in all that Lieutenant Andrews, our current communications officer, said to him.

"Captain, we have some pinging at two-five-zero degrees True," reported Lieutenant Andrews. "We're at one-third speed, course zero-nine-zero. We're coming up to periscope depth."

"Very well," replied the captain. "Up periscope. Sound, what's the bearing now?"

"One-six-one."

As the scope came out of the well, Hammond stooped over, caught its handles and snapped them down into their horizontal position. He put his eyes into the rubber light mask at the eyepiece and followed the scope up until it stopped. As soon as the glass broke the water he spun around, quickly searching the sky and then the horizon. He carefully searched back in the direction of the pinging.

"Down scope," he ordered. As he slammed the handles up against the periscope body, he added, "Mark your heading."

"Zero-nine-zero," I called out.

"Sound, what's the target bearing now?"

"One-six-two."

"All ahead standard. Come left to course two-seven-zero."

We stayed at periscope depth and every few minutes Hammond called for the 'scope to be raised so he could look for the pinging ship. The pinging was getting progressively louder. Fifteen minutes after the initial sound contact, the captain sighted masts of an enemy convoy poking up over the horizon.

"All ahead full. Battle stations submerged," he called out.

Bong! Bong! Bong! Bong! The call to action exhilarated the crew, who ran to their posts. A target at last!

After another fifteen minutes passed, three ships with two escorts hove into view. They drew north of us on a zigzag course at high speed, apparently headed for Takao or the Pescadores Channel. Takao (now Kaohfiung) is a town located at the northern end of a bay near the southern tip of Formosa. The Pescadores Channel is about seventy-five miles northwest of Takao, between Formosa and the small island of Pescadores. We changed our heading to the convoy's calculated base course and continued tracking.

It soon became clear that we could not close to firing range while submerged. When the fast convoy disappeared from view, we secured from battle stations. The captain called the radar tracking party to the conning tower, surfaced, went to full speed on four main engines, and initiated an "end around" maneuver. As soon as we surfaced, I established radar contact at 27,000 yards, a clear indication that the ships we were tracking were large ones. To be detectable at that distance, sizable portions of their superstructure had to be sticking up above the radar's 13,000-yard horizon. At this time the Japanese convoy was slightly east of due north from us. The maximum speed we could get out of the boat was only seventeen knots, about four knots below normal because our course took us into the heavy monsoon-driven sea. The boat shuddered each time her bow pounded and twisted into the relentless oncoming swells. Sea spray pelted the bridge, and occasionally water came down the upper conning tower hatch.

Lieutenant Howarth was on the bridge, standing his regular watch as officer of the deck. Lieutenant Schock operated the radar's PPI in surface-search mode, and I operated the A-scope for fire control ranges and bearings. Captain Hammond remained in the conning tower at the raised periscope. He knew that it was going to be hours before we were in position to attack. Even though it was daylight, the northern horizon was too dark for the skipper to see the ships.

I stopped the radar antenna rotation each time it came to the target bearing, switched to manual operation, and read off the new range and bearing for Lieutenant Jennings, the TDC operator. Hammond divided his attention between the periscope and the TDC. The skipper carried on a conversation with the exec, Lt. Commander Johnson, as the situation developed.

"Luther," said Captain Hammond. "I think we have a chance of getting around them into firing position if they are going to Takao. It's about 125 miles dead ahead of us, isn't it?"

"Yes Captain, that's right. Our speed advantage will fix us up, as long as they continue their zigzag course. But if they stop zigzagging we may lose our advantage."

"Now if they're planning to go through the Pescadores Channel, they will have to turn north, away from us," responded Hammond. "That will produce a more difficult problem. Let's hope that their destination is Takao."

Hour after hour our end around run continued on the surface. Amazingly, no aircraft were flying cover to bother us. We slowly moved ahead, east of the convoy beyond their horizon. Every time Jennings saw that the convoy had "zigged," he reported the TDC results to the captain. It looked as though we were going to soon be in a position to attack the ships. Suddenly, Jennings realized something was amiss.

"Captain," he said, "it looks like they've changed their base course. They're moving north."

"Very well," came the reply. "Tell me what the new course is when you get enough data."

"I've got it now, they're zigzagging around a base course of zero-five-zero. Their rate of advance on the base course is still fourteen knots."

"Very well, come left to zero-five-zero."

Our slight forward advantage in position evaporated with the convoy's new course. Determined to strike, Captain Hammond continued maneuvering the boat to find a way to get at the enemy. By 7:40 p.m. the sky was beginning to darken as the captain began closing the range to determine the disposition of the convoy's escorts. At about 22,000 yards, intermittent pips revealed two escorts covering the starboard flank. Captain Hammond's patrol report picks up from here:

2007 Range to leading ship in column, 15,000 yards. We now had a total of seven ships on the radar screen, three large ships in close column formation and four escorts. Continued tracking and end around, maintaining range of not less than 15,000 yards from leading ship and 12000 yards from nearest escort.

2029 Disposition of convoy as follows: One large AP [transport] and two large AP-AK's in close column formation, one DD [destroyer] escort about 3,000 yards on starboard bow of leading ship, one DD patrolling approximately 3,000 yards on starboard beam of center ship, one unidentified escort on port side of convoy, and one small unidentified escort trailing at a range of about 4,000 yards. Since time was not available to reach a more favorable position on port flank before convoy reaches Pescadores Channel, it was decided to go in from present position. Chances of getting inside the two starboard escorts without detection was slim. Planned to shoot three bow tubes at the beam escort and remaining bow tubes and stern tubes at second and third ships in column—or to accept any favorable shot. With range to leading ship 14,000 yards, headed in at seventeen knots.

As we closed the range on the convoy, we went back to battle stations. The captain stayed at the periscope, his demeanor cool and decisive.

"Quartermaster, make a notation in the log," instructed the skipper. "One of the ships just flashed a red light. Radar, mark range to the nearest target."

"9,500 yards, sir." We were getting close.

"It looks like he's firing at us. Yes, again—and again. Their deflection is right on, they're splashing right on our bearing, but falling short. Did you see the splashes, radar?"

"No, sir, but the sea returns are out to 4,000 yards. They could have masked the splashes."

"Give me a range to the leading ship."

"11,500 yards."

One minute after the escort opened fire, we heard three distant depth charges. The blasts were probably from the other escorts, joining in to create confusion. The night was dark, the sky overcast, and the moon was not due to rise for two hours. According to the captain, he could see only dim blurs of the large ships, but he could not see the escort at all—either before or after he saw the gun fire. The enemy, he reasoned, could not have sighted us either. "This escort was undoubtedly equipped with efficient radar,"Hammond concluded in his patrol report. He came to that conclusion, even though our *APR search receiver had not detected any enemy radar over its entire tuning range. Personally, I think they tracked us by homing in on our SJ radar signal.

However, they found us, the Japanese escort closed range on us for about ten minutes, forcing us to turn away from the convoy. After she returned to her station with the convoy, we headed back and resumed tracking. About that time we entered an area we called a "blind bombing zone," which allowed Task Force 38 planes to attack any submarine without giving warning. It was a dangerous place for *Guardfish* to be running about on the surface.

Reluctantly, Hammond reached the conclusion that it was no longer feasible to follow the convoy because the channel was classified as "restricted waters." That meant the area was mined by the Japanese. We would have to stay on surface and follow behind the convoy to keep from getting tangled with the mines. But since it was clear the enemy was tracking us and there was no maneuvering room for evasive action in the mined channel, the captain wisely appreciated the odds were not in our favor. We continued tracking while moving northeastward, however, so that if the convoy changed course toward Takao, we would be in position to attack. At 10:00 p.m., the enemy ships entered the channel and we lost contact. Hammond sent a contact report to ComSubPac for benefit of submarines or American planes north of the channel. As we reversed course and returned to our patrol station, despondency enveloped the boat.

Task Force 38 returned to Convoy College on January 3 with aerial attacks on Formosa. Our lifeguard assignment was southwest of Takao. We remained submerged, using our raised SD radar mast as a communications antenna, over which we monitored the aircraft frequency. We spent the next day on the surface, south of the blind bombing zone and still on lifeguard duty. Lieutenant Schock manned the SD air search radar, keying it on only five seconds out of every minute so as not to vector Japanese planes to our position. He also monitored the *IFF transponder to see if any American planes interrogated us; none did.

About 9:25 a.m. the junior officer of the deck spotted a submarine periscope northwest of us at about a range of 3,000 yards. We evaded at high speed. A while later the radar detected an aircraft closing in on us, so we made a quick dive, then reversed course in an attempt to engage the submarine. The captain thought that the sub might surface and trail us since we were probably out of sight before submerging. The submarine, however, was not seen again. A "cat and mouse" game between opposing subs was a nerve jangling experience. When both boats were submerged, the game was more like blind man's buff.

The next morning we received a radio message that we had missed the previous day. The submarine periscope seen the day before was probably that of USS Aspro. We were in her assigned patrol area!

January 5 found us still on lifeguard duty, but with our station moved to a position southwest of the Pescadores Channel. We noted a great deal of aircraft activity on the radar, but nothing approached us and we did not pick up any calls for help. About 10:00 p.m. we received instructions from ComSubPac to move to a new lifeguard station south of Hong Kong. By the following day we were about seventy miles off the coast of China, part way to our new station, battling following seas and monsoon winds. About the middle of the 8:00 to 12:00 night watch, SJ radar reported a contact southwest of us at a range of 25,000 yards.

Lieutenant Schnepp, the officer of the deck, called for the captain. Following standing orders, Schnepp changed course to head toward the target. When Hammond arrived in the conning tower, he viewed the radar screen for a short while and then ordered, "Man the radar tracking party."

When we began the tracking there were three strong pips at a range of 23,000 yards. By the time the range dropped to 18,000 yards, still beyond the SJ radar horizon, two more targets appeared. It quickly became apparent that the targets' course was due northeast, running into the wind and parallel with the Chinese coast at a speed of five knots. In addition to the detection range, the pips had other characteristics common to radar returns from large ships. As the radar "viewed" the targets from different angles, the tops of the largest pips separated into two peaks on the A-scope, as if the ship had two large masts or superstructure features. Weak radar interference from the target bearing appeared on our SJ radar screens. The interference patterns on the A-scope convinced me they were not from American radar. The three largest targets were running side by side, with a constant separation of 800 yards. The smaller targets were in the lead.

The formation made Captain Hammond suspicious. He got us in position ahead of the target group and reduced speed so we could use our sound gear effectively and listen for other clues. We heard nothing. At a range of 10,000 yards the largest pips reached their maximum saturation height on the A-scope. We continued to close range, but nothing was visible from the bridge at 8,000 yards, even though visibility conditions were relatively good.

The captain left the conning tower, went to the wardroom and conferred with the other officers. He became convinced that our targets were really radar decoys, perhaps drawing us into a trap. Lieutenant Schock came up to the conning tower and showed me a Naval Intelligence department publication that pictured a typical radar decoy. It was a barge on which a large wire screen stretched between masts to produce a very efficient radar-wave reflector. Such a screen had low visibility and low wind resistance. Thus, a sea-going tug could tow one or more such decoys quite nicely, even during monsoon winds. Perhaps it was the wind that kept the tethered barges precisely separated.

Back in the conning tower, Hammond seemed indecisive and confused. He stood at the raised periscope, with his head drooped down between his arms as they hooked over the periscope handles. Then, strangely, he called for battle stations. We closed range to 2,800 yards and without ever seeing anything, fired three torpedoes. Hammond hoped to hit one of the supposed towing vessels. It was a futile effort, and all three torpedoes missed. He toyed with the idea of tracking the group until daylight, to make a submerged inspection, but realized that the decoy's course would draw us into dangerously shallow waters. On January 7 at 2:34 a.m., Hammond decided to disengage and resume the course to our new lifeguard station. After the patrol, Hammond's superiors criticized him for not getting closer before firing torpedoes at unseen shallow-draft targets, or "radar ghosts."

The next week American forces made history. As Task Force 38 swept into the South China Sea and battered the entire perimeter of Convoy College, American forces invaded the Philippine's main island of Luzon. We spent that historic week on lifeguard station, battling gale force winds and high seas. Raging sea water continued to make our life miserable, pouring over the bridge and down the conning tower hatch. The salt water disabled our forward periscope when it grounded out its electrical panel in the conning tower. The pounding sea bent our forward radio mast and caused both radio communications antennas to be carried away. Men went topside again, risked their lives in the raging seas, and rigged temporary antennas in order to maintain our communications link with other boats and ComSubPac. On January 14 we sighted another floating mine but were unable to keep track of it because of the high sea. The SJ radar went out of commission for the better part of the next day. Hammond submerged the boat so Joe Masters and I could work on it in the quiet deep. We really appreciated that, and we got the radar operating in time for me to go on the next day's early watch.

That evening, January 16, we received orders from ComSubPac to return to base. They cautioned us to be on the lookout for Japanese submarines known to be patrolling the sea lanes around Guam, our destination.

Chapter Eleven

Submarine Alert

Before leaving our station on January 17 to return to base, Captain Hammond radioed ComSubPac to ask for an extension of the patrol. Radioman Brink Brinkley found it difficult to get the message off because the sea was repeatedly crashing over the transmitting antenna. Ultimately, he succeeded by keying the transmitter only when the boat's bow was on the crest of the sea swells, with the antenna out of the water. Hammond wanted to stay on surface to be able to receive the answer, but when an unidentified plane drove us down in the midmorning, he decided to stay down for a while to give the crew a rest from the battering sea. Morale was very low and the sea's constant pounding didn't help matters.

Returning to base with an unsuccessful "dry run" mortified the crew because most of us believed this was the first unsuccessful patrol for the famous *Guardfish*. Owing to the "sea story silence," we did not know that the fourth patrol, under the illustrious Burt Klakring, had also been unsuccessful. In an effort to boost morale, Hammond decided that the time was ripe for a renewal of the boat-wide cribbage tournament. The games took place over several days while we were submerged. Someone regularly announced the current standings over the boat's speaker system. The chief of the boat, Earl Beasley, soon replaced Ojay Johnson as the new *Guardfish* champ.

We found the weather was not much better when we surfaced. Waves continued to break over the bow radio antennas, making reception impossible. I remember Brink's frustration over our inability to copy the fleet ("Fox schedule") messages transmitted from Pearl Harbor, or even those automatically relayed through Guam. Out of desperation, he asked permission to disable the SD radar so he could use its mast as a receiving antenna. His plan worked, and the radiomen happily copied Fox with comparative ease. They focussed their attention on traffic to submarines. A flurry of messages came through addressed to boats around Guam and Saipan warning them of the presence of hostile submarines. In the evening, our radio watch copied the awaited message to *Guardfish* from ComSubPac: the brass refused to allow us to extend the patrol.

During the dark morning hours of January 18, the ravenous sea again devoured our bow antennas, and when daylight came our men again went topside to replace them. During this daunting task, we took so much water down the conning tower hatch that the search periscope's electrical panel in the conning tower was permanently shorted out, preventing its further use. As we approached Formosa later that day, a Japanese radar plane repeatedly forced us to submerge. Shortly after returning to the surface, we struck a solid object with such force that it resounded throughout the ship. The lookouts couldn't see anything from the bridge. Was it submerged wreckage? A dud mine? A log? A faulty enemy torpedo? We will never know.

As we went east through Luzon Straits on January 19, we spent the daylight hours submerged. I always felt peaceful and safe when we were submerged. Most of the scary things seemed to happen on the surface. For example, on the very next day, January 20, we were running on surface northeast of Luzon when the diving alarm went off by itself. It took everyone completely by surprise. "Ah-oo-ga, Ah-oo-ga," rang through the boat, but nobody was near any of the alarm contactors (switches). The officer of the deck had not called "Clear the bridge" and he had not called "Dive! Dive!" over the loudspeaker system. Watchstanders throughout the boat knew they were not supposed to act in response to the alarm unless it was preceded by the "Dive! Dive!" call. But everyone was afraid not to act, for fear that we were about to be bombed. So we dove anyway. Fortunately, we did not go down with the conning tower hatch open and nobody was left topside. Electricians later said they located a "ground defect" in the diving alarm circuit on the bridge. They disconnected the circuit so a bogus alarm would not take us by surprise again.

In the late afternoon of the same day we received a message from Guam, addressed to *Guardfish*. The communication gave the captain instructions about the courses to take and where to rendezvous with the ship that was to escort us into the harbor five days hence. Guam also warned us once again that enemy submarines were patrolling around the island and that one had fired three torpedoes at *Queenfish* that day. Captain Hammond pointed out to his officers the message's warning: if you run into an enemy submarine, "be sure to shoot first."

Aerial activity seemed to be increasing on January 21, so the captain insisted that the SD radar be reactivated. Of course, that meant that the radiomen had to use the uncertain bow antennas for communication, in seas that were again increasing in height. Shortly after dawn the officer of the deck sent men topside again to make adjustments to the battered antenna mast. One of the huge waves crashed over the bridge and knocked several lookouts down. First class Electrician's Mate Dominic J. (Chico) Policicchio received severe bruises on his chest, left arm, and hip. During the night, when the sea trashed the antennas again, the radiomen reconnected the SD mast for communications reception and promptly received a message addressed to *Guardfish*. The submarine wolfpack command at Guam reported the position of a Japanese submarine, located by *RDF (radio direction finder), to be about 500 miles northwest of Guam. That was slightly north of where we were scheduled to be in two days.

The unrelenting sea continued to pound the boat. Amidst the raging waves and the black of night, men went up and rigged temporary antennas from the bridge to the ailing bow mast. Late on January 22, sea water flooded and damaged one of the main engines in the forward engine room. The next morning, sea water cracked another piston, this time in the after engine room. Our entire force of machinists worked for two days repairing the engines. That afternoon huge seas injured another lookout, Seaman Aloysius E. (Mac) McCarey. The Pharmacist's Mate reported that Mac received severe lacerations in his scalp.

Three hours after McCarey's injury, the bow antenna mast "gave up the ghost." Heavy waves, repeatedly breaking over the front of the boat, sheared the mast off flush with the deck and took both long-wire antennas down at the same time. Now we only had the SD radar mast for use as a communication antenna. That meant, of course, that we could not use the SD radar, or its associated IFF equipment, to detect or identify aircraft. We had to rely on our lookouts to spot high flying planes, which the SJ surface-search radar could not detect. I recall feeling very uneasy about this development.

As the 4:00 to 8:00 evening watch changed, Lieutenant Schock, the officer of the deck, passed the conn to Lieutenant Schnepp, then went below into the conning tower to sit at the radar PPI and watch the screen for a while. Although he was the radar officer and a member of the radar tracking party, it was unusual for him to man the radar during a normal watch. But Schock knew we were close to the location where that Japanese sub was reported to be operating, and he was concerned about it.

Schock remained at the radar for over half an hour. He was getting ready to go below and get a cup of hot coffee when he thought he saw a "pip" on the radar screen. He waited for the antenna to come around again to that point and sure enough, it was there again.

"I have a pip on the radar, bearing three-zero-zero degrees, range 11,000 yards," he announced.

"Captain to the conning tower," responded the officer of the deck.

Schock was keyed up. In a calm sea, the SJ radar normally detected a fully surfaced submarine near the radar's horizon of 13,000 yards. However, the detection range was 11,000 yards or less when only the target's conning tower was out of the water (the normal patrolling mode). Depending on the condition of the sea and the synchronization between the antenna rotation and the ocean swells, the detection range could be much less than 11,000 yards. We had not received notification that we were about to cross the path of any other American submarine. In addition, since all independently operating American ships utilized *ten centimeter-band radar, and Japanese submarines did not, the lack of radar interference made this target very suspicious.

"Captain, I think we may have found that Jap sub we've been warned about. Look at it on the screen here, there are no radar indications."

Hammond, with a furrowed brow, studied the screen for a while and then replied. "You could be right, but remember we are in a joint zone, so that could be one of our own boats—or it could be a small friendly surface craft with its radar out of commission. We'll track it and see what we can find." He turned to the man operating the 1MC speaker system. "Man the radar tracking party."

The captain went to the bridge and found the sea much calmer than it had been only hours earlier. There were light rain squalls and an overcast sky, but the moon broke through occasionally. He had us close range to about 10,000 yards and, after careful scrutiny, commented that he could sometimes see an indistinct blur at the target bearing. He moved us away as the exec went below to calculate our position and prepare a contact report. We stayed at 12,000 to 13,000 yards, the maximum radar range, so as to not disclose our own presence to the target while we were communicating with ComSubPac.

Captain Hammond was perplexed. Because our regular radio antennas had been carried away by the sea only hours before, we had to use our SD air-search radar mast as a radio antenna for the urgent radio communications he was about to initiate. Thus, we were essentially blind to the presence of high flying radar-equipped planes except for our APR radar search receiver. But since we were only a couple of days out from Guam, it was unlikely that they would be enemy planes. We did have our IFF transponder activated, so if friendly planes used their IFF interrogator units, they would know they were passing over an American submarine—unless they ignored our IFF returns, as so many American planes had done in the past. Of course, without the SD radar we also could not use our IFF interrogator. But, Hammond figured, so what? Practically everything about that IFF system was a joke. And, to make things more ironic, the word was out that the Japanese were using captured American IFF gear to deceive U.S. forces.

Brink Brinkley had difficulty tuning up the shortwave radio transmitter using the SD mast antenna. Normally, the most reliable radio link was to send the message to Guam, and have them retransmit it to ComSubPac at Pearl Harbor. But the radar mast antenna was too short to operate properly on the low frequency normally used for strong signal communication with Guam. Brink had to tune-up on a higher frequency channel where the antenna produced such a low-angle sky wave that the signal skipped right over Guam. Thus, he had to try to communicate directly with Pearl Harbor. After repeatedly calling Pearl and listening for a response, he finally established contact. Even though his signal was very weak in Hawaii, he got the message through. Before encoding the serial number-nine message, it read:

AT POSITION 15-11 NORTH 137 EAST WE HAVE RADAR CONTACT
ON SMALL SHIP POSSIBLY SUBMARINE X NO RADAR INDICATIONS
X COURSE 270 SPEED 11 X COULD IT BE A FRIENDLY SUBMARINE X
WE ARE TRAILING XX

While Brink was sending off the contact report, Captain Hammond
moved *Guardfish* around the stern of the target to its other side. That
positioned us in a darker background, reducing the chances that the
target could detect us.

When Brinkley was finally available, the captain ordered him up to
the conning tower to man our underwater sound receiver in order check
if the target was using sonar. The captain also had the communications
officer, Lieutenant Andrews, carefully tune the APR radar search receiver over its entire range to look for any evidence that the target had
radar. No pinging or radar signals of any kind could be detected.

We were en route to Guam in a "joint zone," a sea lane designed to
protect us and friendly surface craft from being attacked by friendly
ships or aircraft. It seemed strange that a small, friendly surface craft,
without radar or sonar, would ever be this far away from base without an
escorting vessel. If it was a friendly surface ship or submarine, it would
stay within the joint zone as a matter of naval discipline and self protection. But as midnight approached, the exec reported to the captain that
the target's course was taking it out of the joint zone, directly toward the
northern boundary of Luzon. This was a new ball game. Regulations
allowed us to leave the protected zone if we were in hot pursuit of a
potential enemy, but we had to give ComSubPac notice that we were
doing so.

After being relieved from the sound watch by Joe Masters, Brinkley
went to the radio room to transmit another message to ComSubPac. He
repeatedly called *NPM, Radio Pearl Harbor, without any response.
After an hour of calls, he received an answer from a navy station in
Darwin, Australia. Those operators took the following message, to relay
to Pearl:

REFER TO MY SERIAL 9 X UNLESS OTHERWISE DIRECTED WILL
MAINTAIN CONTACT AND ATTACK WHEN POSITIVE OF ENEMY
CHARACTER X POSITION IS 15-30 AND 136-30 X COURSE 280 SPEED
10.5 XX

A little over an hour later the wolfpack's Task Group Command (CTG 17.7) at Saipan radioed the following message to *Guardfish*:

AM INVESTIGATING POSSIBILITY OF FRIENDLY SURFACE SHIP AND WILL ADVISE X CONTINUE TRACKING X NO FRIENDLY SUB SHOULD BE THERE XX

Ten minutes later, we received a message from ComSubPac at Pearl:

THERE ARE NO FRIENDLY SUBMARINES IN YOUR VICINITY AS SHOWN BY OUR BOARD EXCEPTING SEADOG WHOM YOU KNOW ABOUT AND PLAICE AND SCABBARDFISH WHO ARE ABOUT 400 MILES FARTHER EAST IN ACCORDANCE WITH CTG 17.7 DISPATCH 220351 X IF CONTACT IS SURFACE SHIP IT PROBABLY IS A FRIENDLY SINCE YOU ARE INSIDE OF JOINT ZONE XX

At about 1:30 in the morning on January 24, Hammond instructed the radar tracking party to break off and get some sleep. He told the watch officer of the deck to maintain our distance from the target at the maximum radar range and to notify him of any obvious change in target course. Since it was my regular watch time, I stayed on the radar.

Fred Jennings and Dick Schock recently told me that the wardroom was filled with officers bristling with emotions after Hammond and his entourage came down from the conning tower. The captain's plan was to wait until it was almost dawn, submerge, and visually identify the target as the enemy before launching any attack. Jennings claimed they all admired Hammond, but "there was a strong feeling that our lack of success was due solely to the timidity with which the patrol had been conducted."

Jennings, Schock and others tried to persuade him to attack. The target has left the joint zone and is heading to northern Luzon, thus it is not one of our subs, they argued. If it were a friendly surface craft, it would not be out here with no radar, no sonar, and no escort; the radar range and everything else point to it being an enemy submarine probably headed to Luzon to battle the American invasion forces; or, the target might be going to evacuate key Japanese personnel, as they had done in other places after American forces invaded. Now is the time to attack, they continued, while the submarine was on the surface. If we wait until dawn, we will miss our opportunity because he will dive and then we might be the target.

Their arguments failed to sway Hammond. At 3:38 a.m., however, we received another message from the Task Group Command at Saipan that changed the skipper's mind:

YOU ARE IN A JOINT ZONE X THERE IS NOTHING FRIENDLY KNOWN IN THE VICINITY 15-11 NORTH 137 EAST XX

Hammond went to the bridge and ordered battle stations at 3:45 a.m. Contrary to the last message from Saipan, we were well outside the joint zone. The captain ordered the boat to pull ahead, northwest of the target and to prepare for a submerged approach. As the target closed in, we would be far enough ahead by dawn to have sufficient visibility for identification. But he realized that, if it was an enemy submarine, it might dive before sunrise. Thus, he did not want to get too far ahead.

It took us two hours to get into the leading position. We submerged 13,600 yards ahead of, and approximately 2,000 yards from, the oncoming track of the target. About twenty minutes later Brinkley picked up screws on the underwater sound equipment and shortly thereafter the captain spotted it through the attack periscope. The range was about 6,800 yards.

The sky was completely overcast with intermittent light rain squalls. Through the periscope the oncoming target's silhouette contrasted poorly against the dim glow of the predawn, eastern sky. As it approached, Captain Hammond strained to discern its features. Johnson, the exec, called out the periscope bearings and ranges to the TDC, and at the same time reminded Hammond of the periscope exposure time, so as not to be spotted by the oncoming vessel.

Drawing closer, the target moved southeast of us, all the while the sky growing progressively brighter. During four prolonged observations through the scope, Hammond called for the three Office of Naval Intelligence silhouette books stored in the conning tower. Without revealing what silhouette he had selected, he told Johnson to view the target and identify it. They both independently selected the same page from the same book: it was the Japanese submarine *I-165*.

"Quickly, before he submerges, do we have a firing solution?" asked Hammond.

"Yes, captain."

"What's the firing setup?"

"Range 1,200 yards. Angle on the bow, fifty degrees starboard. Torpedo run 600 yards. Track angle seventy starboard."

"Prepare to fire four fish with a two degree spread."

"Commence firing."

Johnson fired torpedoes number one through four and counted the running time aloud by his stopwatch. One minute and eighteen seconds after firing the first torpedo we heard the first one hit and eight seconds later the second one. Hammond raised the periscope, saw the target surrounded by smoke, and watched it sink.

"Prepare to surface. Gun team to the conning tower. Prepare to pick up prisoners."

According to the book *Submarines of The Imperial Japanese Navy*[6], *I-165* was quite similar in appearance to an American fleet boat. It had about the same displacement, length, breadth, and speed. However, it had tall radio masts fore and aft of the conning tower and a differently-shaped conning tower, farther aft than our boats. It was one of three Japanese submarines called the KD5 type, which included *I-166* and *I-167*, both of which were lost before 1945.

Strange feelings and thoughts filled me as I ran from my submerged battle station to my spot in the conning tower. I felt elation, because we overcame the enemy one more time, but mixed with feelings of sorrow and loss. We sank a submarine, one very much like ours, and its crew went down in their steel coffin—just like ours. "I wonder why the old man thinks there will be prisoners?" I recall thinking to myself. "Well, maybe there'll be a few survivors from the bridge watch. It's likely that nobody from inside the boat got out alive."

As soon as we surfaced, both the captain and the exec hurried to the bridge. We moved in toward the point where the enemy boat went down. Gunner Rose and Willy Hill, the gun team, were topside to protect our crewmen during the rescue of potentially belligerent survivors.

In the conning tower, Yeoman Joseph (Joe) Koch, who kept the Ship's Log during battle stations, went to the periscope; it was still in its

---

[6] *Submarines of The Imperial Japanese Navy*, by D. Carpenter and N. Polmar (Naval Institute Press, Annapolis, MD, 1986).

raised position. He looked through it and described what he saw to the rest of us. "There's lots of floating debris. . . And I see a bunch of guys in the water, too. . . . Hey, do the Japs have blacks in their crews?" Then he cried out in alarm, "Don't shoot!"

I was dumbfounded when the dripping, oily, voiceless survivors began streaming down through the conning tower into the control room. I could not believe my eyes: they were Americans.

Thankfully, the visibility had improved markedly and the water was relatively calm as we searched for survivors. During the search we picked up a total of seventy-three men, including the ship's commanding officer, Lt. Horace M. Babcock. The ship proved to be *USS Extractor* (ARS-15), an Auxiliary Rescue and Salvage vessel. The head count indicated that six men were missing. We continued searching around the wreckage and to leeward at slow speed. After three hours, both Captains Babcock and Hammond concluded that it was futile to search any longer.

As we departed the search area, a pall of gloom and anxiety encased the crowded boat. Captain Hammond composed a message to ComSub-Pac about the tragedy, but our radio transmission was repeatedly interrupted by the hostile approach of American airplanes. Each time as we submerged we fired recognition flares into the air, hoping to prevent further attacks. Finally, slightly before noon, we got the message off and all settled in for the awkward two-day trip to Guam.

Before half a day had passed, a message arrived from Vice Admiral John Howard Hoover, Commander of the Forward Area at Guam:

IN THE CASE OF GUARDFISH AND EXTRACTOR A COURT OF INQUIRY HAS BEEN ORDERED XX

Guardfish's Tenth War Patrol
and Extractor Sinking Location

Map 5

Chapter Twelve

USS Extractor

The navy commissioned *Extractor* on March 3, 1944 in Stockton, California, an inland deep water port some eighty miles due east of San Francisco in the agriculturally rich San Joaquin Valley. Ocean-going ships put in there through San Francisco Bay and the San Joaquin River. From the late 1800s, Colberg Boat Works, *Extractor*'s builder, had been a respected yacht and small boat yard. The nationwide mobilization during World War II swept Colberg into a new mode of operation. It constructed large wooden vessels, such as minesweepers, as well as six diesel-electric ships like *Extractor*, each 183 feet in length and displacing 1,089 tons.

The first contract for ships of *Extractor's* configuration was actually from Great Britain and utilized British design drawings. However, when the United States Navy found an urgent need for wooden (nonmagnetic) salvage vessels to counteract the enemy's use of magnetically detonated mines at harbor entrances, Colberg temporarily set aside the British order. The first three hulls (ARS-13, 14, and 15) became U.S. Navy ships, while the subsequent three hulls went to the Royal Navy.

Extractor's "homey design," serviceable, rugged and yet decorative, was appreciated by her crew. "Her hull was heavily built. . .almost antique," remembered Lt. (junior grade) Semmes Chapman, the ship's salvage officer and head of the salvage diving team, "with sawn ribs in the order of eight to ten inch cross section." Her planking, he continued, was almost as heavy, and was caulked in an old style, by hand. Her superstructure was welded steel, with interior trim showing yacht-like mahogany doors and built-ins. The galleys and mess hall, ship offices and Chiefs' quarters were on the main deck, with crews' berthing below. A well equipped machine shop was forward, preceded by an open cargo hold of two decks. A smaller cargo hatch was aft, beyond the engine room. Two heavy wood masts carried working booms of ten-tons forward and five-tons aft. The towing bitt at the stern had a power reel with two and a quarter inch diameter wire hawsers. . .Deck cargo included two four-ton salvage anchors lashed down forward, and two on the fantail—in addition to heavy ship's anchors. Holds had salvage pumps and compressors, four sets of hard hat diving gear in oak chests, and smaller utility compressors. Ship based diving was supplied with air from the engine room. . . .

Extractor sailed into the Pacific on May 8, 1944, the same month I left San Francisco aboard *Guardfish*. Commanded by a mustang, Lt. (junior grade) Leslie C. Oaks, *Extractor*'s initial assignment was to escort two civilian seagoing tugs, each with two concrete barges in tow, to remote Eniwetok atoll in the Marshall Islands group, about 1,000 miles east and slightly south of Guam. The atoll, captured from the Japanese three months before *Extractor*'s arrival, was slowly filling with a vast armada of U.S. and Allied ships.

From the time *Extractor* dropped anchor in Eniwetok harbor on June 6 until she departed two months later, she was in constant demand for emergency rescue missions and salvage operations. At any moment's notice her squadron commander expected her to be ready to go to the assistance of a vessel in distress, even if it meant putting herself at risk. Such was the case when a minesweeper was sinking outside the harbor. *Extractor*'s order from her squadron operations officer was to leave, "regardless of her [*Extractor's*] condition," and that is what she repeatedly did throughout her brief life. *Extractor* gained a reputation for being a real workhorse, one result of which was the promotion of her skipper to the rank of full lieutenant.

Lieutenant Chapman discussed with the author some of the invaluable work performed by *Extractor*. "A major assignment at Eniwetok was refloating the [merchant ship] SS *Sea Flyer*," Chapman remembered. *Sea Flyer* was "stranded on an entrance channel reef with a full combat load of marines and equipment." The ship was off-loaded by

USS Extractor sister ship. *National Archives*

SeaBeas and stabilized with two heavy anchor sets. *Extractor*, with others assisting, "laid other anchors astern for bodily dragging the ship clear. *Sea Flyer*, disabled, was rigged for towing. . .back to the West Coast [of the United States]."

A week after *Guardfish* completed her eighth war patrol at Midway, *Extractor* headed eastward from Eniwetok in a six-ship convoy. The group included *Sea Flyer*, towed by the civilian tanker *SS Gulf Star*. While en route to Hawaii, the bloody battle for the control of Guam ended. Seventeen uneventful days later, *Extractor* and company arrived at Pearl Harbor. While the others went their various ways, *Extractor* stayed for work assignments in the harbor.

The ship's captain, Lieutenant Oaks, left for a new assignment on September 9. The ship's original executive officer, Lt. (junior grade) Horace M. Babcock, fleeted up to skipper. Ten days later the ship was at sea again in another six-ship convoy. We were "westbound again," explained Chapman, and "*Extractor* was burdened with a tandem tow of an army drill-barge and a barge loaded with 400 tons of dynamite. This was dropped back on the longest wire hawser available!"

Their destination was again Eniwetok atoll, where the ship arrived on October 7. Five days later, *Extractor* was assigned to a 14-ship convoy, each with one or two other vessels in tow plus a formidable naval escort team of three destroyers. The group reached its destination, Ulithi atoll, on October 21. The United States had occupied that island, located about 400 miles southwest of Guam, less that one month before *Extractor* and the other ships arrived.

An urgent call on October 28 caught *Extractor* with only two of her four diesel engines in operating condition. *USS Viburnum* (AN-57), a net tender, was in serious trouble at the harbor channel entrance. The tender had struck a mine, which shattered her hull and killed two men. The emergency was deemed worth the risk, and the squadron operations officer ordered *Extractor* to go to her assistance. Fortunately, the powerful fleet tug *USS Arapaho* (ATF-68) also arrived to take the foundering vessel in tow.

October 1944 witnessed the United States landing on the southern island of Leyte in the Philippines, where American forces engaged in a battle that continued into December. As related earlier, the Japanese surface fleet was destroyed in the Battle of Leyte Gulf. Appreciating the seriousness of their situation, the enemy defense of the island became even more desperate, and submarines and kamikaze suicide planes were utilized to attack the American invasion fleet.

Urgent orders on November 4 directed *Extractor* and two oceangoing tugs to depart from Ulithi. Their operating orders specified that they were to proceed to a mid-ocean location, and further instructions would be sent by radio during the voyage. This emergency mission also caught *Extractor* with an equipment problem: her single radio communication receiver was not working properly. As a result, *Extractor* had to stay close to the tugs, relying on them to lead the way as they received new radio instructions.

The salvage group was going to the aid of *USS Reno*, a light cruiser limping back from the Leyte campaign. A torpedo from a Japanese submarine had almost cut *Reno* in half, blowing a cavernous hole in the warship from one side to the other. When the group located the cruiser on November 6, *Extractor* supplied pumps, shoring material, her salvage officer, and a skeleton crew to help keep the stricken ship afloat, while the two tugs took *Reno* in tow. Together with *Extractor*, three destroyers, and a mine sweeper, the slow convoy made its way back to Ulithi, arriving near midnight on November 10.

Ten days later as *Extractor* was on her way to an assignment inside Ulithi's central anchorage, an explosion split the early morning air. A manned Japanese suicide torpedo (kaiten), launched from a large submarine, had hit the *USS Mississinewa*, a fully loaded fuel oil tanker. *Extractor*, the first to take station alongside the stricken vessel, was quickly joined by three other fire fighting vessels. Together, they streamed water onto the conflagration and rescued many survivors. The burning vessel capsized after two hours and sank with the loss of about twenty percent of her crew. At one point during the action the roaring flames engulfed *Extractor* and burned two of her men, Machinist's Mate Francis J. Flaherty and Boatswain's Mate George (N) Molnar. *Extractor* transferred her injured to the hospital ship *USS Samaritan*, where Flaherty subsequently died.

Following recovery from his burns, Molnar rejoined *Extractor*. According to Lieutenant Babcock, *Extractor's* skipper, the dismembered and badly decomposed body of the Japanese kaiten pilot was delivered to his ship for informal burial at sea on Thanksgiving Day.

The courageous actions by *Extractor's* crewmen did not pass unnoticed. Babcock, as well as several officers and enlisted men, received official kudos from the Commander of Service Squadron Ten:

You are commended for your performance of duty in connection with fighting the fire aboard the *USS Mississinewa* on November 20, 1944. The action of your vessel contributed to the combined efforts made to save the USS Mississinewa and rescue its survivors, and it is felt that your performance of duty was in accordance with the highest traditions of the United States Naval Service. Well done.

Shortly afterward, Horace Babcock was promoted to the rank of full lieutenant.

Extractor spent much of December underway in convoys sailing from Guam to Tinian to Saipan, and then back again. Whether in port or at sea, she was always in company with other ships. There was, after all, safety in numbers.

Admiral Halsey's Third Fleet (Task Force 38) continued to batter the perimeter of Convoy College. On the morning of January 21, 1945, his planes hit airfields on and around Formosa. Good flying weather allowed flight operations to continue throughout the day. Elements of the fleet reached a point about 100 miles due east of the southern tip of Formosa, a refueling zone known as "Area Diesel." In the early afternoon, as one of the battleships of the fleet refueled a destroyer and as carriers launched and recovered flights, a group of Japanese planes swept out of the clouds headed for the aircraft carriers. One of the planes lobbed a bomb onto *USS Langley*. Seconds later a kamikaze suicide plane smashed into aircraft carrier *USS Ticonderoga* at a steep angle. The flaming wreckage crashed through the flight deck and exploded inside the hanger deck, igniting a dangerous fire. Two more kamikazes targeted *Ticonderoga*. Anti-aircraft gunners shot down the first one, but the second slipped through, crashing into the carrier's starboard side near the ship's "island."

Ticonderoga was in dire straits, listing badly and engulfed in flames. The explosion and fires caused serious damage and killed or wounded more than 100 crewmen—including the ship's captain and executive officer. All of her communication gear was put out of commission except for one portable, low powered VHF radio transceiver. The engineering officer assumed command of the ship and radioed the Task Group Commander about the disaster. The Task Group leader passed word to Admiral Halsey's flagship, which radioed the following urgent message to the logistic support group, Service Squadron Ten, in Ulithi:

REQUEST YOU SAIL TOWARD CENTER AREA DIESEL ALL AVAILABLE FLEET TUGS AND ARS'S X ADVISE SPEED OF ADVANCE AND TIME OF DEPARTURE XX

Three hours later the Commander of Service Squadron Twelve, located at Guam, received an urgent call for assistance from his superior at Ulithi:

IT IS REQUESTED YOU SAIL TOWARD CENTER AREA DIESEL LATITUDE 16-10 NORTH LONGITUDE 129-30 EAST ALL ARS'S AVAILABLE X TUGS TO GUARD NPM PRIMARY FOX UNTIL 0000Z 23RD THEN SHIFT TO SECONDARY FOX X ADVISE NUMBER SAILED AND ETA ALL INFO ADDEES XX

Extractor's crew was enjoying a movie on the deck on the quiet Sunday evening of January 21. The surrounding water glistened with a myriad of lights from ships packed into Guam's Apra Harbor. A blinding signal light directed at *Extractor* flashed repeatedly and shook the men out of their peaceful weekend mood. The deck officer called for Signalman Joseph Beers to hurry topside and copy the message. It was a call from Lieutenant Commander Seymour V. Dennison, the squadron operations officer, for Captain Babcock to report immediately aboard *USS William Ward Burrows.*

When Babcock returned he had handwritten orders to depart on an urgent mission as soon as he was ready for sea. The captain alerted his officers to prepare for immediate departure and to report any problems to him. One of the first they discovered was that their *SO-1 surface search radar was not working, even though visiting radar technicians had overhauled it only a week earlier. However, Babcock's exec, Lt. Chester W. Lebsack, who was also the navigation and radar officer, told the captain that the ship's radar operators probably could fix the SO-1 while underway. That satisfied Babcock, especially since the radar did not impress him all that much. The lookouts often spotted surface vessels before the radar picked them up. Besides that, they had their *IFF transponder to identify them to friendly craft. Babcock notified the squadron operations officer that *Extractor* was ready to leave, noting that a few problems would be corrected while at sea.

The departure orders given to *Extractor* gave some of her crew pause for thought. "There was something eerie about those orders that Sunday night," Ensign Beattie remembered. "No instructions, no escort, just a spot in the Pacific." The ship's crew "had become restless and irritable with too many lazy days in port and the possibility of the next invasion ahead of us. . .I overheard one of the chiefs remark that maybe this would be the last trip for 'old' *Extractor*."

She was directed to proceed from Guam without escort—something she had never done before. She was to travel about four days to an open sea area some 500 miles east of the northern tip of Luzon, and get further specific instructions by radio. Nobody on board really knew the purpose of the mission. "Our orders were devoid of any information concerning our task at the designated latitude and longitude," Ensign Thomas A. Beattie, the ship's gunnery officer, later recorded in his diary. "The crew was enjoying a movie on the deck when the orders arrived." They did know about the imminent American invasion of Luzon, and many thought they were off to support the invasion forces. Anxiety was rampant throughout the ship. "Why were we sent out all alone this time?" wondered some of her crew. "Will they get the radar working before we get into enemy waters?" "We are sitting ducks, we hardly have any way to defend ourselves. What will we do if we are attacked by the enemy?"

Captain Babcock, however, suspected they were being sent to assist a ship in distress—as when they went to help the torpedoed cruiser *Reno*. *Extractor* surely would not be alone for very long. Many friendly and well armed ships would be attending the stricken vessel, or so he believed.

Extractor carried three radar operators. Under Lt. Chester Lebsack's supervision they worked hard and long trying to get the SO-1 back in commission, to no avail. The radarmen knew how to operate the radar and interpret its performance, but they had received little maintenance training. Lebsack recently made the following observations to me about their inoperative radar. "We didn't have any technicians or anybody to fix things like that," Lebsack recently admitted to the author. "Odds and ends. . .we could do, like [replacing] fuses and that stuff, but that was about it. I think I was the more educated aboard, and I am not an expert, believe me. I knew how it was supposed to work, but if it went kaplunk, that was it. I had three days of radar school, that's how I became a radar officer."

"We left port at 2300 Sunday without an escort and 900 miles between us and our destination," recalled Ensign Beattie. "We did not have time to take on provisions or water, and that alone offered the prospect of an uncomfortable trip. Our radar was not in operation and we had no underwater sound gear." The first day of the voyage was clear and hot with a calm sea. "After a layover in port," explained Beattie, "the first day is a quiet one with most everyone keeping to themselves, until the monotony of the sea forces you to seek diversion in another's company. We stood our watches quietly and ate sparingly as is usual the first day out. We were making about twelve knots and with the exception of an inoperative radar were proceeding as expected." Rough weather greeted *Extractor* on the second day of her solo voyage. "Constant rain squalls with heavy clouds and some rough sea made the trip uncomfortable and depressing. Our radar was still out and we now had a troublesome main engine exhaust."

Ominous signs of trouble continued to plague *Extractor*. According to Ensign Beattie,

A message finally came through, addressed to us. . . .An attempt to decode the message was unsuccessful. The first part of the message was missed by the radioman and several remaining parts were garbled. At that time we began to worry. The message might have been a change in course or destination and without radar we were a ship afloat, not sure of our destination and without protection. The officers on the *coding board tried many times without success to decode the message. Our radiomen copied messages continuously, hoping for a repeat, which never came, and we could not break radio silence to ask for a repeat message. . . .

The garbled message did not surprise Semmes Chapman, *Extractor*'s salvage and communications officer. "One of the 'Murphy's Law' events [on this trip] was the selection by operations/communications [Admiral Halsey's staff] to send the expected message encoded in the clumsy 'strip board' system," he complained in a letter to the author. It was a cumbersome decoding mechanism and all but guaranteed problems. As Chapman explains it,

> *Extractor* had *ECM and all messages I handled as communicator were broken on the machine. Since ECM use was restricted, only Lebsack, the previous communicator, and Lieutenant Chapman were qualified on it. Two senior enlisteds, Storekeeper [Cecil G.] Collins and Yeoman [Andrew] Dobos were designated to handle the "strip board." With indicators garbled, the "lost" message was turned over to them with an outside chance of solution, which did not occur. They worked hours futilely. . . .

Chester Lebsack, the ship's navigation and radar officer, "never did find out what the garbled message really was until long afterwards." Everybody had a shot at it, he explained, "but we flunked and flunked and flunked. . .By that time we were out at the edge of one of those 'no safe areas,' a kind of a 'no man's land' at sea, so to speak. . .We decided that they would probably send a repeat—but they didn't."

The garbled message went out about 5:00 p.m. on January 22, one day after *Extractor* departed Guam. The decoders aboard the ship recognized only three things in the message: it came from the commander of their squadron in Guam; it was action-addressed to *Extractor*; and one "information addressee" was the Port Director at Guam. Lieutenant Babcock reasoned that since they sent the Port Director an information copy, the subject was not to alert *Extractor* of an impending danger, such as an enemy contact. Furthermore, he suspected that he was going to the aid of a ship that was probably in tow. If that were the case, he expected to be notified daily of the location of the ship. Following this logic, there would certainly be more messages as *Extractor* approached "Area Diesel." If not, Babcock planned to make a thorough search of the area when he arrived. If he was unable to find a stricken ship, he would break radio silence to get further instructions.

What Babcock and everyone else did not realize was that the garbled message instructed *Extractor* to return to Guam. Their inability to properly decode the message set the stage for *Extractor's* tragic meeting with *Guardfish*.

Chapter Thirteen

Torpedo Blast

Extractor was three days out from Guam on January 24, 1945, traversing the deep waters (15,000 feet) over West Mariana Basin. Matters had not improved aboard the ship. "As time wore on our appetites diminished and it was obvious that the crew was jumpy," Ensign Tom Beattie later penned in his diary:

> We kidded with some uneasiness about contacting the enemy. I tried to read, but my concentration was poor. I had the 1200 to 0400 watch and turned in about 2000 for a few hours sack time. When I took the watch the sea was rough and the sky was black. The moon and stars came out occasionally for a few minutes. By 0300 it was pitch dark. We were steaming at standard speed and at times I could not see the bow of the ship, and that was an uneasy feeling. Without radar to detect other vessels the thought of collision crept into my thoughts, unlikely as it seemed.

A wide-awake Beattie was relieved from watch duty at 4:00 a.m. and went into the communication shack to "see if there was any change." An hour later he climbed into his bunk and fell into an uneasy sleep. After tossing and turning, the young ensign left his cabin about 6:00 a.m. and wandered out to the starboard boat deck to check on weather conditions. "The sky," he recalls clearly, "was overcast and the sea was choppy. I could see some of the crew down on the weather deck waiting to get into the mess hall for their morning chow." Beattie also noticed "some commotion among them as ["Leo" Damasze] Gagnon, our Gunner's Mate and security watchstander, pointed to what seemed to be a spray of water some yards off our starboard quarter." Beattie recorded the terrifying scene in his journal:

> I heard one of our Boatswains say there were no whales or dolphins in the area. A second later I saw another spray of water closer to our starboard quarter. In that flash of a second I hoped against hope that it was not what I thought, but before I had a chance to act I saw a torpedo eight or ten feet from the ship drive into our forward hold. I turned my head and the concussion and noise from the explosion was terrifying. I was stunned and numbed. I then looked forward. Smoke was pouring out of the superstructure and splinters and debris were falling everywhere. The bow of the ship was already under water.

The officer of the deck at the time of the explosion was the junior salvage officer, Lt. (junior grade) Carl Philip Burman. "At 0350 I took the watch for the communications officer who was breaking messages," the lieutenant later reported. "As far as our ship was concerned, it was a heavy sea coming off our starboard quarter tending to keep us to the right of our course. The weather was with the sea about ten knots. Visibility somewhere between one thousand and fifteen hundred yards to the best of my knowledge." Burman was in the wheelhouse on the starboard side when the *Guardfish* torpedo slammed into *Extractor*:

> It was sometime between 0615 and 0630. The weather was dry. The Quartermaster was on the bridge sweeping down. He was also on the starboard side of the bridge. It was daybreak, we had already lighted ship. Approximately one hundred and fifty feet away I saw what looked like some splashes, which later proved to be a shallow torpedo whose torpedo wake had caused these small geysers. I was confused, it could not be a bomb fragment but that is what it appeared to be at first. There were no bubbles after it and I did not think it was a torpedo. Took a second look, ran to ring the general quarters alarm and back to the window to take a second look. Then, as I was about to go back to ring it again, I felt the explosion. I saw about two tracks at first and then one the second time I looked. That is all I saw and then the explosion occurred.

As soon as the blast rocked *Extractor*, Burman rang general quarters—"as soon as I recovered from the deck," he added. "I was standing about ten feet from the general quarters buzzer when I first saw the tracks. The space of time of all this was something like five seconds. I understand that some of the men felt something rub against the side of the ship before the explosion. It may have, at any rate it did not register with me. I was too busy watching the tracks."

A few of the early risers, like Kenneth M. Eby, had already eaten breakfast and were lounging around topside, quietly chatting with shipmates. According to Eby, he remembered the torpedo striking "about 6:30 a.m., when one of the other divers, Chester Konopka, and myself were sitting back on the fantail smoking a cigarette." The hit sounded like "a big thud," and struck the starboard side near the engine room and "shook the ship," reminisced the shocked sailor. "I looked out over the fantail and I saw one [torpedo] going by and it missed the fantail about six or eight feet. Right after that I glanced up and I got a glimpse of the one coming that took the bow off, just before it hit."

Almost everyone who was awake aboard *Extractor* heard or felt the ship quiver when the defective torpedo crashed into her hull. Few, if any other than Eby and Konopka, realized that the stern was almost hit by another torpedo. According to Semmes Chapman, the salvage officer, the ship was carrying 4,000 gallons of gasoline in a tank near the stern. "A torpedo explosion at the stern of the ship would have been totally disastrous for the crew."

Arthur T. (Art) O'Grady, a first-class Ship Fitter, was on lookout watch in a starboard aft gun tub with Boatswain's Mate Edward C. Schoeffel when the first torpedo hit:

We felt a bump and then about ten or eleven seconds later we saw, like a dolphin coming toward us in the water. Then Ed said, 'I'd better go and get my life jacket.' So he jumped down and ran forward. In a few seconds the whole front of the ship blew up. General quarters started ringing, but after a few seconds it stopped. . .

For Ken Eby (and probably for most of the crew that fateful day), time and events merged into a blur. "She wheeled over on her starboard so fast that I grabbed the bulwarks and walked up and stood on the port side of the pilothouse," he remembered. "I kicked the life raft and I walked down the side of the hull and went over the side." Years later discussing the events of that morning, Eby remembered seeing many of the items he used regularly as a member of the ship's skilled diving team:

> I swam underwater away from the ship as far as I could and when I came up she was standing straight up in the air. The screws were still turning, so the engines were running. There was a fire hose wrapped around the port screw and it was slapping the hull. She went down right away from the time that fish hit. Everything was flying; all our beaching gear, cables and anchors and all that diving gear that was kept in the forward hold. The explosion bumped big reels of two-inch cable forty or fifty feet in the air, I'll bet. It went way up there. I would say that from the time that fish hit, took her bow off, there was no more than probably two minutes until she went down. We were still running full speed and when it took the bow off she plowed herself under.

Although he had safely gotten clear of the ship, Eby was enough of a sailor to know that he was still in grave danger:

> One thing that worried me was that I wanted to get away from the area. I could see all that wood as she broke up shooting to the surface and hitting me. I swam out and there was a water keg floating out there that I was highly interested in and I grabbed it and swam over to the life raft. I don't know whether there was two life rafts. I think that's the one that I had released. There was a lot of flotation stuff around, and I swam over with the water keg to the life raft. All of us were hanging on around and some were in it. How many I don't know. . .I don't remember seeing another life raft.

A surprised Eby watched in horror as a large submarine surfaced "right away. . .not very far off and it sort of went around us a little bit. A first-class Gunner's Mate by the name of Gagnon. . .had been on subs and he said it was an American sub. Of course, nobody would believe him." The men began taking bets on the nationality of the boat. "He must have made a slew of money," concluded Eby. "I don't think we were in the water more than 25 or 30 minutes, it wasn't very long."

Today, Arthur S. Gorny is a retired orthodontist living in Cheyenne, Wyoming. In 1945, he was an Electrician's Mate. Dr. Gorny recorded one of the most detailed accounts of the sinking of *Extractor*:

On that morning at approximately 0625, I was awakened for early chow to then go on duty to take over the throttle watch from the electrician who had been on the watch since 0400. The ship was a twin screw ship, driven by two electric motors, and an Electrician's Mate and a Machinist's Mate manned the two separate throttles, on a four hours on, and four hours off schedule. "Motor Macs" were in charge of the four diesel engines on the lower level of the engine room

Gorny had just climbed out of his bunk and was pulling on one leg of his pants when he "heard a loud 'thud' against the ship." As he lifted his other leg to pull up his pants, "a very loud explosion occurred, and I was thrown back against another bunk and knocked to the deck. I got up, pulled up my pants, and without shirt or shoes scrambled up the ladder as fast as I could, with one thought in mind—to get to the aft steering hold to get the life jackets I had stashed there over a period of months, since I could not swim."

Gorny had been thinking ahead and had routinely collected life jackets, which were always found strewn about the ship. If he ever had to abandon ship, he reasoned, he was going to have more than one life jacket for such an occasion. The life jackets were stashed in the aft steering hold since that was his assigned battle station during General Quarters.

"When I first reached the main deck from the crew's compartment, I observed the crew abandoning ship from all areas, some with and some without life jackets." For Gorny, who could not swim, the decisions he made over the next several seconds meant the difference between life and death:

I still had to make my way to the aft steering hold to get those life jackets, as there was no way I would go over the side without them. The bow of the ship was sinking rapidly, so it was an uphill climb, and being barefoot on a wet deck, I fell again. As I reached the aft steering hold and started down the ladder, one of my shipmates who was also part of the aft fire control party yelled, "How about me?" I thought he wanted me to hand him a fire axe, extinguisher or some other fire fighting equipment, and I thought if he wanted to be a hero and die with an axe in his hand, he could get his own. He later told me that he was asking me to hand him a life jacket, since he knew I had extra ones stashed in that hold. He was an excellent swimmer and when I came back up the ladder to the main deck, he had gone over the side and I found myself there alone. Other crew members already in the water were yelling at me to "jump," knowing that I could not swim and probably sure that I had panicked and was frozen to the ship and would go down with it.

In reality, Gorny had kept his wits about him and was thinking very clearly:

I had gathered up two "Mae West" Kapok jackets and two inflatable belts around my waist. I put on one "Mae West" jacket with the second one over one arm. Oddly enough at this point I was reasonably calm and remembered not to inflate the belts until in the water, and to hold down the collar on the "Mae West" and cross the other arm over my chest to keep the jacket from becoming dislodged, and to hit the water feet first. The stern of the ship was now high in the air and my first attempt to get up on the rail resulted in another fall and my feet ended up in the water that had now swallowed up about two-thirds of the ship. That experience did panic me and with more strength than I thought I had, I managed to pull myself up and got on the rail and went over the side.

I abandoned the ship feet first as the good book said, rolled over on my back and attempted to swim away from the ship, with what little bit of back stroke I could remember from boot camp days. I was unable to get away from the ship and was looking up at the two propellers, which were now high out of the water, and still running at whatever speed they were running when the engine room crew abandoned ship. I knew my number was up if those propellers came down on top of me as the ship continued to sink. At that point, as scared as I was, I found myself extremely homesick for the dry "terra firma" of Nebraska. Why a stupid thought like that crossed my mind at a time like that, I will never know. Then a hand grabbed me by the collar and a voice said, "kick your feet" and although I was probably dead weight, I thought my feet were churning up a real wake. I was towed to the nearest life raft by the Chief Warrant Bos'n [David J. McCafferty] and he took off to help other crew members who needed help. If there was anyone deserving of a hero's medal, it was this man who helped so many people and was the calming influence for the whole crew.

Gorny never forgot McCafferty's bravery. "I would like to be able to locate that Chief Warrant Officer who actually saved my life," he explained to the author. "As a young enlisted man, conditioned to almost breathe none of the officers' air, and to speak to them only when they gave an order, I didn't have the couth to thank him. Now years later, and much smarter, I hope, if he is still living and can be located, I would sure call him to extend my belated thanks." [As it turned out, David McCafferty was alive and well, and the author was able to arrange for them to get them together on the telephone.]

By the time Gorny reached the nearest life raft, *Extractor* rolled over on her side and disappeared beneath the surface. The young Electrician's Mate hung on to the life raft for everything he was worth, hoping help would arrive. It did, but not in a form he could have imagined: a large submarine was approaching on the surface. "We all thought it was a Japanese submarine and that our number was up, since we could see two crew members standing on deck with what appeared to be machine guns." According to Gorny, he and his mates suddenly came to the realization that "those damn Japs don't plan to take any prisoners." Just as they thought it was over for them, "one of the regular navy 'old salts' on our raft said, 'Hell, that's an American submarine!'" From Gorny's vantage point low in the water, "the submarine looked 500 feet tall. . .and very threatening with those two 'dudes' with the machine guns standing on the bow." If that's an American sub, Gorny thought, "I hope they identify us rapidly to know we are on the same side, before any trigger fingers get nervous."

In a recent conversation about the sinking, *Extractor's* ex-skipper Horace Babcock revealed he was also awed by the selfless heroism of his other Chief Warrant Officer, the oldest man on the ship. "Frank V. Fabbre, the engineering officer, was in his second navy tour, near sixty years old," said Babcock. "When the abandon ship order came, instead of jumping overboard, he ran down into the innards of the sinking ship to the engine room. Only when he was sure that all of his men were out of the compartment did he go topside himself, where he and others valiantly struggled to release the port lifeboat."

Art O'Grady, who was on duty as the starboard lookout when the torpedoes hit, had an series of experiences similar to Arthur Gorny's. The bow was sinking quickly as he made his way aft through about a foot of water:

> We got word to abandon ship. We released a couple of life rafts, one on starboard and one on port, and tried to release a lifeboat on the port side, but it capsized because the ship was listing bad. I ran aft and saw that the port screw was out of the water, and the starboard screw in. I jumped off the back and immediately was dragged down by the turbulence caused by the starboard screw, which was still turning. I fought and fought to stay up and swallowed a lot of water. I didn't have the sense to take my shoes off before I jumped in, so in the water I struggled and finally kicked them off. My life jacket was one of those you have to blow up by mouth so it didn't do me any good. I was barely able to stay up and breathe. Another guy; [Monroe A.] Edwards, who was also a diver; had a life jacket that blew up by itself, and he grabbed me and told me to hold on. We got to the life raft and it quickly filled up. Guys were hanging on, all around in the water.

Like Gorny, O'Grady and the men around him believed the submarine flew the rising sun of Japan:

> Pretty soon the sub came up and we all got scared that it was a Jap sub. Then men came out on the deck of the sub with guns in hand. With their jackets on we couldn't see 'em very well. Some of the guys in the life rafts jumped back in the water, trying to look like floating debris, like the wood from the *Extractor*. But then one of our guys, who was familiar with American subs said, "Hey, that's not a Jap, that's an American sub!" The sub went around us for a while, then finally they started taking us aboard. They threw a Jacob's Ladder down to us so we could climb up.

Richmond L. Marsh, an Apprentice Seaman, had come aboard *Extractor* in Hawaii in August 1944, apparently directly out of boot camp. "I had the twelve midnight to four watch," he remembered, "and when I got off watch I went to the mess hall for some chow, then I hit the sack." Marsh never forgot the next several minutes:

The next thing it felt like we hit something. By the time I got off my bunk, the water was about knee deep. When I got topside, somebody had thrown life rafts overboard. I jumped over the starboard side of the ship into the water, then got on one of the life rafts. I didn't have a life jacket on. We sat in the life raft for, I don't remember how long. Then the sub surfaced. It sure scared me. Didn't know if it was a Jap sub or not. Then I stood up in the life raft and, using *semaphore, made hand signals for "USN." I did that a couple of times, but somebody told me to "quit doing that, or else—." I don't know if I did any good or not.

The shipboard duties of Semmes Chapman, *Extractor's* salvage and communications officer, included being in charge of the ship's diving team, standing deck watches, and decoding the messages his radiomen received. His watch, as officer of the deck that morning, was from 4:00 to 8:00 a.m., but another officer relieved him so he could decode a radio message:

I was sitting at the *ECM next to my bunk in the 'sea cabin' behind bridge, with door open to adjacent chart room on port side. Ship was blacked out and ports closed. Alerted by the blast, I reached into desk drawer for flashlight and went to bridge. It was then barely light and could see ship's bow already down. I have no recollection of seeing or talking with anyone, but returned to chart room in dim red light.

I called to [William M.] Neylon, Radioman, to come up on radio, and asked [Winsor S.] Nuhfer, Quartermaster-striker, as to our last dead reckoning position. I had a pad and wrote a message that we were being "shelled." The ship lurched sharply, rolling down to starboard, and I shouted something like "Get the hell out of here." I led the way to bridge, out and down onto the port life raft. A few moments delay to try to free the stopper hitch, and I jumped perhaps ten feet down into water. For some reason, I thought eyeglasses were more secure gripped in my teeth, but lost them on impact. I was wearing work dungarees, tee shirt and no shoes.

The ship went down, propellers still turning but several hundred yards from me. I possibly had an inflatable belt looped on waist, but did not blow it up. I swam to the other life raft, which was overloaded, and was in water alongside with my head diver, [Arthur T.] O'Grady. Too many to attempt to muster, I called up and asked if there were any injured. The only officer in this group was Bos'n [David J.] McCafferty, who happened also to have the only known injury among the crew, consisting of a broken little toe. . . .Everyone else was afloat hanging to debris as available. I recall hunks of timber, apparently short pieces blown from the foot of the main mast, a fir timber some eighteen inches diameter.

Chapman remembered that the water at that time was "moderately rough," and visibility was limited through swells three to five feet high. "My time in the water was certainly one hour, as scattered people were being gathered to the sub. My first sight of this was without recognition of the type, and the first persons on deck seen with machine guns was not encouraging." Thankfully, the water was warm and did not produce any discomfort. "My strongest recollection," concluded Chapman, "was that 'home' had been lost—and what had happened would never be reported to shore."

Another officer who was near the bridge at the time of the torpedo blast was the ship's executive officer and navigator, Chester Lebsack. When I finally located him for an interview, I was surprised to learn that he lives in the town where I was born and raised: Redwood City, California. We had a long telephone conversation about *Extractor* harrowing ordeal. "I was in the chart room, which was next to the bridge on *Extractor* like a lot of those smaller ships," recalled Lebsack. At the time, he and Chief Quartermaster [Winfred R.] Benson were trying to figure out what kind of stars and planets [see *Star Sight] "we might have gotten in the morning."

Something thumped against the hull of the ship, and Lebsack asked Benson, "What in hell did we find to bump into out here?" He managed only about three steps, with the Chief right behind him, when the torpedo struck the bow of the ship:

I saw the mast disappear and he and I got blown back into the chart room. Benson was kind of a typical navy chief, weight-wise; he'd put on a few pounds. He was my bumper; he hit the bulkhead and I hit him. We had little splinters and things from the explosion but nothing really serious. . . At that stage I knew the game was over. The bow went up and it went down and it was gone. The mast was gone and the whole ship was going forward and it filled up with water like you wouldn't believe.

Lebsack still remembers that the radioman "was in the radio room trying to send a message but the mast was gone." Determined to get off the dying ship, Lebsack, in company with [Virgil M.] Kling, "walked down the hull of the ship into the water. It was already flat on its side, right before it capsized." Although he was off the ship, Lebsack's problems were far from over. "One of the boats had floated off, upside down, about fifty yards away from the ship. I had one of those inflatable life jackets. . .but some kind of a splinter punctured it, and I got in the water—and sank." He remembers thinking to himself, "Well, its up to you now." Gathering their strength, Kling and Lebsack swam over to the boat, "a whaleboat type of a salvage boat. . .floating upside down." The men thought they could right it with some additional help. "We finally decided the hell with it," explained Lebsack, "so we swam over to where the rafts were, which was maybe a hundred yards away. They were all full." Lebsack and his comrades, "the last to be picked up," clung to the mast and waited for assistance:

Can you imagine that? You see this was a wooden hulled ship and the mast was wooden and it was floating upside down, with the snapped-off end sticking out of the water. I had been hanging on to the side of a raft and the weather was calm but Captain Hammond was backing [the submarine] and the backwash pushed several of us away from the raft. This was down toward the tail end of the pickup operation and there were three of us. I can't remember the names of the other two who got washed away. The raft went one way and we went the other way and the closest thing to hang onto was the mast. It was floating upside down.

Two days after the sinking, Ensign Tom Beattie conscientiously recorded his memories in his diary of what he experienced after the torpedo ripped into the bow of *Extractor*. "The bow of the ship was already under water," he penned,

I ran around the boat deck hoping to release the port life boat. Two of the crew were already there. I knew I needed a life jacket, so I climbed down the after ladder of the boat deck to the main deck where we stored life jackets against the superstructure. At that time the ship lurched heavily to starboard. I decided not to go forward to the life raft, for fear the ship would capsize. I climbed onto the bumper guard on the port quarter and prepared to jump. The stern was now out of water and I could see the port screw still turning over. I moved forward several yards to avoid the screw, if the ship settled back in the water. I picked a clear spot in the water and jumped. When I surfaced I was about twenty yards from the whirling screw. Fear gripped me that I would be sucked into the screw, if the ship went under. I saw a life raft some twenty yards away and started to swim.

Beattie had gone only about thirty feet when he heard someone shouting his name. "I looked back and saw our Gunner's Mate [Leo Gagnon] about ten yards away. He was in trouble, as his arms were tangled in his life jacket." Beattie swam to him and grabbed his right arm, hoping all the while Gagnon would not panic and pull him under water. Thankfully, recorded Beattie, Gagnon "kept his head and helped as much a possible. We reached the raft in a few minutes." Several men were already on the raft and others soon joined them. Beattie looked back at *Extractor*, whose "stern was still out of water and the port screw still turning. A piece of line was now caught in the screw and made a loud slapping noise each time it hit the water."

Their situation did not look good. About thirty people were on or clinging to the raft. Others struggled in the water hanging onto pieces of wood, debris, and boxes. The rest of the crew had abandoned the doomed ship from the starboard side and at this time were on a raft about a hundred yards or so away from the raft that carried Tom Beattie. "About that time our ship listed heavily to starboard and then slowly slid beneath the surface. We heard a few muffled underwater noises. It was gut wrenching to see your ship disappear in such a few minutes."

Beattie and his comrades decided to join with the other raft,

so we all kicked and pulled as best we could. Some were half clothed and cold. In spite of our plight, we halfheartedly kidded one another in an attempt to keep up our morale. We had gone but a few yards when someone spotted a periscope and part of a sub superstructure, as we bobbed up and down in the water. Some part of an hour had probably elapsed since we were hit, and I'm sure each of us were hoping the sub would not surface. When we saw the sub we were sure the jig was up. The sub began to circle us and close in at the same time. By now we could fully see the sub. We saw several men emerge from the sub hatch. They had machine guns and were loading clips into them. The past hour had so drained me that the thought of dying did not really get through to me as I was too occupied with the sub.

According to Beattie, "no one got panicky, although you could hear an occasional whimper or deep sigh." Someone suggested the boat looked like an American sub, "but not many really thought so." Thinking ahead, Beattie untied his life jacket, "as I knew the only chance to survive was to stay under water if they began to shoot." Thinking along the same lines, several of the crew left the raft. "I had not decided what to do," he explained, "as I wanted to wait for the shooting." "The sub," continued Beattie, "headed directly for our raft and I thought they were going to ram us." The men began circling the raft, keeping it between them and what they thought was an enemy submarine. The sub angled off to the left and, to Beattie's surprise, the men on its deck began waving to the crew on the other raft. "Our hopes heightened when it looked like the sub crew were wearing dungarees," was how he recalled the moment. When the strangers began throwing lines to the other raft, the stranded sailors knew they were going to be saved:

> We yelled and laughed and some cried. The sea was rough and the rescue work took several hours, which seemed longer, as everyone was anxious to feel the sub deck under their feet. Our raft was the last to be rescued. The sub's first approach to our raft was unsuccessful as we missed the heaving lines. The sub backed down and made another approach and drove into the raft. We scattered to both sides and all hands managed to grab lines and pull themselves aboard.

The horrible ordeal suffered by the crewmen of *USS Extractor* was finally over; Captain Hammond's was just beginning.

Chapter Fourteen

Mixed Feelings

For Albert T. Babb, *Guardfish's* Baker on her tenth patrol, the sinking of *Extractor* will remain vividly in his memory forever—even though he remembers little else about his four and a half years in the navy. Babb was in the galley when word came down to pick up the prisoners from the water. "The first two to pass the galley were covered with oil and could easily have passed for Japanese sailors," he explained. The third one to pass him, however, demanded, "What the hell is going on?" When Bab "saw U.S.N. tattooed on his arm," his heart sank.

Virtually everyone, whether a survivor or submariner, has a vivid recollection of the men pulled aboard *Guardfish*. I was so embarassed at what we had done I carefully avoided the *Extractor* guys the whole time they were aboard. I was afraid they might be hostile and remember thinking, "What can I say if one of them collars me?"

When *Extractor's* crew began to climb down the ladder into the control room, Fred Jennings, *Guardfish's* commissary officer, remembers "an eerie silence prevailed as the magnitude of the tragedy began to sink in." Most of us said nothing "beyond giving the survivors directions on where to go and the necessary communications to run the ship." The survivors remained silent, recalled Jennings, "except for a few men I heard express their great relief that we turned out to be friend, not foe." Jennings and others aboard *Guardfish* were grateful their reaction was not the rage they were expecting, "and did not 'push our luck' by volunteering any conversation with *Extractor* people." According to the commissary officer, "after they had several hours to think about it, I believe the two commanding officers, mindful of the inevitability of a Court of Inquiry, decided to keep inter-crew communications to an absolute minimum, and word to that effect was passed and generally obeyed."

While Jennings felt some relief, Patrick J. McDonald, lead torpedoman in the forward room, suffered an anxious moment when one of the survivors met him in the bow of the boat. "One of the *Extractor* guys, about seven feet tall," he remembered "stepped though the hatch into the forward room, and asked, 'Is this the end that did the business?'"

Being aboard a submarine was a new, uneasy, but interesting experience for most of *Extractor's* crew. Ken Eby remembered that a short while after the sub had rescued the survivors, "they picked up a plane on the radar. They got us all down and, you talk about a bunch of guys going crazy, throwing levers and turning valves. . ." as the boat submerged. Art Gorny had some other observations:

> After we were picked up by *Guardfish*, we found the crew most eager to get us dry clothing, and pairing us up with those our size who furnished us with shoes, socks, etc. that we were without when we had to abandon ship. Although we were very crowded, everyone managed to share the facilities of the sub,. . .and in general I thought we were treated very well by everyone of the *Guardfish* crew. It was quite an experience traveling submerged, and we were allowed a certain amount of freedom to move about the sub, without getting in the way of the crew's required duties.

George D. Lawrence, a first class Motor Machinist Mate on *Guardfish*, was in charge of the forward engine room. "I turned over my bunk to the survivors and then catnapped in the engine room. I never left there, except to go to the head, until we reached Guam." Lawrence ate crackers, sardines, and D-rations stored in the room. "I don't know how the cooks managed to feed the survivors. As I recall there was standing room only throughout the boat."

Like many of his fellow *Extractor* shipmates, Art O'Grady also has clear memories of his first few hours aboard *Guardfish*. "After I got in the sub I went aft and one of the guys gave me some dry clothes and told me to get in his bunk to sleep. I was exhausted, I'd taken down so much salt water." But when he got in the bunk, what he saw startled him. "I saw two of those big torpedoes right above me, they must have weighed a ton each, rolling back and forth—the weather was rough. I couldn't sleep with those things above me, rolling around, so I got up and went to the mess hall I stayed there for the whole time, BS-ing with the guys. I didn't sleep the whole time."

"Our food supplies were almost extinct, after having been at sea almost two months," recalled Al Babb, who shared the work with the cooks. "We did have a large pot of vegetable soup already made, when the survivors came aboard. I added red beets, the only vegetables we had left, to the remaining stock. That went quickly." Babb spent much of the forty hours it took to get to Guam baking bread—138 loaves, six at a time. "The survivors tore them apart as soon as I dumped them out of the pans. . . .I didn't sleep in my bunk for the remainder of the cruise, choosing to catnap at one of the tables in the mess."

After slipping into dry clothes and downing hot coffee, Tom Beattie began taking in his new accommodations aboard *Guardfish*. "We were very crowded with some seventy men added to the sub crew. We slept on the deck of the torpedo room and anywhere we could find space and for the most part we ate sandwiches and coffee." The submariners, he added, "were in shock at having torpedoed an American ship, and did everything possible to make us comfortable." The journey to Guam lasted two days. During the trip to Guam, Beattie, "in disbelief, thought about the *Extractor* at the bottom of the Pacific along with six of our crew. For the most part though, I guess the warmth of being rescued, and the companionship and operation of the submarine, kept my mind occupied."

Chester Lebsack, *Extractor*'s executive officer, made a headcount of the survivors after the rescue. The following men were missing:

IN MEMORIUM
Walter Stanley Bahrey, Seaman second class
Bob Roy Burgess, Radioman third class
Tomme L. Frazier, Electrician's Mate third class
Alvin Charles Orgeron, Ship's Cook third class
William Henry Taylor, Seaman first class
Raymond E. Thompson, Seaman second class

Often, crew members from small ships, as in other walks of life, usually develop close associations with only a few others. Generally they remember only those with whom they worked regularly. "We had mixed emotions [aboard *Guardfish*]," explained Art Gorny, "as we were happy to be out of the water but saddened by the loss of six shipmates, even though a lengthy search was made of a large area before we left for Guam." Gorny was particularly distressed by the loss of one of his closest friends, Tomme Frazier. Like Gorny, Frazier could not swim well either. "Tomme was the electrician I was to relieve on throttle duty on the next watch. I thought he might have become trapped in the engine room, as rapidly as the sea water rushed in." It was only later that Gorny learned that his friend had succeeded in getting out of the engine room. George Molnar helped Frazier inflate his life jacket, but as Molnar towed Frazier to a raft, a wave separated them. Nobody saw Frazier after that.

There is some discrepancy as to how some of the men died. The formal Missing Personnel reports submitted to the Navy identified four men as having been "killed instantly" because they were "sleeping in forward hold where torpedo struck": Bahrey, Burgess, Orgeron and Thompson. Some survivors, however, remember it differently. John R. Thompson, for example, claims that Radioman Burgess was not sleeping in the forward hold at the time of the blast. "I came to know Bob Burgess quite well and he was the last one I saw get off of the ship before it sank," reported Thompson. "I don't know if he could swim or not and he may have been sucked under with the ship."

Chester Lebsack's memory of the event in question also differs from the official report. "We had an American Indian boy, I forget his name, and he was on the boat deck, his abandon ship station." Lebsack saw him leave, but "knew he was not going to make it. . .He was standing there, kind of frozen like a statue. The executive officer hollered at him, "Get away from the boat and get the hell off the ship!" and he jumped from the boat deck. Sadly, explained Lebsack, no one ever saw him again. Lebsack's memory is supported by testimony from Andrew Chemycz, a Shipfitter first class on *Extractor*. Chemycz holds that the "American Indian boy" was a Cherokee named Bill Taylor. He and Taylor worked on the same repair team. Andy also saw Taylor jump from the boat deck. According to a formal report, Taylor "was seen going down by Eby, K.M., MM1c(DS), USN, who attempted to rescue him but could not get to him soon enough."

Although Art O'Grady didn't know personally any of the men lost in the tragedy, he came within a hair's breadth of making a decision that would have cost him his life:

The only ones I was really close to were the other divers. I was a deep sea diver. The *Extractor* was an auxiliary rescue and salvage vessel, that's what the ARS stood for. I was a Shipfitter first class and did repairs on ships. About a week before *Extractor* left Guam, before the sinking, another Shipfitter, Andy Chemycz, and I were told to install some new bunks up forward in the ship. After we finished, we were given the chance to each take one of the new bunks for our own use. We didn't want 'em though. It was too hot up there and the smell of the stored rope was too bad. If we had taken 'em, that's right where the torpedo hit.

Richmond Marsh had a somewhat similar recollection about the new bunks in the forward hold. In fact, one of them was assigned to him. Before the ship left Guam, however, he traded the bunk with a man who had one in the regular crew space. He does not remember the name of the man.

I learned while interviewing various members of *Extractor's* crew that the sinking included three undocumented casualties. The first has already been mentioned, namely the injury to Bos'n Warrant Officer McCafferty. He purposely avoided reporting his broken little toe because he did not want to get a Purple Heart medal for that. "It would be too embarrassing to have to explain to people what I received the decoration for," he said.

Art Gorny had a different reason for not reporting his back injury. He said that he did not want "to make waves," for fear that he would lose his survivor's leave. On his way back to the States, however, he changed his mind:

My back was giving me a real bad time, either from being knocked against a bunk rail when the torpedo hit the ship or from the falls I took before abandoning ship. I was determined to tough it out, in order to get that survivor's leave. But when blood showed up in my urine, I decided to check in at sick bay and the great navy medical establishment took over. They shipped me off to the naval hospital in Shoemaker, California. I went through a long series of tests, torture, and confusion. I was loaded up on pain pills, antibiotics, traction, and a lot of double talk from young medics. They finally got me up and about, and on June 9, 1945, they gave me a medical discharge from the navy.

The third undocumented casualty involved an unlisted member of the crew: the ship's mascot "Lucky," a black Scottish terrier. Some of the crewmen thought that he belonged to the captain, "because no enlisted man could get away with having a dog aboard ship." When asked, however, Babcock denied it. He did admit that he silently approved of the dog being aboard, even if it was a breach of naval regulations. Recently, Semmes Chapman told me that "Lucky" originally belonged to the first skipper, Lieutenant Oaks, who left the dog on the ship when he was transferred. Leo Gagnon, the Gunner's Mate, took over "Lucky's" care. The dog was a close friend to everyone aboard. Whenever they played movies on the main deck, "Lucky" nuzzled his way among the crew, accepting pats, hugs, and snacks from anyone kind enough to offer them. Some members of the crew worried about what would happen to their dog if the ship were to ever go down. According to Andy Chemycz, at Guam they used to throw "Lucky" into the water and dive in after him "to teach him to swim in case we ever got sunk."

A newspaper article quoted Leo Gagnon that "Lucky" slept under his bunk each night. In preparing to abandon ship, Gagnon said, "I ran to the stern and stood there a few moments waiting for my dog to join me, but he never showed up." Andy Chemycz told me he picked up "Lucky," threw him into the water, and jumped in after him. Unfortunately, "Just as we taught him," explained Andy, "Lucky" turned around—and swam right back to the ship only to be sucked under with it."

Chapter Fifteen

Court Convened

At 8:00 a.m., January 26, 1945, *Guardfish* made a mid-ocean rendezvous with *USS George* (DE-697), her escort to Guam. Six hours later at the entrance to Apra Harbor, *Guardfish* furtively transferred her cargo of *Extractor* survivors into small boats waiting to receive them. An hour more and she tied up alongside the submarine tender *USS Sperry*. There was no brass band to greet *Guardfish* this time.

Clay Blair, a submarine veteran of WWII and the author of many popular books, including the magnificent history *Silent Victory*, was one of the men waiting to greet Hammond and his crew. "I came aboard the *Guardfish* [to join the crew] when you put into Guam for refit, immediately after sinking *Extractor*," he wrote me after the war. Clay had been in a relief crew on *Sperry* since she sailed from Pearl to Guam, about October 1944. As he explained it, "I was temporarily serving in the *Sperry* bridge watch as quartermaster and signalman, a busy job, and I arranged for the dispatch of the liberty launches or landing craft to take off your *Extractor* survivors. . . .Although all this was SECRET, we of the bridge watch surmised what had happened."

In order to minimize contact with others, Captain Hammond restricted his crew from going aboard the tender, except on ship's business. Although word came down that we were not to divulge anything about what happened on the patrol, rumors were out already circulating and our embarrassed admissions to their truth spread the stories like wildfire.

Art O'Grady, first class Shipfitter on *Extractor*, pointed out that the "secret" was common knowledge. "It was funny," he said, "all around the base they already knew about the sinking, but we could not talk about it."

The treatment the returning *Extractor* crew received shocked them. There was little concern or compassion shown as a result of their ordeal. "No restrictions were placed upon us about conversing with the *Guardfish* crew, and I think we talked quite freely while aboard," Electrician's Mate Art Gorny explained. "However, as soon as we reached Guam and left *Guardfish*, we were instructed not to talk to anyone about the sinking incident. We were placed under marine guard and marched as a group like boot camp recruits, to the barracks, to showers and treated in general like POW's."

The executive officer of *Extractor*, Chester Lebsack, in a recent conversation said this about the reception:

> We were off-loaded and all bundled into some LTVP's and brought ashore. There were marine guards, down at the little dock at the foot of where the old fort was, and we were incognito. Boy, you said it. We were locked up in the backs of trucks and taken up to the top of the hill and guards posted. My gosh! We couldn't figure out what the hell we had done, because we were sort of in jail in two Quonsets up there. We didn't have any clothes, nothing. As a matter of fact, we had nothing to eat. I had a pair of dungarees on [probably donated by "Sam" Brewer of *Guardfish*]. Somebody had bleached on the name "Sam," which I acquired as a nickname. There were marines patrolling around us, but I got out of there anyway. I'd previously befriended a supply officer up in Guam and I promoted a jeep from him. I went down to. . .the shore headquarters, and raised hell. I reached the point that I didn't give a damn. If you want to court martial me, whatever the hell, but this kind of crap has got to stop, because the crew was up there and everybody all locked up. . .

Lebsack was successful in prodding headquarters into getting his crew fed that day. Nevertheless, the inexcusable "prisoner of war" treatment continued, for both enlisted men and officers.

The day after our arrival at Guam, there was a buzz of activity aboard *Guardfish*. Everyone was packing up, preparing to pass the boat over to the care of the *Sperry* relief crew. That group was responsible for repairs, new equipment installations and resupplying of the sub in preparation for our next war patrol. A bus picked up the *Guardfish* crew, one load at a time, and took us to Camp Dealey for R&R. The camp was located on a beautiful beach amidst a stand of palm trees several miles from Apra Harbor. Lieutenant (junior grade) Dick Schock, the radar officer, my boss, found me in the crew's quarters. He told me that I had to delay my plans about catching the bus to the camp. He said that I had been called to testify in the Court of Inquiry and that I should be ready to leave immediately.

Navy ships of all sorts and sizes filled Apra Harbor. Small landing craft and launches were constantly racing from ship to ship, churning up the calm water. Schock arranged for one of *Sperry's* launches to transport us to the seaplane tender *USS Curtiss* (AV-4). Lieutenant (junior grade) Fred Jennings, the good-natured six-feet, five-inch tall commissary officer joined us on the taxi ride. He had served on the radar tracking party, operating the torpedo data computer.

Curtiss was a large, handsome ship, displacing over 8,670 tons, with a length over 527 feet. She looked something like an ocean-liner, with her sleek lines and tall smoke stacks. Commanded by Captain Scott Ernest Peck, Curtiss was flagship for Vice Admiral Hoover, who had convened the Court of Inquiry.

When Schock, Jennings and I boarded *Curtiss*, a sailor escorted us to the top deck, starboard side, aft of the bridge. Most of the off-duty *Guardfish* officers were already there when we arrived. They were standing together in an empty gun tub next to the officers' wardroom, where the Court was taking place. Brink Brinkley, the boat's lead radioman was also there. He was glad to see me, another enlisted man, because he was uncomfortable being alone with the officers. We waited interminably to be called. There was no sign of the *Extractor* crew.

The official records show that the Court of Inquiry convened at 1:00 p.m. The Judge Advocate, possibly Vice Admiral Hoover's staff lawyer, initiated the proceedings by reading the "precept," the order, issued by the admiral, to have the hearing. The precept named each member of the court, and identified Commander Hammond as the "Defendant." It stated that the investigation was to follow the procedures detailed in the naval lawbook, *Naval Courts and Boards*. The fourth paragraph of the precept states:

The Court will thoroughly inquire into the matter hereby submitted to it and will include in its findings a full statement of the facts it may deem to be established. The Court will further give its opinion as to whether any offenses have been committed or serious blame incurred, and, in case its opinion be that offenses have been committed or serious blame incurred, will specifically recommend what further proceedings should be had.

The members of the Court then went to the ship's fantail, where the *Extractor* survivors were assembled. In conformance with the steps listed in the lawbook, the Judge Advocate instructed the *Extractor* skipper, Babcock, to read his narrative about the loss of the ship to the survivors.[7] The Judge Advocate then asked the survivors, who were under oath, if the captain's statement was truthful, or if they had any objections to it or any complaint about any officer or crew member regarding the sinking. No one registered a complaint.

Even though the crew made no dissent, Lebsack told me that Admiral Hoover probably did. He remembered:

When we first came on the *Curtiss* for the beginning of this Inquiry we were the most motley looking crowd you've ever seen. Apparently Admiral Hoover took one look and said, "Get these guys some clothes. We're not going to have a Court of Inquiry with this kind of a setup." We looked like refugees from the Solomons. Things happened the next morning. Here comes a bunch of doctors and guys with clothes. . .

After the reading of Babcock's statement and questioning of the assembled survivors, most of the enlisted men returned to their barracks ashore under marine guard. The Court then named Lieutenant Babcock an "Interested Party," and instructed him to join them in the wardroom, present information during the hearing, examine witnesses, and introduce new matter pertinent to the inquiry in the same manner as the Defendant. Only he, the members of the Court, the Defendant plus his counsel and the court reporters were present during the entire closed hearing.

---

[7] See "Commanding Officer's Statement in the Appendix at the end of this book, where Babcock's remarks are reprinted in their entirety.

While the Court was aft with the *Extractor* crew, we waited outside the wardroom wondering what was happening. Then I saw a group of senior officers walking forward toward us, engaged in spirited conversation, arms waving and faces flushed. We snapped to attention and gave our best submariner salutes to the group of "scrambled egg" bearers—Admirals, Captains, Commanders—and their entourages. We were seemingly invisible to many of them, as they crowded through the wardroom doorway. What an assemblage it was! I had never before seen so much gold braid in one place. The only one I knew was our skipper, Commander Hammond, but my boss, Lieutenant Dick Schock, also recognized one of the admirals.

Recently I visited Dick Schock in his home in Escondido, California. During the course of our long conversation, I asked him who he had recognized that day. "I remember Admiral Lockwood walking by," he said, "but I don't know whether he entered the room. We snapped to. . . . I recognized him because he came aboard the *Guardfish* to see Captain Ward one time." The admiral he was referring to was Vice Admiral Charles Andrews Lockwood, Jr., Commander Submarines, Pacific (ComSubPac). Lockwood had only transferred his command from Pearl Harbor to Guam the day before, arriving on the *USS Holland*. Doubtless he came to the Curtiss as a show of support and encouragement for Hammond, the *Guardfish* skipper, but there is no mention of Lockwood in the court record.

The other admiral, also a "three star," was John Hoover, Commander Forward Area, Central Pacific, who initiated the Court of Inquiry under his action-title as Commander, Task Force 94. He had been based on *USS Curtiss* since June, 1942. Holder of the Navy Cross for action in World War I, he was an organizational and tactical dynamo. Early in World War II he received the Distinguished Service Medal for his leadership in combating German U-boats in the Atlantic and Caribbean. Later he received his second and third Distinguished Service awards as Commander of the Forward Area, Central Pacific for ". . . operations which have secured control of the Central Pacific through the Marianas." Like Admiral Lockwood, Hoover did not attend the proceedings.

Three others in the "scrambled egg" team were Members of the Court; Captain Scott Ernest Peck, Captain John Mylin Will and Commander Herbert C. Behner. Captain Peck, President of the Court, entered the navy as an enlisted man, advanced to the rank of Warrant Officer and then to commissioned officer in naval aviation. In 1942, after twenty-four years of naval lighter-than-air duty, he advanced to the rank of Captain and became head of the navy's airship division. He took command of the USS Curtiss, Vice Admiral Hoover's flagship, in October 1943.

Captain Will, an Annapolis graduate [1923] with a Master of Science degree, was Commander, Submarine Squadron 28 and also Commander Task Group 17.10 headquartered at Guam. Will had the reputation of being an extremely capable, "no nonsense" engineering and repair specialist.

Commander Behner, captain of USS Bowditch, was a communications and hydrographic specialist. He was a member of the Institute of Radio Engineers, known in postwar years as the Institute of Electrical and Electronic Engineers (I.E.E.E.).

The fourth officer of the Court was Lieutenant Commander Simon K. Uhl, the Judge Advocate. His job was that of prosecutor, examiner of witnesses and legal aid to the other Court Members.

The skipper of Guardfish, Commander Douglas Hammond, entered the wardroom with his two-member counsel, Captain George L. Russell and Commander Thomas B. Klakring. Both had illustrious careers in the submarine navy. Captain Russell commanded both Submarine Squadron 10 and a Submarine Task Group, with headquarters aboard the sub tender USS Sperry. He held a Bachelor of Laws degree and twice had served on the staff of the Judge Advocate General in Washington, D.C. (Later he actually held that high office himself.) Commander Klakring was in charge of Submarine Division 102. He was, of course, the shrewd, courageous, and highly-decorated first skipper of Guardfish.

Another member of the entourage we saw approaching the wardroom was Captain Oliver F. Naquin, operations officer of Admiral Hoover's Forward Area staff. Ironically, he had been in another Court of Inquiry six years before, but in that one he was the Defendant. However, the strangest twist to this case of deja vu was that the previous hearing also involved a submarine and a salvage vessel. He had been the skipper of the submarine USS Squalus, which in 1939 accidentally sank in 240 feet of water, about ten miles off the coast of New England, due to a faulty *main induction valve. Naquin was cited for his heroic leadership during that ordeal. USS Falcon (ARS-2) rescued thirty-three men from the submarine, but was unable to get to the twenty-six other crewmen who had already perished in flooded compartments. Thereafter, *Falcon* successfully raised the sub and towed her to shore for reclamation.[8] Afterward, *Squalus* was renamed *Sailfish* and served actively throughout WWII.

Possibly another member of Admiral Hoover's staff was in the group outside the wardroom. Ken Eby of the *Extractor* crew told me that he saw Henry Fonda, the motion picture idol, aboard the *Curtiss*. Fonda was Hoover's intelligence officer and assistant operations officer from May 1944 to August 1945. Eby probably saw Fonda during the reading of Babcock's "Commanding Officer's Statement." Probably referring to Fonda's dark beard and unpressed khakis, Eby said, "He was a crummy looking officer."

The Court of Inquiry was in session for four days, and its 110 page official record contains some 40,000 words. After each witness was sworn in the first interrogator was usually the Judge Advocate. Next in line were Members of the Court, the Defendant (Hammond) and the Interested Party (Babcock) who carried out examinations and cross-examinations of each witness. When there were no further questions, the Court offered each witness the opportunity to make any relevant statement to them. As the witnesses were released, the Judge Advocate warned them to not divulge anything said or heard in the proceedings.

The first day of hearings disturbed Babcock, the *Extractor's* skipper. Golden dolphin pins (the insignia of the qualified submarine officer) were everywhere—even on the chest of a member of the Court. Babcock had the feeling that the "deck was being stacked against him." A lack of counsel compounded the problem. There he was, all alone, while Hammond had two top-notch counsel members at his side. At the close of the first day's session, Babcock asked Lieutenant Commander Uhl, the Judge Advocate, to obtain counsel to represent him and Uhl came through for him. As proceedings began on the second day of the Inquiry, Babcock introduced his own counsel to the assembly, Lieutenant Timothy A. Johnson. Babcock did not know Johnson before the hearing, nor did he ever see Johnson afterward. He said, "Both Lieutenant Johnson

---

[8] For full details of this incredible underwater rescue, the first of its kind in history, see *Blow All Ballast!*, by Nat A. Barrows (Court Book Company, New York, 1940).

and I felt a bit intimidated by all the big brass. I sensed that they were more concerned about protecting the navy brass than they were about what had happened."

On day two the Court interrogated *Guardfish* personnel: Three officers, and two enlisted men; Brinkley and me. The questions covered weather and sea conditions, navigational position-fixing, navigational operating zones, warnings received about enemy submarines, SJ radar target contact and tracking, underwater sound target observations, visual target observations and identifications, description of the torpedo attack, SD radar and IFF equipments, and the reliability of IFF.

As I entered the wardroom that second day I was apprehensive, but curious. The *Curtiss* wardroom was huge, compared to the one on *Guardfish*, with dimensions approximately thirty feet by forty feet. The witness chair was on the forward side of the room, facing aft. There was a long empty table on the right side of the witness chair. The members of the Court, Hammond plus counsel and Babcock plus counsel, sat behind three long tables that arced around, facing the witness chair. The court reporter sat by himself, between the witness and the starboard table of the arc.

I was not aware of the presence of the court reporter until he interrupted my testimony and asked me to repeat something. Perhaps he could not understand me because I did not speak loudly or clearly enough. More likely, it was because of my nervous stammering.

The Judge Advocate only asked me a few questions about my training and the operating condition of the radar. My testimony was inconsequential, but it was the memory of that court reporter that caused me to wonder, almost fifty years later, if the court record still existed, a curiosity that ultimately led to this book.

On the third and final day of testimony, the Judge Advocate addressed his queries to the staff of *Extractor*'s squadron leader and to Vice Admiral Hoover's staff. The topics focused on radio messages to, or about *Extractor* or *Guardfish*, the plotting of *Extractor*'s position, and any actions taken as a result of those plots.

The members of the Court spent the fourth day enumerating their Findings, making a list of their Opinions based on those findings and, finally, listing their Recommendations for subsequent action by appropriate authorities.

Chapter Sixteen

Communcation Errors

Achronological review of events covered by the Court's Findings demonstrates that the sinking of *Extractor* was the result of a string of interconnected errors. If any one of them had not happened, it is probable that the tragedy would not have occurred.

The radio message in Court Exhibit Six reveals that four ships in addition to *Extractor* were sent to assist the stricken *Ticonderoga*. Two vessels, *USS Munsee* and an unnamed Task Unit 30.8.19, were dispatched from Ulithi, while a third, *USS Shackle*, steamed from Saipan. The fourth, *USS Sarrano* (whose skipper did not consider his ship seaready when Admiral Halsey ordered her out), also left from Guam, but considerably later than *Extractor*.

The fact that *Extractor* left Guam with an inoperative radar and no technician aboard to repair it was the first critical mistake in the sequence of events leading to the sinking. If her radar had been operating when she met *Guardfish*, it is unlikely the torpedo attack would have taken place. Even if *Extractor's* radar had not detected us, *Guardfish* probably would have detected her radar signal with either the SJ radar or the APR radar search receiver. The result is that Captain Hammond would have known the target was friendly and let her pass.

Horace Babcock testified that he did not know his radar was inoperative when he received urgent verbal and handwritten mission orders from his squadron's operations officer, Lieutenant Commander S. V. Dennison. Babcock testified that in repeated experiences under similar circumstances, his operations officers told him that he should leave "regardless of [his ship's] condition." Dennison, however, when cross-examined by Babcock on this point, disagreed:

Babcock: In an emergency such as was considered to exist, would it have been considered advisable to hold a ship for say ten hours for repairs to radar or radio equipment?

Dennison: In this specific instance, if the radar was out and it was reasonable that it could be repaired in ten, possibly twelve hours, we would probably have held the ship. I could not say specifically. That would be a decision for Captain [John David] Reppy.

The Court's opinion was that Babcock "should have reported to his immediate superior in command. . .that *Extractor's*. . .radar was inoperative."

The next critical blunder occurred on January 22. On that day, the garbled and incomplete message ordering the ship to return to Guam was "received." Unfortunately, it was so defective *Extractor's* personnel found it impossible to decode. The operator who received the message was Bob Roy Burgess, Radioman third class, one of the six crewmen who perished in the sinking. After a considerable amount of questioning and testimony, the Court concluded that Radioman Burgess was probably not responsible for copying errors, even though the transmission's sending speed was much faster than normal. Two independent and corroborating witnesses identified the actual source of the garbling to be at "Radio Honolulu" (Pearl Harbor).

Captain Lawrence W. Frost was the communications officer on Vice Admiral Hoover's Forward Area staff. Frost was intimately familiar with the radio communication system that provided the navy with radio coverage over the entire Pacific area. In fact, he was responsible for establishing the efficient communications system in use in the Forward Area, a task for which he received a Legion of Merit citation. Captain Frost spent a substantial amount of time describing the trans-Pacific network in some detail during his testimony.

Short wave radio communication frequently suffers from severe, random fluctuations in signal strength (fading). Experience shows that received radio signals fade by different amounts and at different times on different radio frequencies. A *frequency diversity* communications system combats fading by simultaneously sending out the same message from two separate radio transmitters, which operate on different frequencies. The receiving station tunes to the two signals on separate radio receivers. Then, when the outputs of the two receivers are combined, the perceived signal strength is relatively constant.

During WWII, combining of the receivers' outputs was accomplished with split earphones. That is, with the output of one diversity receiver connected to the earpiece on the operator's left ear, and the second receiver's output connected to the right earpiece. Frost's system had an added complexity; both frequency signals from Pearl Harbor were instantaneously, automatically rebroadcast from Guam on *another* set of frequencies. Rebroadcasting boosted the signal strength for ships in the westward reaches of the Pacific.

The frequency diversity system worked well for those ships equipped with two receivers. Unfortunately, *Extractor* and many other small ships had only one receiver, and thus their incoming signals were not protected from the effects of fading.

The Court Record demonstrates *Extractor* was also affected by another defect in the system. Her lead operator was William M. Neylon, Radioman second class. What follows is an excerpt from the Court's exchange with him. The examiner first established that if one shortwave receiver were in use and it was tuned to an unreadable channel, an excessive amount of time would be required to tune it to the second channel. The net effect, of course, would be that a portion of the message would be lost. The mention of "tape" in the proceedings refers to paper tape used in an automatic Morse code sending machine that simultaneously keyed both of the frequency diversity radio transmitters. The tape contained punched holes or inscribed lines, representing the dots and dashes of the message, with which the machine automatically keyed the radio transmitters. (*NPM is the call sign of Radio Pearl Harbor.)

Court: With equipment you had, could you have guarded more than one frequency circuit?

Neylon: No, sir, not more than one high frequency circuit.

Court: How long did it take you to change from one frequency to another?

Neylon: About a minute.

Court: After the message was being received and it appeared that there was difficulty in receiving, how much time would it take to change to another frequency in an effort to get the correct and entire message?

Neylon: I would say about three-fourths of a minute or a minute to change and tune in the signal.

Court: Did you have difficulty in receiving NPM Primary?

Neylon: Yes, sir.

Court: Why?

Neylon: Because of the transmission from NPM and there was interference.

Court: Was there any remarks made by the operator, Burgess, to you?

Neylon: Yes, sir. When he showed me the message, he complained about the tape and also the speed of the transmission.

Court: What difficulty was encountered with the tape in the operation?

Neylon: Letters were being combined, groups being combined, and the "dits" were confused with the "dahs."

Court: This message, which was addressed to the Extractor and which she was not able to break and was incomplete and garbled, came in about 5:30 p.m. on the 22nd?

Neylon: Some time in the late afternoon.

Court: What time, Item [Extractor's local] time, did that dispatch come in?

Neylon: To the best of my knowledge it came in just before evening chow.

Court: What time was evening chow?

Neylon: 4:30.

Court: You relieved the man [Burgess], who received this dispatch, immediately after that?

Neylon: Yes, sir.

Court: What were the conditions that you found regarding the other traffic on circuits you were guarding?

Neylon: It was unusually fast for a Fox circuit and I would say that on an average of every other message that tape fouled up and caused the transmitting station to remove the tape and send again.

Court: Did that procedure happen with this particular message?

Neylon: The message addressed to the *Extractor* I could not say.

Court: During the period of that day you were the supervisor, you maintained a radio log of the traffic, did you not?

Neylon: Yes, sir.

Court: Were many of the dispatches, recorded during the periods you were guarding Primary Fox, garbled and incomplete?

Neylon: Yes, sir.

Even though the Judge Advocate called most of those who testified, it was Lieutenant Babcock who summoned a witness from Vice Admiral Hoover's radio communications staff aboard *USS Curtiss*. Granville Baker, Radioman third class, U.S. Naval Reserve, ComFwdArea Staff, had the same third class rating as Burgess, the *Extractor* operator who received the garbled message.

Babcock: Did you copy message H3624 on Primary Fox on the twenty-second?

Baker: Yes, that is what I have down here.

Babcock: Did you have any trouble copying this message?

Baker: Yes, I had quite a lot. I was using two receivers, as I have 8530 and 8230 *kilocycles. I was copying off two different frequencies.

Babcock: Will you state the reason for using the two receivers?

Baker: The relay was sticking, the signal was bad, that is why I was using both phones.

Babcock: Can you say anything about the speed of the transmission?

Baker: If I knew just what time of the day it was, I don't remember. I judge it was being sent about twenty-two or twenty-three words per minute.

Babcock: Do you have any difficulty copying at that speed?

Baker: No.

Babcock: But you say the signal was bad?

Baker: Yes, sir.

Babcock: Noise level?

Baker: There wasn't so much noise, it was an S-4 signal.

Babcock: Tell what you mean by S-4 signal?

Baker: S-5 is good, S-4 would be fair.

Babcock: What is the best signal?

Baker: S-5.

Babcock: Down to what on the scale?

Baker: S-1, that is signal strength. Of course the reception could be bad.

Babcock: So your signal strength was 4. What about interference, if any?

Baker: I have interference off and on but I can't recall. Sometimes I have local interference.

Babcock: Do you recall anything concerning interference on this particular message?

Baker: Nothing that I can recall. Could be local interference from the broadcasting station.

Babcock: Did I understand you to say the tape was slipping?

Baker: Yes, sir. It could have been the relay. You can be sending along and send half a character and you won't hear the rest.

It is important to keep in mind that Baker was copying the signal directly from NPM at Pearl Harbor. If he had been tuned to NPN in Guam, the signal would have been an S-5 (i.e., very strong, since he was also at Guam). The keying problem—probably a sticking keying re-lay—had to be associated with one transmitter, not with the code tape machine. If it originated in the tape machine, the same problem would arise on both transmitter frequencies, and the use of two receivers would not have helped Radioman Baker on *Curtiss*. But Radioman Burgess on *Extractor* only had one receiver, and he had unfortunately tuned it to the defective transmitter's frequency. A helpful analogy to a sticking keying relay is a person's mouth erratically sticking shut while he is speaking; the result is unintelligible garble. All of this explains why Burgess could not make out what was being sent, and why *Extractor* did not receive her orders to return to Guam.

Even though one of the Court members was a radio communications engineer, neither he nor the Court as a whole seemed to recognize the full significance of the problem at NPM. "The radio transmissions from NPM [Pearl Harbor], wrote the Court, were ". . .definitely unsatisfactory and extremely difficult to copy." The Court should have written that the signal was impossible to copy.

The next logical question to be asked is why did NPM not repeat the important message? Rear Admiral Norvell Ward, *Guardfish's* second skipper, explained to me that it was not up to the radio station to deter-mine whether to resend a transmission. "The navy wide practice," he explained, was that the command originating a message determined the number of times a message should be broadcast. All messages to submarines were sent at least three times. The directive "Acknowledge" was always included in the message when the commander wanted the submarine to "break radio silence" and acknowledge the message. If it was not acknowledged, the commander had the message rebroadcast a second and a third night, in order to cover all nonreceipt possibilities.

Even though Capt. Oliver Naquin of Vice Admiral Hoover's staff was also a qualified submariner (and the former skipper of *Squalus*), transmitting a change of ship's orders only one time seemed manifestly reasonable to him:

Court: As an operations officer handling movement of ships, do you consider that one transmission of a Fox schedule to a ship the size of the Extractor *is sufficient to be assured they receive vital information?*

Naquin: Yes, normally I consider that is sufficient. If we did not assume that, then the entire concept of the Fox system would be questionable. We normally do business on that basis in the navy.

The Court did not formally express an opinion about Vice Admiral Hoover's practice of only sending vital Fox messages once, and not requiring an acknowledgment by the recipient.

Given all that transpired, it is logical to wonder why Babcock did not break radio silence and ask for the message to be repeated. The Judge Advocate and the Court queried several officers from different commands about the practice of breaking radio silence. Testimony on this issue revealed that the subject came up more than once aboard *Extractor*. The following exchange occurred during the testimony of *Extractor's* communications officer, Lieutenant (junior grade) Semmes Chapman:

Court: Did you suggest to the commanding officer that a retransmit should be requested?

Chapman: I had requested the executive officer—he had brought up the point. In fact, the captain had first asked as to the custom of breaking radio silence—to get our opinion.

Court: Was your opinion asked for?

Chapman: Yes, sir.

Court: What was your answer?

Chapman: That radio silence was broken only for enemy contacts.

The following is an exchange on the subject with Captain Frost, the most authoritative source present and the communications expert for Admiral Hoover's ComFwdArea.

Judge Advocate: As communications officer are there any instructions in connection with what is known as breaking silence by ships while in operation?

Frost: Yes, I am familiar with instructions. The question of whether or not to break radio silence is a tactical decision of which has to be made from time to time by every commanding officer, and it is usually specifically covered in operation plans and orders. In general, ships at sea normally maintain radio silence unless a tactical situation indicates that it should be broken, which again comes back to the decision of the commanding officer whether or not he should break it.

Judge Advocate: In other words, there is no ironclad rule covering the situation but it is entirely up to the discretion of the commanding officer of the ship?

Frost: It is entirely up to the commanding officer's discretion, the normal situation is to maintain radio silence unless in the opinion of the commanding officer warrants breaking it.

During his second appearance in the witness chair, *Extractor's* skipper, Lieutenant Babcock, had the following question put to him:

Court: Were you given any specific instructions as to radio silence prior to your departure on this mission?

Babcock: No, there was none.

The Court expressed the opinion that "a small ship such as the *Extractor* . . . required to operate independently in waters in which both friendly and enemy submarine craft can be expected to appear should be more carefully briefed and instructed in proper communication procedure than was done when *Extractor* was sailed on her last mission." The Court also concluded that "the commanding officer of the *Extractor* should have broken radio silence to ask for a retransmission of the operational priority dispatch. . .which he was unable to break."

The next miscalculation in the sequence of events leading to *Extractor's* demise was the report that there was "nothing friendly known in the vicinity" of *Guardfish*. Why did the plotters tracking the movement of American ships fail to realize that *Extractor* was a potential *Guardfish* target?

Chapter Seventeen

Identification Errors

The first radio message Captain Hammond sent to his superiors about the radar contact (which later proved to be *Extractor*) inquired whether the target could be a friendly submarine. The question set ComSubPac, Pearl Harbor, and Commander of Task Group (CTG) 17.7, Saipan, into motion, checking their plotting boards and radio messages for the locations of Allied submarines in the general vicinity of *Guardfish*. Their responses indicated that *Guardfish* was the only friendly submarine in the area. CTG 17.7 also reported there might be friendly surface ships and they were checking on that possibility. The Court's Exhibit 10 recorded the urgent message from CTG 17.7 to Commander of Task Force (CTF) 94, Vice Admiral Hoover in Guam, as follows:

AT 15-11 NORTH 137 EAST COURSE 270 SPEED 11 GUARDFISH REPORTS A SMALL SHIP POSSIBLY SUB X ARE THERE ANY FRIENDS THERE XX

Less than an hour later CTF 94 responded with the succinct but erroneous reply: "NEGATIVE." The incorrect but decisive response from Vice Admiral Hoover's command prompted CTG 17.7 to cautiously inform *Guardfish* that her target was very likely an enemy vessel.

When the Court realized the CTF 94 error, it called key members of Admiral Hoover's staff as witnesses. Testimony revealed that it was the operations officer and former *Squalus* skipper Oliver Naquin who composed the terse and ultimately fatal "negative" message. Captain Naquin was called as the next witness and grilled on the matter:

Judge Advocate: Will you give the Court the reasons which you had for sending out the message stating there was nothing in the area?

Naquin: The message I sent was based on my plot in the operations room. The *Extractor* was ordered out and reported as sailing at 2100 [Guam local] time on the twenty-first. She was ordered later by Commander Third Fleet [Admiral Halsey] to turn around at 2100 King [Guam local] time on the twenty-second if no other orders were received. This message was filed at 1049 on the twenty-second by Commander Third Fleet which placed this vessel well clear of the area in question.

Judge Advocate: What was the possibility of the Extractor not having received the Commander Third Fleet directive to return to Guam and was that possibility considered?

Naquin: There is always possibility that any ship or station may not receive communications but plots cannot be run on conjectures.

Judge Advocate: Is it the practice of the operations officer at any time to take into consideration the advance movements of the ships that there might be a possibility of two ships running courses where they would converge?

Naquin: Yes.

Judge Advocate: And was that done in this case?

Naquin: Yes.

Judge Advocate: If that was the case, then how do you explain the message that said there was nothing in this area?

Naquin: That message is based on my plot. To have sent any other message would have been based on conjecture and supposition. To do so would have possibly prevented a submarine from attacking an enemy ship.

Judge Advocate: Does Commander Task Force 94 keep a plot of every ship moving through the area in which the Extractor was sunk?

Naquin: Yes.

Judge Advocate: There is testimony in the record to the effect that the Extractor was approximately 600 miles from Guam when she was sunk. Did you know this?

Naquin: I did not know that at the time. I don't know on what basis that computation is made.

Judge Advocate: Do you know how long overdue the Extractor was?

Naquin: No. I would have to make allowances for wind and current in order to arrive at a definite answer.

Judge Advocate: Can you give the Court any idea as to that time?

Naquin: It might amount to a couple hours or less.

Captain Naquin's cross-examination was conducted by the defendant, Commander Hammond:

Hammond: Was there anything done to ascertain her position, either by radio or air search? In other words, was there anything done by operations to check her exact position?

Naquin: No, I saw no reason for making such a check at the time.

Hammond: Captain Naquin, how many other ships operating under the cognizance of Commander Task Force 94 ship movements office were in the area where the Extractor was sunk?

Naquin: According to my plot there were none.

Hammond: Then the Extractor was the only vessel plotted in the ship movements office which should have been in that area?

Naquin: I believe there was another tug but she was also turned around.

Hammond: When orders of this type, that is orders that are sent out to operating vessels requiring a complete cancellation of their former orders, is it customary or proper to require the ship to acknowledge?

Naquin: No, it is not. It is neither customary nor proper. I would not say it is improper but it is my understanding this was sent out on a Fox schedule which is a normal frequency for transmitting information to ships at sea.

Hammond: Then your plot is run on the conjecture that all messages sent are received?

Naquin: I know of no other way of running a plot.

Hammond: Are you aware that vessels ordinarily locally assigned such as the Extractor enter Apra Harbor at night as well as during the day?

Naquin: I am aware of that fact.

Hammond: Then there would be no reason for the Extractor to lay off the entrance of Apra Harbor merely because she arrived after dark?

Naquin: That would be entirely up to the port director.

Hammond: Do you know whether the Extractor asked the port director permission to enter Apra after dark 23 January?

Naquin: I do not.

Hammond: Would you have any record in your office which would enable you to determine this?

Naquin: I might have negative information to show nothing was asked. We keep a record of all ships that are reported to us. . .but I might say that there are many that are not reported.

Hammond: You know that the Extractor was sunk several hundred miles from Guam?

Naquin: Yes, I know that.

Hammond: Then, do you think that you can make a presumption that she did not ask permission to enter Apra.

Naquin: Yes.

Hammond: I believe you made the statement that you did not desire the Guardfish to be prevented from attacking an enemy ship. Would your office be willing to run the risk to have a submarine attack the Extractor rather than for an enemy ship not be attacked?

Naquin: I don't see that my office enters into such a concept. I merely made that statement as a general principle that if I had to assume otherwise than that ships were carrying out their orders at sea that my or any one's plot would become confused, would be based on assumption and conjecture. I can conceive of situations at sea where we might miss out on the enemy by telling a ship to lay off just because we were guessing at the ship's other orders and we were guessing at the ship's action rather than conducting our plot according to what the ship's orders read.

Hammond: Did the possibility of a communication failure with respect to the Extractor receiving orders to turn around occur to you?

Naquin: No, I believe I have covered that in stating that I assumed that the ship received her orders.

Hammond: When you were asked if there were any ships in the area, did it occur to you that she might not have received it?

Naquin: No.

Hammond: You have stated that the possibility of communication failure is always present?

Naquin: Yes, I think that is always possible, but in this case they had over ten hours to get this message.

Hammond: You did not feel it was necessary to qualify your answer?

Naquin: I did not.

Hammond: When you were asked by dispatch if the area was clear of friends, you did not know for a fact that the Extractor was clear, did you?

Naquin: No more than I would know for a fact that any other ship at sea was in a definite location.

Hammond: None the less, in answer to that dispatch you made a positive statement, did you not?

Naquin: I made a positive statement to a positive question. The question was "are there any friends there." My plot indicated that there were not and the answer was in the negative. I had no reason for giving an affirmative reply to the question.

After hearing this exchange, together with other testimony, the Court eventually made the following statement: "That when surface contacts are reported in areas where no ships are known to be, more careful investigation should be made into the possibility of ships under-way in that general area being out of position and the possibility of communication failures considered before a positive statement is made that the ship could not be friendly." Walking a fine line, the Court managed to escape without a finding that either Captain Naquin or Vice Admiral Hoover deserved any blame for *Extractor's* sinking.

Although the mistake in dealing with the garbled transmission, as well as Captain Naquin's "oversight" can be reasonably explained, the issue of the faulty visual identification of the target by *Guardfish* is not as easily rationalized. Indeed, of all the mistakes made, it is the most difficult to understand. How could anyone possibly mistake a salvage and rescue vessel for a submarine?

The psychological pressure from repeated warnings of enemy sub-marines may have had something to do with it, and a considerable amount of circumstantial evidence pointed to the target as fulfilling those admonitions. Still, both Captain Hammond and his executive offi-cer, Lieutenant Commander Luther Johnson, were mistaken in the iden-tification of the target. What caused them to a be completely convinced that the vessel was the Japanese *I-165*, or a submarine at all? Johnson was the first *Guardfish* witness to testify. The Judge Advocate asked him about the periscope approach:

Judge Advocate: Will you explain to the Court just exactly what you saw at that time.

Johnson: I will insofar as I said it was a silhouette. I could not make any distinguishing lines, flat structure more or less. The silhouette appeared to me in such a way that I was positive it was a submarine. I saw merely a part of the deck line. It seemed to be a long, practically straight deck line and what appeared to me to be an *I-165* class Jap sub, a radio mast or antenna. The forward part of the bridge curved down to the deck and gradually sliding down to the after deck.

Judge Advocate: At this point when the observation was made, what would you say was the height of the periscope from the surface of the water?

Johnson: At the time I made the observation the periscope was about four or five feet above the surface of the water.

Judge Advocate: Is that the usual or the average that is needed under those circumstances?

Johnson: On that range we wanted to show as little periscope as possible in order to remain undetected and in order to identify the actions of the target.

Judge Advocate: Did you attempt to identify this object by anything that you might have had on board, such as the ONI 54 [an Office of Naval Intelligence publication]?

Johnson: We had. We used the ONI 54. We did this in connection with the possibility that it might be a surface craft. I examined the ONI 41-42 and we observed it was a submarine and I looked at the submarine section and saw a silhouette of what was in the periscope.

Judge Advocate: Did it occur to you at any time that it could be a surface ship?

Johnson: It had occurred to us during the night tracking. That was the reason for sending the messages that were sent, in order to find out if possible its identity.

Judge Advocate: When you say it had occurred to you, what reason do you have for making that statement?

Johnson: The reasons I had for making that statement is just what happened. We wanted to identify any craft in this vicinity because we were in a joint zone and we were supposed to be positive that the target was an enemy before firing.

Commander Hammond was the last to testify during the second day of the hearing. He requested that he be called to testify on his own behalf. Although the record seems to indicate he put the questions to himself, they were actually proposed by one of his lawyers:

Q: When you looked at the target through the periscope, did you notice any characteristic which would convince you that the target was not a friendly submarine?

Hammond: On the first look my impression was that it was a submarine. On the second look, which was primarily to check for our own submarines, we were familiar enough with our own silhouettes to know that there was nothing to indicate it was one of ours.

Q: What did you estimate the height of the waves to be?

Hammond: Estimated to be in the vicinity of four feet. Set the torpedoes to run at six feet, based on this assumption.

Q: At any time after you came to the conclusion that the target was an enemy submarine was there any doubt in your mind?

Hammond: Not the slightest. I would like to make it even stronger than that. I didn't have the executive officer check me on the identification, I had him look just to see what we were looking for, for his own information so he could know what we were doing. He is responsible for holding the whole attack party. The identification part was his own.

Q: If there had been any doubt in your mind, what would your procedure have been?

Hammond: Procedure at that time would depend on the degree of doubt. If there had been a possible doubt I had another officer in the conning tower at the time who has made seven or eight war patrols, I would have asked him to look, probably. If there had been considerable doubt enough in my own mind to seriously question it, being where I was, I think I would have debated.

The Judge Advocate cross-examined Commander Hammond:

Judge Advocate: How long an interval elapsed between the time you ordered to commence firing and from the time from which you last saw the target by the periscope?

Hammond: Possibly three seconds. The procedure followed was normal routine followed on the *Guardfish*, wherein the commanding officer advises the control party in advance when we are ready to shoot, give the torpedo data computer operator orders to standby for firing.

Judge Advocate: At the time you made this observation prior to firing, what were the weather conditions as far as the sea, the weather itself, and the distance that you were able to identify an object?

Hammond: The condition of the sea I have stated the estimated waves to be approximately four feet high, I set the torpedoes based on that assumption. I could see this particular ship at 6800 yards, as determined by a post firing plot. The time the target was first sighted was approximately twenty-four minutes prior to sunrise. The sky was overcast. Passing rain squalls, there was a definite pre-sunrise light in the east which placed the target between the *Guardfish* and this light area in the east.

Judge Advocate: What did you see at that time?

Hammond: I saw what to me was definitely the conning tower and bridge structure of a submarine which closely resembled the *I-165* class submarine. This bridge structure was a horizontal straight line from the forward part of the bridge, a sharp drop and a lower section bridge aft. The conning tower structure forward tapered down until it met the deck line. There was a similar taper aft, only not as marked as that forward. There was one antenna mast at the after end of the conning tower structure and what appeared to be a raised periscope with the necessary supporting sheers at the forward part of the conning tower bridge structure. On at least two observations I observed what appeared to be a straight line deck of a submarine extending both directions from the bridge conning tower structure.

Judge Advocate: How many times was the object sighted through the periscope?

Hammond: The object was sighted by me at least four times, as determined by recorded bearings—possibly one or two more wherein no bearings were taken. Was observed by the executive officer on two separate occasions.

Court: Did it occur to you in any of these observations that it might have been a surface craft?

Hammond: Not the slightest indication. It never occurred to me at one time.

It is obvious that both Hammond and his executive officer saw only the silhouette of *Extractor's* superstructure and an occasional trace of the line of her deck. This was probably because the periscope, which looked across the crests of all the waves between the vessels, was purposely kept low to avoid detection. According to both officers, on the last observation before firing, the range to the target was about 1,200 yards, and *Extractor* presented approximately a fifty degree starboard angle on the bow. When I first read this testimony, it seemed strange to me that the Court failed to make any comparisons between the silhouettes of *Extractor* and the I-165. Out of personal curiosity, I constructed such a comparison, which is shown in Appendix Two. The display shows the silhouettes of the two ships from their deck lines up.

"The commanding officer of the *Guardfish*," concluded the Court, "through a very serious error in identification failed to establish the enemy character of the ship which he attacked beyond the possibility of a doubt and thereby made a fatal and tragic mistake which resulted in the sinking of the *USS Extractor* and the loss of six members of her crew."

Guardfish's skipper, executive officer, and radar officer (Dick Schock) were questioned at length about why the electronic target identification (IFF) system was not used. Each took great pain to point out that the system was originally incorporated on American submarines to protect them against attacks by American airplanes. Thus, the submarine high command ordered that IFF units on every boat be connected to the sub's SD air search radar, rather than the SJ surface search radar.

Lieutenant Babcock, *Extractor's* commander, questioned Captain Hammond on this point:

Babcock: Is the current submarine doctrine not to use IFF to identify surface ships?

Hammond: To the best of my knowledge and belief it is.

Babcock: Therefore, it would not occur to you to use IFF for that purpose?

Hammond: If there had been indication of another radar in the vicinity it is possible that the IFF equipment might have been used, but I seriously doubt that it would be.

Babcock: Your IFF, is it regularly used for aircraft identification?

Hammond: When in areas where friendly planes can be expected, it is.

Babcock: To the best of your knowledge and belief, do the Japanese have any equipment in their planes by which they can trip IFF equipment?

Hammond: To my knowledge our submarines have received proper recognition by planes closing the range and have been bombed immediately thereafter by Japanese planes.

It is important to understand that since the air search SD radar could only detect objects above the horizon, had it been used while target tracking it would not have detected *Extractor*. However, if we had simultaneously interrogated *Extractor's* IFF transponder, a "friendly" response would have appeared on our otherwise blank SD radar screen. Unfortunately, we could not use our IFF interrogator because heavy seas had carried away *Guardfish's* bow mast and communications antennas, so we had to use the SD radar mast as a radio antenna to obtain instructions from high command. The need for those urgent communications preempted use of the mast until we received the "Nothing friendly known in the vicinity" response about four and a half hours later. We received that message about three hours before dawn.

Given this unusual situation, it is not surprising that Hammond failed to envision utilizing the aircraft identification system to try to identify a surface target. During World War II, few officers had sufficient knowledge of electronic equipment to be able to creatively employ that technology in any situation, much less on a pressure-filled combat patrol.

Much to the relief of both Douglas Hammond and Horace Babcock, the Court's general conclusion about the sinking of *USS Extractor* was that no criminal offenses had been committed by any party involved. Its conclusions were set forth as thirty separate "Opinions," which filled three legal-sized pages. The Court's final pair of observations set forth two instances of "serious blame," as follows:

Opinion 29. The Court is of the opinion that serious blame was incurred by the commanding officer of the *Guardfish* in that he did not use his. . .[IFF] equipment to assist in identification, and in that he failed positively to establish the enemy character of the ship he attacked, beyond the possibility of doubt.

Opinion 30. The Court is of the opinion that the commanding officer of the *Extractor* incurred serious blame in that he failed to take steps to obtain a complete copy of an operational priority dispatch [the garbled message] addressed to him for action.

The last page of the Court of Inquiry Record listed the Court's Recommendations. Unfortunately, the copy provided to me by the Navy was blacked out. Although I later attempted to acquire a complete copy by citing the Freedom of Information Act, the Navy deemed it to be privileged information.

Theodore Roscoe, in his book *Pig Boats: The True Story of The Fighting Submariners Of World War II* (p. 391) wrote that, in accordance with Opinion 29, the "Court of Inquiry voted a reprimand for the commanding officer of the submarine," Douglas Hammond. The same source also blamed the sinking on "the failure of the operations officer [Oliver F. Naquin] at Headquarters, Commander Forward Area, to check *Extractor's* whereabouts at the time the submarine reported contact." Since this information was not included in the Court Record, it must be concluded that one or more of Roscoe's official Navy contacts had access to the unabridged Recommendations page from the Court Record. Roscoe does not mention any action taken as a result of Opinion 30.

One of the Court's recommendations should have been for Radio Pearl Harbor to repair the transmitter that caused the garbling of the message to *Extractor*. Some two months after the end of the Court of Inquiry, however, the defect had apparently not yet been repaired. During *Guardfish's* next (eleventh) patrol, the communications officer complained in the patrol report about the repeated garbling of the keying from one of the navy transmitters.

In spite of the Court's final two opinions, the navy allowed Douglas T. Hammond to retain his command of *USS Guardfish*, and Horace Babcock was given his choice of another ship to command.

Chapter Eighteen

The Last Patrols

The sinking of *Extractor* marked the end of the glory days for *Guardfish*, one of the top scoring submarines in the Navy. After the tragedy, our proud submarine even became an object of derision. The first evidence of this came shortly after the Court of Inquiry, while we were on R&R at Guam's Camp Dealey.

The main activities at the camp were beer guzzling, swimming, table tennis, softball, sleeping—and beer guzzling. Hundreds of enlisted men crowded into the beer garden during the scheduled open hours. As we swilled our brew, we swapped sea stories about our previous patrols. Although our officers had instructed us to not discuss the *Extractor* friendly-fire sinking, it appeared to be common knowledge and it was not long until the hazing began.

At first the ribbing was good natured: "Hey, *Guardfish*, when are you going to add an American flag to your Battle Flag?"[9] As the beer pitchers emptied, though, the taunts became increasingly bellicose.

---

[9] The battle flag was a pennant which displayed the name and graphic representation of the boat, together with symbols representing various battle actions, such as a small Japanese flag for every ship torpedoed by the submarine. Ours had a caricature of a Guardfish, a long fish with a sharp beak, surrounded by twenty-six Japanese flags, for the six warships and twenty cargo ships we claimed.

George Lawrence, one of our engine room gang, remembers that one exchange led "almost [to] a brawl. Then somebody came up with the idea to settle it on the baseball field in a winner-take-all game. A group scraped up all the betting money they could." According to Lawrence, the men managed to gather "about $1,500," which is over $15,000 in today's currency. "*Guardfish*," he remembers proudly, "won the ball game and the pot. There was no more trouble."

Unfortunately, the problem continued to dog many members of our crew. Even some of our officers were antagonized and threatened by drunken officers from other boats. As might be expected, Captain Hammond was the focus of much of it. Although ComSubPac allowed him to remain in command of *Guardfish* following the Court of Inquiry, Hammond knew morale was low on his boat and he expected some trouble, even from his own officers. After the tenth patrol, Lieutenant Jerry Howarth was scheduled to be sent back to a boat then under construction in New London. But, he recalls, "Captain Hammond asked me to change my plans. He said he was going to take the boat out again, that he'd been exonerated, and said, 'Jerry, I'd appreciate it if you'd make another patrol with me. I'm going to need all the support I can get.' Although Howarth told Hammond he would be happy to sail with him again, he did not feel good about it. "I had my fingers crossed," he told me recently. "Maybe I was walking into the last one, you know."

Yes, I did know. And Howarth was not the only one who dreaded going out on another patrol. "The *Extractor* Fiasco," as we called it, made me realize more than ever that we were all vulnerable to the quirks of war. I wondered constantly if I would ever get back home to real life, to ham radio—to girls.

On February 27, 1945, Hammond took *Guardfish* out on her eleventh war patrol. ComSubPac assigned us to an independent run this time instead of a wolf pack. Our destination was Japan, where perhaps there might be a chance to redeem *Guardfish's* reputation. The Japanese-held island of Iwo Jima was under attack by U.S. invasion forces at this time, a bloody battle that would grind on for weeks. On March 1, as we were passing near the island, orders were received to help air and surface units search for downed American airmen. After a three day search, surface ships found the airmen and we continued our northward journey. The next day our watchmen sighted a floating mine. We paused and "Gunner" Rose sank it with his BAR.

Guardfish's War Patrols
Eleven and Twelve

Map 6

During the daylight hours of March 5, four different unidentified planes drove us down. We thought they might be friendly, but none gave an IFF response on our SD radar. That evening we made our first definite identification of a Japanese airplane patrolling the cold gray skies. We detected it on our SJ radar, but also picked up a VHF radar signal on our APR search receiver. The plane passed us by and apparently never spotted us. Since we knew the enemy could home in on our VHF radar signal, and that we were unlikely to find anymore friendly aircraft, we shut down the SD radar.

It was a cold time of year to be patrolling near the Japanese home islands. Thankfully, before we left Guam we were issued cold weather gear, which consisted of dark-green woolen sweaters and canvas jackets with furry collars and linings. Our lookouts wore long underwear, sweaters and jackets, and long, hooded fur-lined canvas overcoats. Their hands, which were already covered with wool gloves, were buried deep into bulky fur-lined leather mittens. With so much clothing on they could hardly move, and when they did they waddled around like penguins.

At 4:00 a.m. the next day, I began my conning tower watch on the SJ radar, and as usual exchanged positions with my watch mates each half hour. It was damp and very cold, and we did not talk much. The dim red lighting, the rocking of the boat, and the sound of the waves made me wish I was back in my warm bunk.

As 5:30 a.m. approached I was at the helm preparing to move back to the radar when a Japanese aircraft jumped us out of nowhere. The first indication we had that the plane was homing in on us was when the pilot switched on his searchlight to scan the water.

Our starboard lookout's shrill voice sliced through the air: "Plane closing fast on the starboard quarter!"

Lieutenant Howarth, the officer of the deck, spun around, verified the report, and immediately shouted, "Clear the bridge! Dive! Dive! Dive!" Given Howarth's premonitions about undertaking another patrol with Captain Hammond, one can't help but wonder what was going through the lieutenant's mind as he watched the aircraft speed toward the boat.

Encumbered by all the cold weather gear, the lookouts stumbled and crashed together at the hatch, rode each other down the ladder, fell in a heap on the conning tower deck, clawed their way to the lower hatch and repeated their collisions and shoulder rides down the ladder into the control room. The junior officer of the deck stumbled closely behind the lookouts, taking control of the dive as the boat plunged down through the freezing brine. Clay Blair, the quartermaster of the watch, jumped through the hatch from the bridge, dropped into the conning tower, and moved aside as Lieutenant Howarth, the officer of the deck, followed close behind him. As he passed through the hatch, Howarth grabbed the lanyard and slammed the hatch cover down with the weight of his body. Something, though, had gone desperately wrong.

Clay recalled the incident in a recent letter to me:

> When we crash-dived, it was my job to step up and dog the conning tower hatch shut with the little wheel in the center of the hatch cover, while the officer of the deck held it shut with a lanyard to prevent sloshing water before the dogs snugged the hatch tight. Thoroughly frightened by the aircraft, I nonetheless went through my routine. We were going down like a rock, but the hatch would not dog-down. A torrent of ice water spewed in through the undogged hatch. Panic and loud shouts. "What the f— is going on?" Somehow I forced my way back up to the wheel through this torrent of water. . .

Captain Hammond arrived in the conning tower shortly after the diving alarm sounded. He stood near the lowered number one periscope, away from the down pouring water. At my helm position I watched as Clay tried repeatedly to dog the hatch closed. Sea water was cascading into the conning tower from around the perimeter of the thirty-inch diameter hatch. It poured down on us and across the deck like a river, and plunged through the lower hatch into the control room. As we submerged the force of the inrushing water increased. Repeatedly Clay tried to snug the wheel tighter but the rush of water overwhelmed him and threw him back. Lieutenant Howarth climbed through the ice water to try and tighten the wheel, to no avail. The situation was critical. If we continued the dive we were going down for good, but if we surfaced, the Japanese plane might get us.

Hammond took command of the situation. "Close the lower conning tower hatch!" he yelled down to the control room. I turned around to my left and looked down through the hatch, into the control room. The waterfall completely enveloped the ladder. It also engulfed Chief Kimball L. (Kim) Young, who was climbing up through it while groping to locate the hatch lanyard. Although unable to see the lanyard, Young managed to grab it and tugged downward with all his might—but it would not move. Once, twice, three times he tried, to no avail.

The captain, who could not see what was happening, called out again, "Close the conning tower hatch!"

Then I saw the problem: the lanyard was looped around and snarled on a ladder rung. I stepped to my left and kicked the lanyard latch on the hatch cover. That allowed the spring loaded hatch cover to drop down to its closed position with a bang, in effect, sealing us in a small flooding compartment. The icy seawater quickly covered the top of the hatch cover and began slowly creeping up the sides of the conning tower.

I was suddenly aghast at what I had just done. "I'm dead," I said to myself as my mind floated away to my mother. I pictured her receiving the news of my death with bitter anguish and deep sadness. I was going to put her through another deathblow. A loud voice over the intercom brought me back to my senses—and erased for the time being the overwhelming sight, sound, and smell of seawater filling our tomb. Someone was calling us from the control room below!

"Conning tower, conning tower, are you OK?"

Captain Hammond went to the intercom control unit, turned the switch, and answered, "Yes, we're all right."

Silence.

The seconds ticked by. More silence. A bitterness rose in my constricted throat. The water continued to pour in.

Finally the intercom crackled again. "Please answer. Are you OK, Captain? What shall we do?"

Hammond calmly responded, "Make the depth 100 feet."

The control room intercom switch came on and we heard a mumble of confused voices, arguing about what to do. "They must all be drowned up there," we heard. "We'd better surface. Blow all ballast, take her back to the surface."

The confusion in the control room infuriated Hammond, who called out, "Belay that order! This is the captain speaking! Belay that order!" The boat's bow angled upward; we were heading toward the surface. Were the control room personnel unable to hear the captain, or was someone simply refusing to honor his order?

In retrospect, it seems ironic to me that Douglas Hammond gained a reputation as one who lacked courage. Other submarine skippers who intentionally forfeited their lives to save their boat and crew received the Congressional Medal of Honor for heroism. But nobody outside our conning tower knew that Hammond was willing to sacrifice himself (and us) to save *Guardfish.*

As the boat rose and we drew close to the surface, the reduced pressure lessened the force of the flooding water, which allowed Clay to stay on the ladder while trying to locate the cause of the leak. Initially he could not budge the hatch, since the weight of the water on top of it was too great. Finally, when it did open, the cause of the problem became clear: one of the lookout's heavy leather mittens was laying across the hatch coaming.

The episode was a shattering experience for me. Now that I had been rescued from an almost certain death, I had to know what had happened. Why had the control room watch disobeyed the captain's order and surfaced the boat? After things calmed down, I examined the 1MC intercom control unit and found that someone had accidentally flipped a hidden switch. With the switch in that position, the control room could speak to the conning tower, but not visa versa. Hence, the diving officer had not heard the captain's order repealing the order to surface.

Fortune was indeed smiling on our boat. When we broached the surface, everyone braced for the bombs that would surely be dropped upon us. The Japanese airplane, thank God, was nowhere to be seen.

While one woolen glove had almost cost all of us our lives, an oversight by another sailor in Guam saved those of us trapped in the conning tower. Notwithstanding the large quantity of water that had poured through the hatch, the water level in the tower never climbed higher than several inches above the deck plates. As Hobby Hoblitzell explained to me, when we left Guam someone failed to close the drains at the bottom of the periscope wells, even though this is required by naval regulations. The sea water simply drained down from the conning tower through the periscope wells, into the control room bilge. I also wondered why "my" radar had not detected that attacking plane. I checked it out thoroughly but everything seemed to be operating normally. Either the operator doped off and failed to see the pip on the PPI scope, or the plane was too high to detect on that surface search radar.

While the question of our failure to detect the plane will probably never be solved, it did not take long to determine whose glove got stuck in the hatch. Just a few hours later that same morning, as he was preparing to go back on lookout watch, Richard (Dick) E. Cone admitted to me that the errant mitten was his. Someone had stepped on his hand and pulled it off as he was going down the hatch. How could we prevent such an occurrence from happening again? Clay Blair recalled that "some northerner remembered that when he was a kid, his mother used to prevent him from losing his mittens by sewing a single line to each of the mittens and running it up through the sleeves and across the shoulders inside the jacket." Thereafter, continued Clay, "Captain Hammond decreed that all personnel who stood bridge watches were to have their mittens strung in that kid-like fashion—a novelty to a southerner like me. It worked. No one else dropped a mitten."

Although we had dodged a well-aimed bullet, our brushes with death were not over. Every few hours while we were on surface that night, the effectiveness of the SJ radar and the "mitten fix" were both verified when the radar picked up Japanese patrol planes as they drove us down. The next night, while evading yet another attacking plane, we slipped quickly beneath the surface and promptly lost control of the dive. For some reason, we could not blow the negative tank to correct our steep downward angle. *Guardfish* continued dropping into the abyss. In a short time we were appreciably deeper than the boat's 300-foot test depth, although just how deep is still a matter of some debate. We all feared that we were about to discover the boat's true "crush depth."

Clay Blair was in the control room during the hair-raising event and he saw Earl Beasley, the chief of the boat, jump into action. Beasley was in his bunk in the forward battery compartment when the boat dove, and he quickly sensed that something was desperately wrong. He ran, stark naked, into the control room and quickly devised a solution to the problem. A temporary line was rigged from the boat's 200 psi air system and it was used to "blow negative." This quick thinking brought the boat back under control. The initial failure resulted from a defective high pressure air-manifold valve that had jammed and refused to actuate. Without Beasley's quick thinking, none of us would have made it. Years after the war, Clay Blair commented on the "mitten-in-the-hatch" and "jammed-blow-valve" incidents, saying, "Both these terrifying things

Clay Blair (left), noted historian of the submarine war in the Pacific, and author Claude Conner (right) on the deck of *Guardfish* in 1945. Blair and Conner were crewmates during the war's final year. *Photo courtesy of the author.*

happened during my first week on my first war patrol. I thought maybe I was in the wrong branch of the navy!"

Beginning on March 9, our patrol track took us back and forth across the entrance to Kii Suido, the route into the Inland Sea and the cities of Kobe, Osaka, Kure, and Hiroshima, between the islands of Honshu and Shikoku. We remained on this station, twiddling our thumbs within sight of land, for the next twenty-five days. Naval Intelligence suspected that the few remaining major warships of the Japanese Navy were hiding in the Inland Sea. Our primary assignment was to destroy those ships when they came out through the channel. Unfortunately for us, they never came out. Our secondary assignment was to attack merchant shipping—but not a single cargo ship emerged. Following on the heels of the "terrifying things" we had only recently endured, the dearth of targets dragged down the crew's morale further, taking with it any hope of redemption for *Guardfish*.

We continued to make our nightly weather reports by radio to prepare for the B-29 raids scheduled for March 14—and received more attention than we desired from Japanese patrol planes. Then, on March 18, Admiral Halsey's Task Force 38 steamed in and his airplanes plastered the Kobe-Kure area. We were on "lifeguard" duty during those raids.

During my watch in the predawn hours of March 19, we discovered we were not the only submarine on our station. We briefly picked up a target on our SJ radar at the radar horizon, around 13,000 yards distant. Then, about a half-hour later as daylight was beginning to break, the officer of the deck, Lieutenant Howarth, sighted a torpedo speeding toward us. We evaded at flank speed, submerged, and using our raised SD radar mast as an antenna, continued to listen on the "lifeguard" frequency. Several hours later, after being alerted to the presence of downed aviators nearby, we surfaced. Following a brief search, while also looking for periscopes and torpedo wakes, our watchmen spotted two men in rubber boats. We made our way to them and plucked the airmen, Ensign Paul H. Whitford and Radioman Vincent Royal Smith, from their rafts. Clearing the area at full speed, Captain Hammond wrote in his war patrol report that we had "no desire to positively identify a Jap torpedo." The airmen we picked up were from the carrier *USS Hancock*. They were on a mission in the Kobe area when anti-aircraft fire hit their plane. Following instructions, they stayed with their disabled craft until they could ditch in the ocean, where we were waiting to pick them up. They had only been in the water for several minutes before we found them.

On April 3, we left our Kii Suido patrol station and arrived at Midway Islands eight days later. ComSubPac classified the patrol as "successful" even though we did not sink any enemy ships. Hindsight demonstrates that this was justified: we had provided important weather reports for both the B-29s and Admiral Halsey, stood watch for the remnants of the Japanese fleet, and rescued two naval airmen.

After two weeks of R&R at Camp Gooneyville, and two more weeks on sea trials, *Guardfish* left Midway on May 8, 1945, on her twelfth war patrol. That was also Victory in Europe (or VE-Day), the day that the war in Europe ended. That epic moment in history really did not mean much to us. The Pacific War was still grinding away, and this time our destination was Tokyo Bay. All of us wondered if we would ever get back alive, especially after our recent experiences. While en route to Tokyo, another typhoon hit us. Monstrous seas pounded us for days. During the peak of the storm, on May 12, green water repeatedly swamped the bridge. Quartermaster third-class Joseph G. Ward received a couple of broken ribs when the water threw him against a protruding ammunition locker.

We arrived near the entrance to Tokyo Bay on May 17, just in time to take our "lifeguard" station during a massive B-29 air raid. The full width of our SJ radar screen was saturated with airplane pips for a three hours. As the B-29s left the area, we got word by VHF radio that they did not lose a single plane. It was hard for us to believe that the Japanese could not put up a better defensive fight.

The following day we proceeded to a new area in search of targets. We moved slowly northward following the 100 fathom (600 feet) ocean depth curve on our navigational charts, which placed us from seven to forty miles off shore. Our poor luck continued, however, and we did not see anything but sampans, various small craft, and an occasional patrol boat close to shore.

We reached our new patrol area on June 1. It was across the mouth of Tsugaru Straits, the shipping lane in and out of the Sea of Japan, between the islands of Honshu and Hokkaido. In spite of a diligent search, not a single ship was seen. Most of the time on station the boat was wrapped in a pall of dense fog and the weather was very cold. The water temperature was so close to freezing that exposed metal surfaces inside the boat, such as our bunk rails, were covered with a thin coating of ice. Despite the cold, we could not use our electrical heaters because we had to conserve battery power while we were submerged. The only excitement we had while on station happened on June 13, when we spotted a floating mine and destroyed it with gunfire. This time, much to my delight, it actually exploded!

On June 15, we received orders to leave our station and to proceed to Pearl Harbor, by way of Midway. The next day as we ran east on the surface we came upon an enemy craft, a small 100-ton Japanese trawler. Since it was equipped with a radio direction finder, a radio transmitter, and a couple of light machine guns, Captain Hammond identified the vessel as an anti-submarine picket boat. We battle surfaced and easily destroyed it with our deck guns. Even though their vessel was nothing but a pile of floating rubble, most of the Japanese survivors refused to be rescued; two of them, though, did come aboard as our prisoners.

ComSubPac classified this patrol as "unsuccessful." Most of us disagreed with the call, however, since we got through the patrol ALIVE. We arrived safely at Midway on June 19, where we refueled, took on fresh provisions, and another three more prisoners of war (two Japanese and one Korean) for transport to Pearl Harbor. Pearl Harbor was reached a week later and we transferred all five POWs into the custody of the Commandant of the Fourteenth Naval District. Then, we spent two carefree weeks of R&R at the Royal Hawaiian Hotel on Waikiki Beach, swimming, drinking and enjoying life.

When we returned to the boat we learned that *Guardfish* was not going to make another war patrol. We also had a new skipper: Lieutenant Commander Julian T. Burke.

Our new assignment was "school boat duty," under the Submarine Training Command. In her new assignment, *Guardfish* acted as a target for anti-submarine forces. The surface ships practiced finding us with their sonar and then dropping small contact explosive charges on us, called "Hedgehogs." Although they were classified as "Training Aids Only," the Hedgehog explosions were strong enough to put dents in our hull. This duty allowed for a lot of liberty time in Honolulu, and even though there was a severe wartime shortage of females, I learned the romantic art for which sailors are famous the world over: womanizing.

Then, wonder of wonders, the war ended in August following the atomic bomb blasts at Hiroshima and Nagasaki. Shortly after a tumultuous, sardine-packed VJ-Day celebration in Honolulu, we headed back to the States, to the city of New Orleans via the Panama Canal.

Gone was the fear of impending disaster.
Gone was the fear of no tomorrow.
Gone was the fear of life without life.

Postscript

Extractor Survivors

The officer and enlisted crew of *Extractor* boarded the "jeep" aircraft carrier *USS Breton* for transportation to Pearl Harbor on February 5, 1945, six days after the completion of the Court of Inquiry. Marine guards still held them like prisoners of war, completely isolated from the *Breton* crew, forbidden to talk to anyone outside their own group. When they reached Hawaii, officials again ordered them not to talk to anyone.

Extractor's commanding officer, Horace Babcock, his executive officer, Chester Lebsack, and Chief Yeoman Andrew Dobos flew to Washington, D.C. to reconstruct the ship's records. The rest of the crew ultimately boarded a cargo ship en route to San Francisco. Security personnel again advised them not to talk to others on the ship. The wall of secrecy collapsed on March 5, the day they arrived in San Francisco. Newspapers on the dock contained a front page United Press article announcing: "Survivors of the *USS Extractor*, sunk by an unidentified American submarine, arrive in San Francisco today."

In Washington, D.C. on March 18, Babcock held a news conference for the Navy Department about the sinking of his ship. He did not identify *Guardfish* as being the submarine that sank him. "Lieutenant Babcock had no rancor," reported the *New York Times*. "He pointed out that the *Extractor* from water level resembled a submarine, and that the other skipper honestly thought he was sinking a Japanese submarine." The navy gave Babcock his choice of taking command of another ARS, like *Extractor*, or a training ship attached to a school on the Hudson River. He chose the latter, *USS Catbird* (IX-183), which he commanded for almost two years. Babcock left the navy in 1946 and returned to his previous job with the Arizona District Office of the United States Geological Survey. He retired from U.S.G.S. in 1977 as district chief of Arizona's Water Resources Division. In the meantime, he served, by presidential appointment, as chairman and Federal Commissioner for the interstate Pecos River Commission. He also served as a worldwide water development projects consultant for the U.S. State Department and the World Bank until he retired in 1985. He currently resides in Tucson, Arizona.

Guardfish and Her Skippers

In company with three other submarines, *Guardfish* left Pearl Harbor for the United States late in August 1945. At the Panama Canal, we stopped at the city of Balboa to wait for entrance clearance. Given eight-hour shore passes, multiple busloads of sailors patronized La Casa de Amor and other similar establishments, followed by tours through the navy's "production line" chemical prophylactic stations. From Panama we sailed, in company with eleven other submarines, to fabulous New Orleans, Louisiana, where glowing newspaper headlines and Southern hospitality greeted the Navy, but with *Guardfish* as the star of the show. For about a month and a half, as crew members left for their two-week home leaves, the rest of the crew partied. There was no shortage of girls in New Orleans.

Late in October, following the Navy Day celebration, the boat departed for New London, Connecticut, arriving there in early November to prepare for decommissioning. Upon completion of the boat's moth balling, we celebrated with a ship's party that I will never forget. Thereafter, most of the boat's wartime crew dispersed for discharge or new assignments. It took years for us to get back together, but now we have annual reunions.

The navy decommissioned *Guardfish* in May 1946 and stored her with the "mothball fleet" upriver. In June 1948, she was reactivated as a

Naval Reserve Training Ship at New London. During the summer of 1960 she was again taken out of service, supposedly for good. But on October 10, 1961, in the waters off New London, *Guardfish* did the Navy's bidding one more time. After a skeleton crew got her underway, they abandoned the boat and boarded a surface vessel. The submarines *Dogfish* and *Blenny* tracked Guardfish for a while, then fired fully armed torpedoes at her, a fatal blow that sent her to the bottom. The purpose of the war game was to test newly developed torpedoes under actual firing conditions. The news of her final loss saddened me.

Even though she is gone, *Guardfish's* record remains. She is one of the top scoring submarines of World War II. Postwar reviews of Japanese shipping records by a Joint Army-Navy Assessment Committee ranked her in the top eight regarding number of ships sunk. When one realizes that 258 submarines made war patrols, the significance of her service becomes obvious. The postwar review credited her with sinking nineteen enemy ships, seven less than we had claimed. That meant that we only damaged the others, or perhaps the Japanese lost records of those ships. Nevertheless, Burt Klakring and Norvell Ward went down in history as two of the most successful WWII submarine skippers.

Commander Klakring returned to the States after his detachment from *Guardfish* in May 1943. He spent about a year at the Submarine School at New London, Connecticut as an instructor of officers, followed by command of Submarine Division 102 in the Pacific, the job he held during the *Extractor* Court of Inquiry. Eager to get back into combat, he once sailed as commander of a submarine wolf pack. For that special service he received the Silver Star and Bronze Star awards. After the end of the war—by then a full captain—Klakring served in staff positions for the Commander Fifth Fleet and Office of the Chief of Naval Operations. In 1947, he took command of Submarine Squadron Eight and the Submarine School at New London. He retired in 1949 with the rank of Rear Admiral. After leaving the navy, he joined the management team of the Electric Boat Co., a division of General Dynamics Corporation in Groton, Connecticut. He served as assistant general manager, and later as manager of the company's international activities. He died at age 70 in July 1975.

When Commander Norvell G. Ward was transferred from *Guardfish* in the fall of 1944, he joined the staff of ComSubPac as assistant operations officer. He served in that capacity throughout the remainder of the war, and for several months after the cessation of hostilities. Thereafter he transferred to the staff of Commander Submarine Squadron Two. During 1946 and 1947, Ward commanded *USS Irex*, the navy's first snorkel-equipped submarine. For the next year he held a position at the Naval Academy, followed by a year on the staff of Commander Submarine Flotilla One.

During part of the Korean War, from 1951 to 1952, Ward commanded the destroyer *USS Yarnall* in the Far East. He then joined the staff of Commander Second Fleet as anti-submarine warfare and undersea warfare officer and was promoted to the rank of captain. From 1955 through 1958, Captain Ward commanded the oiler *USS Nantahala*, Submarine Squadron Five, and then Submarine Squadron Fourteen. From 1961 through 1964, he served in the office of the Chief of Naval Operations, Washington, D.C.

In early 1965, Ward moved to Vietnam and took the position of Chief of the Naval Advisory Group, United States Military Assistance Command. The following year he assumed the duty as Commander Naval Forces, Vietnam, plus additional roles with the Military Assistance Command. For service in that capacity he received the Distinguished Service Medal. In 1967-1968, the experienced naval officer commanded Service Group Three, during which time he received his fourth Legion of Merit award for "exceptionally meritorious service." During that period Captain Ward also suffered a terrible personal blow: one of his four children, Capt. Alexander K. Ward, USMC, died as a result of wounds received in action.

In 1968 and 1969, Captain Ward served as Assistant Chief of Naval Operations for the Navy Department, earning a fifth Legion of Merit award. In early 1970 he became Commander Caribbean Sea Frontier, with additional duties as commandant of the Tenth Naval District and Commander Antilles Defense Command, located in Puerto Rico. He served there until his retirement from the navy as Rear Admiral in August 1973. He and his wife Elizabeth today reside in Atlantic Beach, Florida.

Guardfish's third skipper, Commander Douglas T. Hammond, left the boat in July 1945 to serve as the executive officer of the battleship *USS North Carolina*. The following year, he served on the battleship *USS Missouri* as executive officer, and a year later became Commander of Submarine Division Twelve, Pacific Fleet. From July 1948 through

October 1950 Hammond was a member of the personal staff of the Secretary of the Navy in Washington, D.C., after which he commanded the submarine tender *USS Sperry*. Naval records show that in September 1952, he was confined at the Naval Hospital in Bethesda, Maryland. Owing to poor health, he retired with the rank of captain in April 1953. Hammond moved back to his hometown of Stephens, Arkansas, where he spent his retirement years raising cattle and playing golf. He died in May 1983, leaving behind his wife, Lucy Smith Hammond, and two daughters.

Naval historians have not been kind to Hammond. In his five war patrols as skipper, two on *Cabrilla* and three on *Guardfish*, he sank only two enemy ships, a freighter and a small trawler, and damaged two others, one of which was an aircraft carrier. Despite these meager results, it was the sinking of *Extractor* that tainted his naval career. In my eyes, however, Doug Hammond was a brave commander—and almost a Medal of Honor candidate because of his heroism in the conning tower incident during the eleventh war patrol.

The Author

Soon after *Guardfish* arrived in New Orleans in September 1945, I went home to California on a fourteen-day leave. Around the end of the month I was back on the train returning to Louisiana. During a stop in Los Angeles, a shipmate, Wilhelm W. (Chuck) Wilkinson, joined me. A few more miles down the track the train stopped in Pasadena—and my life changed forever.

Mary Angela Rahm got on the train. Her beauty and grace enthralled me. She sat down across the aisle from me; an older man appeared to be traveling with her. She was a picture of loveliness; in fact, I could not keep my eyes off her. After a while I followed the man into the rest room and struck up a conversation. When I found that he did not know Mary, it was a signal for the Navy to "move in." The train arrived at Mary's destination, San Antonio, Texas, around midnight of the following day. I got off with her to meet her mother, then boarded the train for Louisiana. I spent the rest of the trip thinking about her.

It was not only Mary's beauty that overwhelmed me but her religious convictions. She was one of the few people I had ever met who really believed, not hoped, in the existence of God. While I considered myself an agnostic, I was getting disgusted with my own way of life and wished there were higher goals to look forward to. I knew before she got off the train that I wanted her for my wife. I even told Chuck, my shipmate, about my hope. Still, I could not see how such a marriage could ever happen. I later learned from Mary that she also talked about me in the train's rest room. A lady she did not know had approached and told her, "You are going to marry that sailor." Mary thought it was far more likely that she would marry one of the tens of thousands of air force men who were stationed in the San Antonio area.

As soon as I reported aboard *Guardfish* I wrote Mary a letter. The next week, I wrote her again. After three weeks, with no reply, I gave up hope of ever hearing from her. But then, well into the fourth week, a short note arrived. Mary and her mother were going to briefly visit New Orleans to see me and check out the October 27 Navy Day activities! Her visit helped cement our friendship and we pledged to write each other every day. Shortly after Navy Day, *Guardfish* set out for the submarine base at New London, Connecticut. Our daily correspondence went on until my Christmas leave. Then, with the aid of government transportation, I flew down to Austin to visit her, where she was attending the University of Texas. While we were having dinner at a restaurant that first night, I asked her to marry me. I was filled with emotion and unable to finish my meal—because she had immediately accepted my proposal! We spent Christmas vacation at her parents' home in San Antonio, laying plans for our future. After I returned to New London, we continued our daily correspondence until I received my discharge from the navy in March 1946. Thereafter we both moved to Southern California, where she moved in with her married sister, Leona Barry, and I rented a nearby room. Our wedding took place on May 5, 1946 at Mission San Gabriel.

Because of the postwar recession, I was unable to find a job as an electronic technician. After applying at nearly all of the electronics companies listed in the Pasadena telephone directory, I went to work for a small company called VacSeal Laboratories. Weltis W. (Wes) Wihtol hired me as an apprentice laboratory glassblower and trained me to build germicidal low pressure ultraviolet lamps. When Wes left the company, VacSeal's major customer, Birtcher Medical Corporation of Los Angeles, hired me to build ultraviolet lamps for them. Two years after the birth of our son Gregory, it became clear that we needed more income, so I renewed my search for a technician job. After repeated failures, Mary turned to her religious convictions and convinced me that we should pray.

I became a believer that God really answers prayers when I got a letter out of the blue offering me a job as a junior engineer for Heintz & Kaufman, Limited, an electron-tube manufacturer 450 miles away in South San Francisco. The letter was from my old boss Wes Wihtol, who was then chief engineer for the company. I immediately accepted the offer and in 1949 we moved to the Bay Area. After four years at Heintz & Kaufman, during which I simultaneously attended college, I advanced into microwave tube engineering development work at Varian Associates, one of the first high technology companies in what is now known as "Silicon Valley." From 1949 to 1958, the rest of our children were born: Catherine, Christine, Michele, and John. In 1962, because of our growing family, we were again financially pressed and Mary again suggested prayer for another job. The result was one more amazing unsolicited offer as an Engineering Project Manager for Warnecke Electron Tubes in the Chicago Area, which we quickly accepted.

Engineering projects come and go. Following job opportunities, we moved to the Los Angeles Area in 1964, where I worked for Hughes Aircraft Company. In 1973 we moved yet again, this time back to the Bay Area where I returned to work at Varian Associates. In 1978, our dear son John, then nineteen years old, died of a drug-related death, whether suicide or murder we do not know. The resulting trauma came very close to breaking up our marriage.

I retired from Varian in 1990, a Life Senior Member of the Institute of Electrical and Electronic Engineers, after working forty-one years in key engineering and management positions—even though I never did get a college degree. We moved to our present home in Rancho Cucamonga, forty-five miles east of Los Angeles, to be near our four surviving children.

On May 5, 1996, Mary and I celebrated our fiftieth wedding anniversary.

Glossary

1MC: Model designation for an electronic intercom system used on American submarines that enabled the transmission of voice announcements or two way voice communications to any, or all, *compartments. The central amplifier control unit, located in the conning tower, also incorporated a shipboard alarm generator. The generator produced three alarm types: the diving alarm (ah-oo-ga, Klaxon sound), collision alarm (rising siren sound) and general quarters alarm (call to battle stations, which was the bong-bong sound of a ship's bell). Actuating switches for each of the three alarms were on the bridge, inside the conning tower, and in the control room.

Air Bank: Heavy steel flasks containing high pressure compressed air. Air compressor pumps filled the air banks with a large volume of the outside air while the boat was on the surface. That air was later used to blow water out of the ballast tanks to surface the boat. There were three independent air banks aboard *Guardfish*, two outside the pressure hull, and one inside.

A-Scope: Type of *radar screen presentation that had a single horizontal line of light across the middle of the "picture tube" face. The distance along the line represented the range of a target from our boat. The position at the left-hand end of the range-line represented the originating ship's location, where a large vertical, flat topped pulse appeared. That pulse represented the outgoing pulse of radio energy. A target *pip appeared along the range-line at a position corresponding to the target's distance from the originating radar. *Fire control radar usually used this type of screen presentation during World War II.

Angle on the Bow: The angle formed by a target ship's direction of travel and the line of sight of that ship from a viewing vessel.

APR: Model designation for a type of radio receiver used to detect and identify radar signals of different frequencies. The use of plug-in tuning units enabled the receiver to cover a very wide frequency range, from *VHF through *UHF. After the receiver was manually tuned to the signal frequency, the built-in pulse analyzer oscilloscope further classified the originating radar.

Blip: See Pip

Bow Plane, Stern Plane: Wing-like fins that extended horizontally from the bow and stern of a submarine. Tilting the fins adjusted the boat's inclination and depth, when used in conjunction with the various control and ballast tanks. The location of the Bow Plane and stern plane operators was in the control room.

Bubble: The bubble in a spirit level type of inclinometer, used to determine the inclination of the submarine's keel to the horizontal.

Coding Board: A manual device used in the encoding and decoding of messages during World War II, instead of using the *ECM. It was a board with many movable strips. All strips had the alphabet, numbers, etc., printed on them. The printing on the strips used water soluble ink so that the coding characters could be removed easily in case of impending capture.

Compartments, listed from bow to stern (see Cross section of a Gato-class submarine, Chapter Two)

1. **Forward Torpedo Room, Forward Room:** Used for storing and firing torpedoes. It also provided bunk space for the torpedomen. The forward end of the room was filled with six torpedo tubes, their loading doors and associated apparatus. The compartment stored a total of sixteen torpedoes ("fish")—six in the tubes and ten in the room. It had heavy storage racks on both sides, stacked two high, for eight of the torpedoes. The room's removable deck plates allowed the other two fish to be stored under the deck. Some of the crew's bunks filled space above and below the stacked torpedoes. Other bunks hung from the overhead and the remainder were on the starboard side, in the torpedo loading pit. The forward room incorporated an escape hatch and a supply of Momson lungs, to provide means for the crew to escape from the submerged submarine in case of an emergency.

2. **Forward Battery, Officers' Quarters:** A battery of 126 large, lead-acid type electric cells, stored in the space below the deck plates, gave the compartment its name. Each cell was four or five feet tall. The officers' quarters, above the deck plates, provided cabins for both the commissioned officers and the chief petty officers. The forward end of the compartment was working space for the two Stewards Mates, the officers' servants. At that time they were always blacks or Filipinos. Their small work area included a coffee urn, storage drawers, food warmers and the like. The captain was the only officer who had a private cabin; all others shared sleeping rooms. All officers shared the single head in the compartment. The wardroom, where the commissioned officers ate and met, contained a table, bunks, and movable chairs. The ship's yeoman had a tiny office on the starboard side, at the after end of the compartment. He was the enlisted man who maintained all of the ship's records.

3. **Control Room:** This compartment contained all the controls used during submerged operations, including the submergence ready light panel (which we called the "Christmas Tree"), *Bow Plane and stern plane controls, inclinometer (*bubble), depth gauges, and *hydraulic manifold. It also contained other critical facilities, such as the

ship's master and auxiliary gyro compasses, an auxiliary steering position, *SD radar, *IFF interrogator, IFF transponder and the radio room. The auxiliary, or pump room, was below the deck plates. It contained pumps, blowers, compressors and motor generators.

4. **Conning Tower:** That portion of a *fleet boat that stuck above the plane of the main exterior deck. It consisted of a tank-like compartment (a separate pressure hull) and its surrounding fairing superstructure. While on surface, the officer of the deck was on the bridge, which was on the topside deck above the compartment. The bridge had a raised platform, on which the officer of the deck and quartermaster stood, looking forward. The forward and after cigarette decks were extensions of the bridge deck. The port, starboard and high lookout watchmen stood on raised platforms, while the after lookout stood on the after cigarette deck at the *TBT. A watertight hatch in the deck on the starboard side of the bridge led below by way of a metal ladder. The ladder dropped into the forward end of the conning tower compartment, where the officer of the deck conned the boat while submerged. This small room contained ship controls (steering, motor speed annunciator, *1MC, etc.), torpedo controls (*TDC, firing console, etc.) and detection equipment (two periscopes, *SJ radar, *QB and QC sonar). A watertight hatch, below foot-level on the forward port side of the compartment, led down into the control room by another vertical ladder.

5. **After Battery, Crew's Space:** This compartment also derived its name from the battery of 126 lead-acid type electric cells stored in the space below its deck plates. The forward end of the compartment, above deck plates, contained the ship's galley. The cooks prepared food for the entire ship's company there. Immediately aft of the galley was the crew's mess hall, containing four fixed tables, with stationary benches on each side. The room seated a total of twenty-four men. Aft of the mess hall was the crew quarters. It contained a total of forty-eight stainless steel framed bunks, stacked in four rows running fore and aft. The crew's duty assignments while at sea were four hours on watch and eight hours off watch, thus there was always someone sleeping. The chief of the boat assigned some bunks, known as "hot bunks," to more than one person, since there were not enough bunks for every member of the crew. That meant that men from different watch times were assigned to the same bunk. A metal door at the after end of the sleeping space, was the entry into the crew's head area. It contained two stalls with heads (toilets), two stall showers and two wash basins. It also held an automatic laundry machine, the first of its kind.

6. **Forward Engine Room and After Engine Room:** Each of these compartments contained two diesel main engines. Each of the engines directly coupled to a high powered electrical generator. Output from the engine-driven generators provided electrical power to operate the electrical propulsion motors in the motor room when the boat was operating on the surface. While on the surface, the generators charged the submerged-power source, the electrical batteries. In the forward engine room, below deck level at the after end of the room, was a small auxiliary diesel engine ("dinky"). It performed as a low power substitute for any main engine. The after engine room

duplicated the forward engine room, except that it had a small machine shop in place of the "dinky."

8. **Motor Room:** The two large electric motors in the motor room propelled the submarine both on the surface and when submerged. Each motor drove a separate screw (propeller) through a rotary speed-reduction gear. The motors derived their electrical power from the diesel engine-driven electrical generators while the boat was on the surface. While submerged, power came from the electric batteries in the forward and after battery compartments. Huge electrical switches, needed to accomplish the change-over from generator to battery power and to establish the charging of batteries by the generators, were located in the "control cubicle," a perforated stainless steel box that measured eight or ten feet on a side. The cubicle was shock-mounted; suspended by springs located at the edges and corners, to isolate the enclosed switches from the potentially disastrous effects of depth charges. Two controllermen actuated the switches from the "maneuvering panel" that was aft of the cubicle, at the after end of the compartment. The controllermen adjusted individual motor speeds as ordered.

9. **After Torpedo Room, After Room:** This compartment was very similar to the forward room, except that it was smaller. There were four torpedo tubes, each with a torpedo stored in it. Four other torpedoes were stored out in the room. Thus, the boat contained a total of twenty-four fish, in the two torpedo rooms. The after room also contained an emergency escape hatch, with Momson lungs, similar to the forward room.

DF (RDF): Abbreviation for Radio Direction Finder, a radio receiving equipment that had a highly directional antenna. The RDF enabled an operator to determine the direction of the origin of an incoming radio signal. RDF "sightings" from two or more locations enabled the determination of the location of the source.

Diving Officer: The officer responsible for stabilizing and controlling the vertical movement of the submerged submarine. Located in the control room, he functioned under the direction of the officer in the conning tower.

DR: Abbreviation for Dead Reckoning, a navigational plotting operation. This technique determined the position of a ship from the composite of courses, speeds, durations and estimated drifts from a known point of origin.

DRAI (Dead Reckoning Analyzing Indicator): A device that automatically plotted the ship's apparent position on a chart. It used course information from the ship's gyro compass, speed from the ship's water speed recorder (Pit log), and time from the ship's clock (chronometer). The navigation officer corrected the DRAI position each time he obtained a reliable position fix.

ECM (Electric Coding Machine): This was like an electric typewriter, the letter coding of which was determined by the code of the day. A group of code wheel setting, inserted into the machine each day, set the electrical interconnections for that day's code.

Fathometer: Equipment used to measure the distance to the sea floor from the keel of the submarine. It did so by measuring the time for a burst of ultrasonic energy to reflect from the bottom and return to the boat, and then converted that time interval into distance.

Fire Control Radar: A *radar system used to assist in the aiming of armaments, such as torpedoes or deck guns. It incorporated features that enabled the measurement of a target's range and bearing with greater precision than was normally found in *search radar.

Fleet Boat: The name given to long-range American submarines built shortly before and during World War II, in order to differentiate them from earlier coastal types.

Hydraulic Manifold Station: A collection of valves that controlled the submerging, surfacing, and attitude of the submarine through the flooding and blowing of ballast tanks and by water transfer between control tanks.

IFF (Identification, Friend or Foe): This electronic system was used to determine if a *radar target was friendly. The most widely used version in World War II was a *VHF pulsed radio system, originally devised by the British. The system consisted of an IFF interrogator unit (on the craft with a searching radar) and an IFF transponder unit located on the friendly target-craft. The IFF system's output appeared on the screen of the *search radar adjacent to the target *pip.

Is-Was: Navy jargon for the Submarine Attack Course Finder, forerunner of the *TDC. One side of the seven-inch diameter circular, multi layer plastic device was used to assist the submarine to reach a favorable firing position or to ascertain whether such a position could be reached. The other side was in the form of a circular slide rule, arranged to resolve enemy speed with data secured during the approach.

JP: An underwater sound listening device located in the forward torpedo room that operated at audio frequencies. Its T-shaped sound head, located above the main deck, was rotated by hand.

KHz: A symbol that stands for kilohertz. This electrical term relates to the frequency of an alternating voltage or current in thousands of cycles per second (Kilo= thousand, hertz= cycles per second).

Kilocycles: A term of electrical (radio) frequency measurement that was in use during World War II, meaning "thousands of cycles (per second)." This term, a number of years after the war, was replaced by "kilohertz," abbreviated as *KHz.

Main Induction: A large diameter air duct that carried outside air to the engine rooms and the rest of the surfaced submarine. Its hydraulically operated valve, used to close the main induction while submerged, was surrounded by the fairing superstructure, aft of the conning tower compartment.

MHz: A symbol that stands for "megahertz." This electrical term relates to the frequency of an alternating voltage or current in millions of cycles per second (Mega= million, hertz= cycles per second).

Microwave: An electromagnetic (radio) wavelength that is a small fraction of a meter long, corresponding roughly to *UHF and *SHF frequencies.

NPM: The call letters of the United States Navy's high frequency ("short wave") radio telegraph station located at Pearl Harbor, Hawaii. NPM broadcasted Fox schedules to navy ships and stations throughout the Pacific area. It transmitted simultaneously on a number of different frequencies to improve the reliability and coverage of widely different areas throughout the year, day and night. It was supported by manual relay stations in Australia and Alaska. After we recaptured Guam, the Navy added automatic repeater transmitters there (radio station NPN) to improve the coverage in the western Pacific.

Periscope Shears: The structure, projecting from the top of the *fleet boat's conning tower, that physically supported the periscopes against sideways forces.

Pip (or Blip): The indication on the *radar screen that represented the radar return (echo) from a target.

PPI: Abbreviation for Plan Position Indicator, a circular radar screen that produced a map-like presentation. The center of the screen represented the location of the ship, as if you were looking down on the sea from above the ship. A target appeared on the screen as a dot or small arc of light, called a "pip" or "blip." The distance of the pip from the center of the screen represented the range (distance) of the target from the ship. The angular displacement of the pip from the top of the screen usually represented the bearing of the target relative to the bow (heading) of the ship.

QB and QC: Model designations for two types of *sonar equipments that operated at ultrasonic frequencies (above audible range). Each device covered a different frequency range.

RDF: See DF.

Radar Indications, Radar Interference: A pattern that appeared on the ship's radar screen as its antenna rotated through the direction of another radar that was transmitting on a similar radio frequency.

Radar: Stands for "Radio Detection and Ranging." This is a radio transmitting, receiving and electronic time measuring system used to locate an object by means of reflected radio waves. In pulsed radar systems, as were used in World War II, powerful radio wave impulses, sent through space at the speed of light, bounced from a target. Electronic measurement of the time for the radio wave to go out and return translated into target distance. The pointing of the directional radio antenna determined the target's angular bearing.

Safety Tank: A ballast tank, totally contained within the submarine's pressure hull.

SD: Model designation for a *VHF, air-*search radar. It was the first radar used aboard American submarines. Its nondirectional antenna, mounted on the top of a periscope-like mast, could be raised out of water while the vessel was submerged. The raised mast alternatively served as an antenna for submerged high frequency radio communications.

Search Radar: A *radar system intended to detect targets at the greatest possible range. Such a radar usually used a *PPI screen presentation and a continuously rotating, directional antenna. Air search radar, used for aircraft detection, had an antenna system that concentrated on objects above the horizon, while surface search radar concentrated on the ocean surface up to the horizon.

Semaphore: One of the requirements for recruits at boot camp was that they learn semaphore signaling. Semaphore is the visual communication system in which two flags, one held in each hand, are put in various positions that represent letters of the alphabet. The only semaphore that I really learned at boot camp was how to signal "USNAVY" with our flagless hands, whenever our company was practicing in the drill hall.

SHF: Stands for Super High Frequency, the term in current usage applies to radio frequencies from 3,000*MHz to 30,000 MHz.

Silent Running: Quiet operation of the boat, typically used during depth charge attacks to prevent detection by listening equipment. All unnecessary equipment that created noise were turned off, including pumps, air conditioning units, fans, and so forth.

SJ: Model designation for a surface *search and *fire control, *SHF *radar used on American submarines. It operated at a nominal radio wavelength of *ten centimeters. The equipment incorporated a *PPI for surface search and an *A-scope for fire control applications.

SO-1: Model designation for a surface *search, *SHF *radar used aboard various small U.S. Navy surface craft. It operated at a nominal radio wavelength of *ten centimeters.

Sonar: Stands for "Sound Navigation and Ranging." An apparatus that detects the presence and location of submerged objects by means of sonic (audible) or ultrasonic (above audible frequency) waves. Active sonar sent sound energy though the water and sensed the reflection of that energy from the target. Surface crafts during World War II mainly used active, pulsed sonar for submarine detection. That equipment sent powerful sound impulses into the water and then measured the time for the return of the echo from the target, which translated into target range. (The "PING. . .ping" sounds heard in wartime movies about naval operations are those of active, pulsed sonar.) Passive sonar, on the other hand, enabled the operator to listen for the sounds produced by a target. Submariners preferred the use of sound equipment in the passive mode and rarely used the active mode. They listened for the sonar "pinging" and screw (propeller) noise produced by the surface craft. (The "pinging" produced by a target could often be heard long before visual or radar detection of that ship.) The pointing of their highly directional electrosonic transducers (sound heads) determined the target's bearing in both active and passive sonar systems.

Star Sight: The visual measurement of the "angular altitude" of a known celestial body relative to the horizon. Multiple star sights enabled determination of one's location in latitude and longitude. The navigational instrument used to perform that was the hand held sextant.

TBT: Target Bearing Transmitter. A target sighting device similar to a pelorus that electrically transmitted the optical pointing direction (bearing) to the conning tower and control room. There were two TBT positions, one at the bridge and the other on the after cigarette deck. They provided bearings for fire control or navigational purposes while on the surface.

TDC (Torpedo Data Computer): A manually operated electro-mechanical computer that established the track that the torpedo needed in order to hit the moving target.

Ten Centimeter Band: This is the nominal operating wavelength of some *radar equipments. The frequency that corresponds to a wavelength of ten centimeters is 3,000 *MHz.

UHF (Ultra High Frequency): This is the term that currently applies to radio frequencies from 300 *MHz to 3,000 MHz.

VHF (Very High Frequency): This is the term that currently applies to radio frequencies from 30 *MHz to 300 MHz.

Appendix One

Statement of Commanding officer, *USS Extractor*:

At Guam, we received orders from Commander Service Squadron TWELVE to proceed to Point "Diesel,"with no indication of exact nature of our mission, but assumed it was regarding salvage work on disabled vessels. No escort was provided. We took departure from No. 1 channel buoy approximately 2300, King, 21 Jan 1945, and set course 281° (T) direct to Point "Diesel." Prior to the departure, all men were mustered and informed that we were proceeding through dangerous area unescorted and that all hands were to have their life jackets readily available at all times.

The ABK (IFF) was set in operation and remained in operation throughout the entire trip. Our SO-1 surface search radar was not operating upon leaving port and we were unable to get it in operation at any time.

On January 22nd, approximately 1630, King, we received a radio message that we were unable to decode. About the first eight code groups were missing and the rest of the message was badly garbled, including the indicators at the end of the message. The radio operators reported that reception was very poor and that the transmission of the message was very fast. Numerous attempts were made to decipher the message using all available effective codes with no results. I did not consider it advisable to break radio silence to request a repeat on the message as I had my original orders which gave my destination and I felt certain that either the message would be repeated or that we would be contacted later as we still had three days to go before arriving at Point "Diesel."

On the morning of the 24th, approximately 0630, Item, I was in my cabin preparing to shave when I felt a slight jar followed a few seconds later by a terrific explosion. I immediately rushed to the bridge in time to see considerable debris fall back into the water and I immediately perceived that we had been hit on the starboard side about in the middle of the forward hatch and the bow of the ship was sinking rapidly. As soon as I came up the ladder, I told the Communication Officer, Lt (jg) Semmes Chapman, USNR, to send out a distress message immediately, which he was unable to do.

The Officer of the Deck, Lt(jg) C.P. Burman, USNR, sounded general quarters immediately following the explosion. The ship was settling in the water evenly and at first I thought there was a possibility that the watertight bulkhead forward of the crew's compartment was holding and that we might stay afloat. A few seconds later, however, approximately two minutes from the time the ship was torpedoed, she suddenly listed to starboard and I gave the order to abandon ship. The word was immediately passed throughout the ship to cut loose the life rafts and abandon ship. An attempt was made to release the port motor launch but it was impossible to crank out the boat boom over the side in time, so the boat gripes were released in hopes that the boat would float free as the ship sank. All hands abandoned ship in a very orderly fashion, and proceeded to the life rafts. Many of the men who were good swimmers helped pull other men to the rafts. A few minutes after we abandoned ship the ship capsized and sank. The total time from the initial hit until the time she sank beneath the water was approximately five minutes

As soon as the ship went down all hands started collecting dried provisions which had floated free and stowing them on the life rafts. We had been in the water about twenty minutes when the submarine, the *USS GUARDFISH*, surfaced about 600 or 700 yards off and started circling around us until they identified us and began rescuing survivors. After picking up all immediate survivors, the *USS GUARDFISH* patrolled around the immediate vicinity for a couple of hours searching for any additional survivors until we were certain that they had all been picked up. It is my opinion that all men remaining afloat were picked up before we left the area.

The visibility was very poor, probably less than a thousand yards and the sea was rough throughout the entire trip. To the best of my knowledge, at the time of our attack we were approximately on our course. There is a possibility that we may have drifted five or ten miles north.

Nearly all of the men abandoned ship with their life jackets and that possibly accounted for the large percentage of survivors. Out of a crew of 79 men and officers, the following six enlisted men were missing: Bahrey, Walter Stanley, S2c, USNR; Burgess, Bob Roy, RM3c(T), USNR; Frazier, Tommie Lemerle, EM3c(GY), USNR; Orgeron, Alvin Charles, SC3c(T), USNR; Taylor, William Henry, S1c, USNR; Thompson, Raymond Edward, S2c, USNR. Of these, four were believed to be in the forward hold at the time of the explosion and were probably killed instantly. Taylor was observed sinking by Eby, K.M., MM1c,(DS), USN, who attempted to rescue him but failed. Frazier, T.L., had a life jacket on and was being towed to a life raft by Molnar, G., BM1c, USNR, when a large wave hit them and separated them and Frazier was not seen since. None of the survivors suffered no more than a few minor scratches and sprains.

> (signed)   H. M. BABCOCK, Lt., D, USNR
> Commanding Officer,
> *USS Extractor*, ARS 15

Appendix Two

This Appendix provides some interesting graphic evidence of the similarities between *USS Extractor* and the Japanese submarine *I-165*. *Guardfish* mistakenly identified the former as the latter.

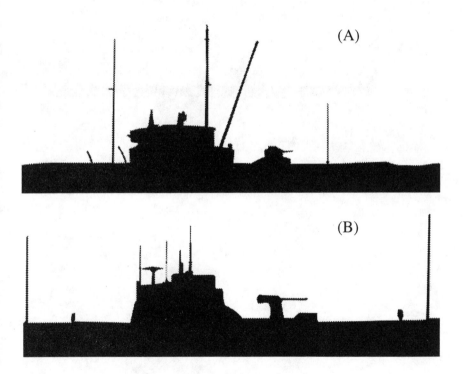

(A)

(B)

USS Extractor (A), and *I-165* (B). The silhouttes above are simulated views of what Commander Douglas Hammond, *Guardfish's* skipper, may have seen through his periscope—without the heavy seas—before mistakenly sending *Extractor* to the bottom.

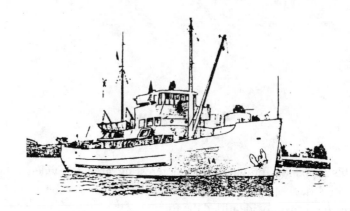

(A) *USS Extractor*, with a 50 degree angle on the bow; (B) Japanese submarine *I-165*.

Bibliography

OFFICIAL DOCUMENTS

Code of Federal Regulations, 32, parts 700 to 799 as of July 1, 1991.
Deck Logs, *USS Extractor* (ARS-15); May 1944 to December 1944. Washington, D.C.: Navy Historical Center.
Deck Logs, *USS Guardfish* (SS-217); May 1944 to June 1945. Washington, D.C.: Navy Historical Center.
Dictionary of American Naval Fighting Ships. Washington, D.C.: Naval History Division, 1968.
Naval Courts and Boards. Washington, D.C.: Government Printing Office, 1937.
Record Of Proceedings of a Court Of Inquiry convened on board *U.S.S. Curtiss* by order of Commander Task Force Ninety-Four United States Fleet [into the] sinking of *U.S.S. EXTRACTOR.* . . . Washington, D.C.: Navy Historical Center.
Selected Biographies and Historical Information. Washington, D.C.: Navy Historical Center.
WWII Diary/Report File, *U.S.S. CABRILLA* (SS-288), NRS-18. Washington, D.C.: Navy Historical Center.
WWII Diary/Report File, *U.S.S. GUARDFISH* (SS-217), NRS-1975-37. Washington, D.C.: Navy Historical Center/
WWII History/Diary/Report File, *U.S.S. TICONDEROGA* (CV-14), NRS-1981-7. Washington, D.C.: Navy Historical Center.
WWII Muster Rolls-1519, *U.S.S. EXTRACTOR* (ARS-15). National Archives of United States.
WWII Muster Rolls-1792, *U.S.S. GUARDFISH* (SS-217). National Archives of United States.

BOOKS

Barrows, Nat A. *Blow All Ballasts! The Story of the Squalus.* New York, NY: Court Book Company, 1940.
Blair, Clay, Jr. *Silent Victory: The U.S. Submarine War Against Japan.* Philadelphia and New York: J.B. Lippincott Company, 1975.

Calhoun, C. Raymond. *Typhoon: The Other Enemy*. Annapolis, Maryland: Naval Institute Press, 1977.

Carpenter, Dorr and Norman Polmar. *Submarines of the Imperial Japanese Navy*. Annapolis, Maryland: Naval Institute Press, 1986.

Feldt, Eric A. *The Coastwatchers*. Garden City, N.Y.: Nelson Doubleday, Inc., 1979.

Guerlac, Henry E. *Radar in World War II*. Tomash Publishers/American Institute of Physics.

Lowder, Hughston E. *The Silent Service: U.S. Submarines in World War II*. Baltimore, Maryland: Silent Service Books, 1987.

Roscoe, Theodore. *Pig Boats: The True Story of the Fighting Submariners of World War II*. Toronto, London, New York: Bantam Books, 1958.

ARTICLES AND REFERENCE SOURCES

The Bluejackets: Manual. Annapolis, Maryland: United States Naval Institute, 1940.

Encyclopaedia Britannica. Volumes 23, 24. Chicago, London, Toronto: Encyclopaedia Britannica, Inc., 1960.

Life Magazine (March 15, 1943).

Register of Alumni; Graduates and former Naval Cadets and Midshipmen. Annapolis, Maryland: The United States Naval Academy Alumni Association, Inc, 1993.

INDEX